On the Place of Linguistics in Northern Afghanistan

SIL Global
Publications in Linguistics 156

Publications in Linguistics is published by SIL Global. The series is a venue for works covering a broad range of topics in linguistics, especially the analytical treatment of minority languages from all parts of the world. While most volumes are authored by members of SIL, suitable works by others will also form part of the series.

Series Editor
Susan McQuay

Editorial Staff
Eugene C. Burnham, Managing Editor
Elke Meier, Proofreader (German)
Eleanor J. McAlpine, Proofreader (English)

Production Staff
Priscilla Higby, Production Manager
Nathaniel Shaver, Compositor (XLingPaper)
Ian McQuay, Compositor (Print and ePub)
Carrie Ann Shaver and Barbara Alber, Cover Design

SESTAVINE:
- 16 svežih ostrig, oluščenih
- 1 skodelica kuskusa, kuhanega in ohlajenega
- 1 kumara, narezana na kocke
- 1 skodelica češnjevih paradižnikov, prepolovljena
- 1/4 skodelice oliv Kalamata, narezanih
- Feta sir, zdrobljen

NAVODILA:
a) V veliki skledi zmešajte kuhan kuskus, na kocke narezano kumaro, prepolovljene češnjeve paradižnike, narezane olive Kalamata in nadrobljen feta sir.
b) Mešanico kuskusa prelijte z oluščenimi ostrigami.
c) Nežno premešajte, da se združi.
d) Postrezite pri sobni temperaturi.

100. Sladice iz ostrig in redkvic

SESTAVINE:

- 16 svežih ostrig, oluščenih
- 2 skodelici narezanega zelja
- 1 skodelica redkvice, narezane na tanke rezine
- 1/4 skodelice grškega jogurta
- 1 žlica jabolčnega kisa
- 1 čajna žlička dijonske gorčice
- 1 čajna žlička medu
- Svež koper za okras
- Sol in poper po okusu

NAVODILA:

a) V veliki skledi zmešajte narezano zelje in na tanke rezine narezane redkvice.
b) Na vrh solate z oluščenimi ostrigami.
c) V majhni skledi zmešajte grški jogurt, jabolčni kis, dijonsko gorčico, med, sol in poper.
d) Preliv pokapajte po solati.
e) Okrasite s svežim kopromom.
f) Postrežemo ohlajeno.

ZAKLJUČEK

Ko zaključujemo naše popotovanje po "Popolna kuharska knjiga ljubiteljev ostrig", se iskreno zahvaljujemo, da ste se nam pridružili na tej okusni pustolovščini skozi svet ostrig. Upamo, da je teh 100 neustavljivih stvaritev sprožilo novo odkrito strast do kulinaričnih možnosti, ki jih te oceanske dobrote prinašajo na mizo.

Ta kuharska knjiga je več kot le zbirka receptov; je dokaz raznolike in niansirane narave ostrig – slavljenje njihovih okusov, tekstur in veselja, ki ga prinašajo tistim, ki cenijo lepoto morske hrane. Ko uživate v zadnjih grižljajih teh kreacij, vas spodbujamo, da nadaljujete z raziskovanjem sveta ostrig ter eksperimentirate z različnimi sortami in metodami kuhanja, da bi našli popolno izkušnjo z ostrigami.

Naj bo "Popolna kuharska knjiga ljubiteljev ostrig" vir navdiha za vaše kulinarične podvige, sprožanje pogovorov in ustvarjanje trajnih spominov za jedilno mizo. Hvala, ker ste nam dovolili, da smo del vašega popotovanja ljubiteljev ostrig. Dokler se naše poti spet ne prekrižajo v kraljestvu slastnih spoznanj, veselega luščenja in prepuščanja svetu ostrigovih užitkov!

www.ingramcontent.com/pod-product-compliance
Lightning Source LLC
LaVergne TN
LVHW021710060526
838200LV00050B/2599

Dedication

This publication offers insights into the linguistic variations of languages spoken in northern Afghanistan. The tribute herein is dedicated to Simone Beck, who dedicated many years of her life to comprehending the linguistic diversity of this remarkable region. Simone's scholarly pursuits extended beyond mere academic research; her focus was on the people behind the linguistics. In addition to her linguistic discoveries, she meticulously documented her ethnographic observations, unveiling the religious and sociolinguistic nuances inherent within the communities she studied. Through this compilation of insights concerning select language groups in northern Afghanistan, we aim to honour Simone's extensive foundational research in this geographical expanse, alongside her valuable theological insights.

Contents

Figures	xi
Tables	xiii
Foreword	xv
Preface	xvii
Introduction	xix
Abbreviations	xxiii

1 Exegese von Jesaja 40:12–31 (Simone Beck) — 1
- 1.1 Einleitungsfragen — 1
  - 1.1.1 Verfasser des Buches – der Prophet Jesaja — 1
  - 1.1.2 Historische Situation – politisches Umfeld — 2
  - 1.1.3 Diskussion der Einheitlichkeit — 3
- 1.2 Abgrenzung der Perikope — 10
  - 1.2.1 Inhaltliche Abgrenzung — 10
  - 1.2.2 Grammatische Abgrenzung — 10
  - 1.2.3 Einheit der Perikope — 10
- 1.3 Kontext — 11
  - 1.3.1 Enger Kontext — 11
  - 1.3.2 Weiter Kontext — 11
  - 1.3.3 Kontext im Buch Jesaja — 13
  - 1.3.4 Arbeitsübersetzung im Überblick — 13
- 1.4 Analyse der Poesie in Jesaja 40:12–31 — 15
  - 1.4.1 Parallelismus in Jesaja 40:12–31 — 15
  - 1.4.2 Metrum oder Rhythmus in Jesaja 40:12–31 — 15
  - 1.4.3 Stil — 16
- 1.5 Diskussion offener Fragen — 18
  - 1.5.1 Wie lautet die Antwort auf die Fragen in Vers 12? — 18
  - 1.5.2 Die Bedeutung von איש עצתו in Vers 13 — 19
  - 1.5.3 Die Bedeutung von מסכן in Vers 20 — 20
  - 1.5.4 Die Bedeutung der Negation in Vers 24 — 21
  - 1.5.5 Der Vergleich mit dem Adler in Vers 31 — 22
  - 1.5.6 Das Problem der Müdigkeit von Gläubigen in Vers 31 — 23
- 1.6 Betrachtung der einzelnen Verse — 24
  - 1.6.1 Jesaja 40:12–14   I Größer als die Schöpfung;
    a) Rhetorische Fragen — 24
  - 1.6.2 Jesaja 40:15–17   I Größer als die Schöpfung;
    b) Folgerung — 26
  - 1.6.3 Jesaja 40:18   II Größer als die Götter;
    a) Rhetorische Fragen — 29
  - 1.6.4 Jesaja 40:19–20   II Größer als die Götter;
    b) Folgerungen — 30
  - 1.6.5 Jesaja 40:21   III Größer als die Machthaber;
    a) Rhetorische Fragen — 32
  - 1.6.6 Jesaja 40:22–24   III Größer als die Machthaber;
    b) Folgerungen — 33
  - 1.6.7 Jesaja 40:25   IV Größer als das Universum;
    a) Rhetorische Fragen — 35

1.6.8 Jesaja 40:26   IV Größer als das Universum;
       b) Folgerungen   35
 1.6.9 Jesaja 40:27–28a   V Größer als die Kraftlosigkeit;
       a) Rhetorische Fragen   37
 1.6.10 Jesaja 40:28b–31   V Größer als die Kraftlosigkeit;
        b) Folgerungen   38
 1.7 Inhaltliche Übersetzung   41
     1.7.1 Jesaja 40:12–17   I Größer als die Schöpfung   41
     1.7.2 Jesaja 40:18–20   II Größer als die Götter   42
     1.7.3 Jesaja 40:21–24   III Größer als die Machthaber   42
     1.7.4 Jesaja 40:25–26   IV Größer als das Universum   42
     1.7.5 Jesaja 40:27–31   V Größer als die Kraftlosigkeit   42
 1.8 Anwendung   43
 1.9 Zusammenfassung   44
2 **Backgrounding and Foregrounding, Prominence, and Highlighting in Afghan Wakhi: A Text Discourse Analysis (Simone Beck)**   51
 2.1 Background information   52
     2.1.1 Geography and population   52
     2.1.2 Previous research about the Wakhi language   52
 2.2 Four genres   53
 2.3 Foregrounding and backgrounding   54
     2.3.1 Narrative   55
     2.3.2 Procedural   61
     2.3.3 Behavioural   64
     2.3.4 Expository text   65
     2.3.5 Summary   68
 2.4 Prominence summary   69
 2.5 Highlighting   70
     2.5.1 Narrative   70
     2.5.2 Procedural   72
     2.5.3 Behavioural   73
     2.5.4 Expository text   75
     2.5.5 Summary   77
 2.6 Conclusion   78
3 **Linguistic Areality in Northeastern Afghanistan (Henrik Liljegren)**   83
 3.1 Introduction   83
 3.2 The region and its linguistic landscape   83
 3.3 Data and methods   85
 3.4 Language classification   88
 3.5 Lexical analysis   92
 3.6 Structural analysis   93
     3.6.1 Word order   94
     3.6.2 Nominal categories   95
     3.6.3 Simple clauses   98
     3.6.4 Phonology   101
     3.6.5 Lexical structure   103
 3.7 Concluding discussion   109
 3.8 Acknowledgements   113

4 Towards a New Analysis of Wakhi Clitics (Erin SanGregory)   119
    4.1 Introduction   119
    4.2 Overview of Wakhi clitics   120
       4.2.1 Clitics defined   120
       4.2.2 Wakhi verbal agreement suffixes vs. agreement clitics   121
       4.2.3 Wakhi TAM clitic   124
       4.2.4 Classifying Wakhi clitics   126
    4.3 Overview of previous analyses   126
       4.3.1 Erschler's AWC analysis   127
       4.3.2 Hughes's application of the DFCF and PI   128
       4.3.3 Fuchs's split analysis   130
    4.4 A preliminary Lexical Functional Grammar analysis of Wakhi clitics   132
    4.5 Conclusion   136

5 Complex Converbal Predicates in Afghan Turkmen (Nathaniel Shaver)   139
    5.1 Introducing converbal constructions   140
    5.2 Varieties of converbal constructions in Turkic languages   140
    5.3 Varieties of converbal constructions in Afghan Turkmen   141
    5.4 Mono-clausality tests for complex predicates   142
       5.4.1 Reflexive and non-reflexive pronouns   143
       5.4.2 Causatives   144
       5.4.3 Passivization and intonation curves   148
       5.4.4 The problem of unmarked coordination   151
       5.4.5 Scope of negation and licensing of negative concord items   152
       5.4.6 Filler gap   154
       5.4.7 Uniqueness of tense and aspect marking   155
    5.5 Auxiliary or light verb   156
    5.6 Characteristic properties of auxiliaries   156
       5.6.1 Auxiliaries are grammatical rather than lexical   156
       5.6.2 Auxiliaries do not assign semantic roles   157
       5.6.3 Auxiliaries and number of arguments in a clause   157
       5.6.4 Auxiliaries have dependent status   158
       5.6.5 Auxiliaries have defective paradigms   158
    5.7 Conclusion   159

6 "How Have You Appreciated the Uzbek Language?": The Role of Language in Afghan Uzbek Identity Formation (Joseph Stark)   163
    6.1 Introduction   163
    6.2 Methods of data gathering   164
    6.3 Summary of the study's key findings   165
    6.4 Losing education and language   167
    6.5 Asserting positive identity as Uzbek people   169
    6.6 Fighting to assert Uzbek identity, culture, and language   175
    6.7 Interaction with other literature   177
    6.8 Summary and applications   178

7 The Questions of *pa* – A Munji Contemplative Question Particle
   (Paul Williamson) **181**
   7.1 Introduction 181
   7.2 Background 181
   7.3 Question formation in Munji 181
   7.4 The meaning of the *pa* particle 182
   7.5 Semantic restrictions on the use of *pa* 182
       7.5.1 The pragmatic use of *pa* 184
       7.5.2 The syntax of *pa* 185
   7.6 Summary and conclusion 186
Language Index 187

Figures

Figure 3.1. Map of northeastern Afghanistan with geographical locations of sample varieties.   84

Figure 3.2. Three hypotheses regarding Nuristani Indo-Iranian classification.   88

Figure 3.3. Language relatedness according to traditional classification.   91

Figure 3.4. Lexical similarities in NEA languages.   93

Figure 3.5. Parents and their siblings: full differentiation, Uzbek (Turkic).   106

Figure 3.6. Parents and their siblings: "uncles-aunts-terminology", Munji (Iranian).   106

Figure 3.7. Parents and their siblings: "mothers-fathers-terminology", Waigali (Nuristani).   107

Figure 3.8. Parents and their siblings: "mothers-terminology", Korangali Pashai (Indo-Aryan).   107

Figure 3.9. Structural similarities in NEA languages.   108

Figure 3.10. Map of northeastern Afghanistan with sample varieties plotted as belonging to one of two diffusion zones.   112

Figure 4.1. C-STR for example (6).   134

Figure 4.2. C-STR for example (38).   135

Figure 4.3. C-STR for example (40).   135

Figure 4.4. C-STR for example (10).   136

Figure 5.1. Ditransitive predicate recipient-marking language patterns.   146

Figure 5.2. Recipient and causee correspondence in Pattern 2 languages.   146

Figure 5.3. Prediction of the causee's grammatical relation.   146

Figure 5.4. Passive promotion patterns for intransitive and transitive base verbs.   149

Figure 5.5. S-STRUCTURE of marked coordinate clauses in Afghan Turkmen.   152

Figure 5.6. S-STRUCTURE of unmarked coordinate clauses in Afghan
    Turkmen. 152

Figure 6.1. Patterns of convergence/divergence tension in Afghan Uzbek
    identity formation. 166

Figure 6.2. The relationship between *millat* (nationality), *millyet* (ethnic
    group), *qaom* (family network), and *til* (language). 170

Figure 6.3. Areas of Afghanistan with significant Uzbek speakers
    indicated by shading. 171

Figure 6.4. Uzbek language use and paternal Uzbek bloodlines compose
    Uzbek identity markers. 174

Tables

Table 2.1. Four genres of discourse	54
Table 2.2. Foregrounding and backgrounding features in the four genres	68
Table 2.3. Features used to indicate prominence in the four genres	69
Table 2.4. Features used to indicate highlighting in the four genres	77
Table 3.1. Language varieties in the data sample	86
Table 3.2. Order of adposition and noun phrase in NEA	95
Table 3.3. Number of cases (based on: A, S, P, R) used by varieties in NEA	96
Table 3.4. Case distribution exemplified with the noun "boy" in Roshani, Chalas Pashai, Ashkun, Sanglechi and Munji	96
Table 3.5. Number of genders in NEA	97
Table 3.6. Case alignment (nouns)	99
Table 3.7. Agreement patterns (verbs in pfv/pst)	101
Table 3.8. Retroflex consonants in NEA	102
Table 3.9. Affricates in NEA	102
Table 3.10. The inventory of dental, retroflex and palatal plosives, affricates and fricatives in Gawar-Bati (Indo-Aryan)	103
Table 3.11. Numeral bases in NEA	103
Table 3.12. Numerals in Ashkun (Nuristani)	104
Table 3.13. The numerals 6, 16, 26 and 36 in seven languages	104
Table 3.14. Kinship terms for one's parents and their siblings in NEA	105
Table 4.1. Subject agreement suffixes	122
Table 4.2. Agreement clitics	123
Table 5.1. Non-defective paradigm of V2 in Afghan Turkmen	159

Foreword

In honouring the memory of Simone Beck[1], we cannot overlook the invaluable contributions of another esteemed colleague, Eberhard Werner[2], the editor of this book. Eberhard's profound insights, scholarly acumen, and unwavering dedication enriched the fields of anthropology and theology, leaving an indelible mark on our academic community.

Tragically, Eberhard passed away on 4 August 2023, before this book reached publication. Yet, his presence resonates throughout these pages, a testament to his tireless efforts to advance scholarly discourse and promote interdisciplinary understanding.

We are profoundly grateful for Eberhard's invaluable contributions to this project. His vision, expertise, and meticulous attention to detail were instrumental in compiling and refining the diverse array of papers presented here. While this volume is dedicated to Simone Beck, we acknowledge with deep appreciation Eberhard's role in shaping its content and guiding its development.

May this publication stand as a tribute to the enduring legacies of both Simone Beck and Eberhard Werner, whose contributions continue to inspire and enrich our academic pursuits.

Wayne Lunsford, PhD
Regional Associate Director
SIL Eurasia
April 2025

---

[1] Deceased 20 May 2017
[2] Deceased 4 August 2023

Preface

The editor, authors, and peer reviewers of this work dedicate this academic publication to Simone Beck, a distinguished linguist, a Christian theologian, and a dear friend to her colleagues and to the people group with whom she worked. The circumstances of her sudden loss and her humble personality encouraged the editor to follow her example by honouring the linguistic and development project in northeastern Afghanistan that she started. Her work aimed at the linguistic description of a language group and its dialectical variations in northern Afghanistan. Those participating in this publication are not just honouring her but also endeavouring to continue the work she started.

The broad variety of the contributions in this volume is dedicated to the people groups of northern Afghanistan. The unique landscape and the diversity of the people groups in their religion and linguistic and cultural orientation are reflected here.

You will find in this research many facets of the above-mentioned diversity. The first two chapters are summaries of the two MA theses that Simone Beck wrote as a theologian and linguist. One concerns a text from the Hebrew Bible and its interpretation. The subject of the other is field linguistics and research on the Wakhi language. Both deal with linguistic and anthropological insights. The Hebrew Bible thesis is about the historical implications of an ancient text for those that follow such a text. Her linguistic Wakhi thesis is about a specific ethnolinguistic people group and includes studies about the Kunar province.

Also included in this volume is a study on Wakhi clitics as well as an overview of the linguistic diversity of northeastern Afghanistan and detailed studies about Afghan Turkmen, Uzbek, and Munji.

Our special thanks go to Simone Beck's family, Redcliffe College, and the Martin Bucer Seminary, who allowed these studies and the work of Simone to be made public. The contributors to this work and the peer reviewers are also heartily thanked for their time in honouring our dear colleague. We also want to express our deepest appreciation to the many linguists and anthropologists whose research into the ethnic groups and their languages in the northeastern part of Afghanistan has benefitted language development, mother-tongue education, and literacy. And lastly, we express our deepest appreciation to the people of Afghanistan, who themselves developed reading and educational material for language use and the education of their children in their and 8 as mentioned in this publication.

It is the hope of the editor that the work started by Simone Beck will be continued and will stimulate more research. Also, our hope is also that the audience of this publication will profit, as much as we did, from the peer-reviewed research presented here.

Eberhard Werner
Germany, June 2021

Introduction

This tribute volume focusses on an interesting linguistic area. The language groups of northeastern Afghanistan not only reflect a variety of many dialects due to being geographically isolated by high mountains and deep valleys, but they also reflect the effects of being in the centre of the many political changes that have overrun the country of Afghanistan since WWII.

Simone Beck was born and raised in southern Germany. She decided to work in linguistics in West Asia. Her interest was in the country of Afghanistan. After settling in Kabul for some years she met Wakhi speakers and became interested in that people group. They are from the northeastern part of Afghanistan, and they also live in areas of southeastern Tajikistan. Simone Beck was also interested in Christian theology and thus studied theology as well as linguistics. A tragic incident took her life in 2017, more than ten years after she had decided to focus on this Asian country. It was a shock to her colleagues and friends as well as to the language speakers with whom she worked, sometimes remotely and sometimes on location in the Wakhi Corridor. Her travels from Europe to Afghanistan became routine to her, but the times in the country were always special, and she spoke many times of her experiences. The book *Ermordet in Kabul*[1], written in 2021, describes Simone's life and work among the peoples of Afghanistan.

The contents of this tribute volume start with two contributions from Simone herself. She worked on two master's theses, one on Christian theology and the book of the prophet Isaiah from the Hebrew Bible with the Martin Bucer Seminary in Bonn, Germany, and the other on Field Linguistics concerning the Wakhi language with Redcliffe College in Gloucester, England. Neither of these theses have been published so far. However, due to lack of space we decided to present the reader with only selections from the full theses, including the conclusions that Simone Beck drew from her research. Thus, the themes of the two master's theses remain in the selections presented here, which represent nearly half of this volume. Readers are invited to obtain copies of the full works directly from the institutions mentioned.

We will now look at the contributions in detail. In her 2006 German MA study on Isaiah 40:12–31, Simone Beck invites us to look at a piece of Hebrew poetry. It is presented as a stylistic description of God the creator in the form of an accusation to an audience that is asked to think over their actions. Her exegesis includes an overview of the introductory questions and historical interpretations of the text, the text structure, writing and text styles, as well as her own literal translation and interpretation of each verse. She investigates the form, redaction, text and literary history of the text and gives an overview of the manifold understandings and classification. As part of what is called "Deutero-Isaiah", chapters 40–55 are understood to be presented by a different author or authors from chapters 1–39. However, there is also evidence that the whole book is written *en bloc*. Simone Beck follows the tradition that in chapter 40–55 there is an obvious change in style and focus, but such a change is absolutely possible in literature, and can often be observed. The main argument is that the object of adoration and the audience in mind do not change throughout the whole book. The passage from verse 12 to 31 of

---

[1] Führer, Heidemarie. 2021. *Ermordet in Kabul: Vom Leben, Glauben und Kämpfen der Simone Beck*. Hänssler Verlag.

chapter 40 is a unit in so far as the storyteller or author praises the superiority of the one God of Israel, who is above all non-Israelite images of gods, who is the creator and who is lastly very personally interested in the well-being of his people. Thus, from the standpoint of adoration-literature this Biblical passage moves from universal praise, down through society and from there down to the individual as the basic element of the community. The audience is made aware of the mighty God as a supreme power at the one end of the continuum and a very individual counsellor at the other. Simone Beck sums up her findings with the impressive implication that the almighty God makes himself small to let his followers participate in his power and magnitude.

In her 2013 MA thesis in the field of linguistics from Redcliffe College, Gloucester, Simone Beck writes on the text discourse of the Wakhi language. After a geographical and ethnographic description of the Wakhi people, information is given about the linguistic classification of the Wakhi language. Following the text discourse analysis of Stephen H. Levinsohn, Simone Beck researched the entire systematics of the features of his text discourse. However, we decided to present only the most outstanding features to give the audience an idea of the many facets of the Wakhi language. The Wakhi people populate the Wakhan Corridor that is bordered by Pakistan, Tajikistan, and China. Their population is estimated at 75,000, and this Indo-European Iranian, Eastern, Southeastern and Pamir Wakhi language has the ISO 639-3 code [wbl].[2] It belongs to a "Pamir-Sprachbund" with Shughni, Ishkashimi, Sanglechi, and Munji. Her research is based on stories that she investigated while she was in the homeland of the Wakhi people in Afghanistan. We present here only the features of foregrounding and backgrounding as well as prominence created by highlighting. Simone Beck's analysis goes much further, but her conclusions on her findings are presented here. These conclusions sum up her impressions on text discourse based on her research.

Henrik Liljegren presents us with the "Linguistic reality in northeastern Afghanistan (NEA)". He last met Simone Beck in 2017 during a workshop. Simone and other researchers joined this workshop on the linguistic reality of NEA along with many nationals and speakers of the languages in this geographical area. His findings presented here are "hot off the press" so to say. It is interesting that he comes up with close to thirty language groups in this area. He advocates two distinct diffusion zones based on his linguistic analysis. He suggests that it is not by coincidence that the diffusion is identical with the influence of Pashto or Dari. The research presented here is part of a wider research project by the Swedish Research Council.

Erin SanGregory presents a paper entitled "Towards a New Analysis of Wakhi clitics", in which she works on the same language group as Simone Beck did. SanGregory focuses on so-called "wandering clitics". She proposes a new phrase structure rule to describe the functionality of these two types of clitics. She uses the linguistic data that she gathered in the language area. She starts using the differentiation of simple clitic and special clitic, before she moves on to suggest other categories. These are agreement clitics and TAM clitics. Her phrase structure rule suggests locating a clitic in 2P, after a non-initial

---

[2] The Language Index gives the ISO 639-3 codes for the languages mentioned in this volume in brackets. Some codes have added letters within parentheses, which are the author's own differential coding.

constituent, or in pre- or postverbal position, and also allows for multiple manifestations of the same clitic within a clause (see her conclusion).

Joseph Stark describes the Uzbek identity formation of the Uzbek language in Afghanistan, based on ethnographic data. He gathered the data in 2017 to 2018 from twenty persons. How does language add to the formation of a national identity? The main pointers of identity formation are education, sustainable use of language and culture change. Stark presents the features that form identity in the Uzbek community. He presents two main identity markers of what it is to be Uzbek, language and an Uzbek father. This has to be weighed against having the same religion, homeland area, and traditions that this language group shares with other Afghan populations. Interestingly, the suppression of the Uzbek language in former times and the recent opening of Uzbek education in school and for adults is a main identity marker, and at the same time leads to a loss of identity based on language, since multilingualism demands strong languages of wider communication for reasons of trade and information-sharing within a nation state. Currently, Uzbek is on its way to becoming the third official language in Afghanistan but it has to be proved by the Uzbeks that this will be realistic in daily life. On the other hand, the distinctive feature of the paternal bloodline has become more important. Stark's research is a welcome insight into the ethnic realities of modern Afghanistan.

Nathaniel Shaver presents a linguistic study on compound verb structures in Afghan Turkmen. Specifically, he examines the syntactic properties of converbal or -IB constructions in Afghan Turkmen. He asks whether these constructions are comprised of one or two clauses and uses grammatical tests to determine their syntactic quality. Shaver's examples in Afghan Turkmen are in Persian/Arabic script, which is evidence of the variety of orthographies and languages present in Afghanistan. Shaver concludes with three research questions that should be addressed in the future, thus acknowledging the complexity of the Afghan Turkmen verbal system.

Paul Williamson is researching the Munji question particle /pa/. Munji, as an Indo-European language, belongs to the Pamir Sprachbund that was mentioned above and is thus related to Wakhi. The Munji-speaking population is around 5,300. The particle /pa/ asserts that neither the speaker nor the listener has the answer to the question. Instead of asking for information, /pa/ is used to invite dialogue, solicit advice, or to exclaim about one's own wonder or confusion.

Abbreviations

-IB	converb ending in -ib/-ub/-ip/-up
1	first person
2	second person
2W	second word
2P	second position
3	third person
A	agent-like argument of canonical transitive verb
ABL	ablative
ACC	accusative
AGRP	agreement phrase
AN	animate
AUX	auxiliary
AWC	almost Wackernagel clitic
BHS	Biblia Hebraica Stuttgartensia
c-str	constituent structure
CAUS	causative
COMP	complementizer
CON	connector
CQ	contemplative question marker
CVB	converb
DAT	dative
DEM1	demonstrative, near
DEM2	demonstrative, mid
DEM3	demonstrative, far (deixis)
DFCF	doubly-filled COMP filter
DP	determiner phrase
EMPH	emphatic marker
ERG	ergative
EZ	ezafa particle
F	feminine/one's father
FB	one's father's brother
FZ	one's father's sister
GEN	genitive
IMP	imperative
INAN	inanimate
INF	infinitive
INTENS	intensifier
INTJ	interjection
IPFV	imperfective

LOC	locative
LVC	light verb construction
M	masculine/one's mother
MB	one's mother's brother
MZ	one's mother's sister
NCI	negative concord item
NEA	northeastern Afghanistan
NEG	negation, negative
NOM	nominative
NP$_{SUBJ}$	noun phrase subject
NR	near deixis (proximal)
OBJ	object
OBJ$_2$	object 2
OBL	oblique
P	patient-like argument of canonical transitive verb
PASS	passive
PFV	perfective
PI	prosodic inversion
PL	plural
POSS	possessive
PP	prepositional phrase or postposition phrase
PRF	perfect
PRS	present
PRSM	presumptive
PSR	phrase structure rule
PST	past
Q	question particle/marker
R	recipient
REFL	reflexive
REL	relative
S-COMP	subordinate clause
S-structure	sentence or clause structure
SBJ	subject
SPEC	specifier
SG	singular (or singular second position)
STV	stative
SVC	serial verb construction
TAM	tense, aspect, and mood
TP	topic phrase
TR	transitive
VP	verb phrase

1

Exegese von Jesaja 40:12–31

Simone Beck
SIL; Martin Bucer Seminar
October 2006
Leitfrage: Wie manifestiert sich die Größe Gottes in Jesaja 40:12–31?

1.1 Einleitungsfragen

1.1.1 Verfasser des Buches – der Prophet Jesaja

Jesajas Name bedeutet „Jahwe ist Rettung". Es liegen nur wenige biographische Angaben über seine Person vor. Folgendes ist bekannt oder wird vermutet: Jesajas Heimatstadt war Jerusalem (Jes 7:1–3). Kaiser (1969:203) vermutet, Jesaja habe aus einer Beamtenfamilie gestammt und eine Ausbildung an einer Jerusalemer Weisheitsschule genossen. Sein Zugang zum König deutet darauf hin, dass er sich in der Oberschicht der Gesellschaft bewegte (Jes 36:13–20); möglicherweise war er selbst adliger oder gar königlicher Abstammung.

Laut Walvoord und Zuck (1998:5) sei er gemäß der Überlieferung der Cousin von König Usia gewesen. Jedenfalls konnte er vornehme Männer um einen Dienst bitten (Jes 8:2).

Seine Frau, auch Prophetin (Jes 8:3), gebar Söhne, deren symbolische Namen Schlüsselbegriffe der Botschaft Jesajas waren: יָשׁוּב שְׁאָר „Ein Rest wird zurückkehren" und מַהֵר שָׁלָל חָשׁ בַּז „Schnell zum Plündern" (Jes 7:3; 8:3–4); laut Kaiser war vielleicht auch עִמָּנוּ אֵל „Immanuel" (Jes 7:14ff) einer seiner Söhne. Jesaja war von einer kleinen Gruppe von Jüngern umgeben, möglicherweise gehörten auch seine Söhne dazu (Jes 8:16–18). Seine kompromisslose Konfrontation mit König Ahas zeigt seinen Mut und seine alleinige Hingabe an Jahwe und seine Berufung (Jes 7). Aber er litt auch, wie viele andere Propheten, emotional unter der Botschaft, die er zu verkündigen hatte (Jes 21:2–4). Pehlke (2002:171) weist auf die Wortgewalt des Propheten hin. Kein anderer Prophet verfügte über einen so großen Wortschatz von seltenen Wörtern. Er verwendete fast 2000 verschiedene hebräische Wörter. Er gebrauchte Gedichte und Lieder (Jes 5:1–7; 42:14), Metaphern (Jes 28:17; 30:28), Wortspiele (Jes 3:24; 17:12), Parabeln (Jes 28:23–29), ein Spottlied in Form eines Leichenliedes (Jes 14:4–23) und andere literarische Formen.

Jesaja wurde im Tempel von Jerusalem von Gott durch eine Vision zum Propheten berufen. Seine Botschaft richtet er an den jeweils herrschenden König und an das Volk. Die Botschaft Jesajas, wie die vieler Propheten, war die Kritik an der religiösen, sozialen und politischen Schieflage in der Gesellschaft, sie betraf besonders die Weisen (für ihre mangelnde Weisheit; Jes 5:21), die Priester (Jes 28:7–10) und das Volk (für seine falsche Anbetung; Jes 29:13). Ungewöhnlich ist Jesajas Interesse an der internationalen Politik. Sein Warnung blieb während des Syro-Ephraimitischen Krieges (Jes 7), während der Invasion durch die Assyrer (Jes 10:5–6) und im Vorschatten der Deportation nach

Babylon (Jes 39:6–7) immer die gleiche: Der mangelnde Gehorsam gegenüber Jahwe wird Konsequenzen haben.

Jesaja predigte diese Botschaften während der Regierungszeiten der Könige Usia bis Hiskia, sie sind in Kapitel 1–39 niedergelegt. Während der Regierungszeit Manasses konnte Jesaja vermutlich nicht mehr in der Öffentlichkeit erscheinen (2 Chr 33:1–9). Seine letzte Botschaft predigte Jesaja wahrscheinlich 701 v.Chr. während der Bedrohung Jerusalems durch Sanherib. In seinen letzten, zurückgezogenen Jahren, als er alt war und verfolgt wurde, legte er laut Webb (1996:24–25) die Botschaften von Kappitel 40–66 schriftlich nieder. Sie vervollständigten sein früheres Reden. Außerdem schrieb er noch eine Biographie über das Leben des Königs Hiskia (2 Chr 32:32). Gemäß Walvoord und Zuck (1998:5 9) schreibt Justin der Märtyrer (ca. 100–165 n.Chr.), dass Jesaja zur Zeit Manasses mit einer Säge in Stücke geschnitten worden sei.[1] Darauf spielt wohl Hebräer 11:37 im Lied über die Glaubensväter an: „Sie wurden zersägt."

Zeitgleich mit Jesaja wirkte der Prophet Micha in Juda, allerdings auf dem Land. Er verurteilte mit Schärfe die soziale Ungleichheit seiner Zeit und sprach vom kommenden Messias, der das Volk retten würde. Im Nordreich wirkte der Prophet Hosea, der Gerichtsbote Gottes, der aber auch an den Bund Gottes mit Israel appellierte und das Volk zur Umkehr aufrief, die Gottes Gnade zur Folge haben würde.

1.1.2 Historische Situation – politisches Umfeld

Gemäß Jesaja 1:1 predigte Jesaja zur Zeit der Könige Usia, Jotham, Ahas und Hiskia. Zu seiner historischen Situation gehört außerdem Manasse, weil Jesaja in seiner Regierungszeit noch lebte und arbeitete, jedoch nicht mehr öffentlich auftrat.[2] Gemäß vieler Theologen entstanden Teile des Jesajabuches erst zu später, exilischer und nachexilischer Zeit.[3] Deshalb werden die entsprechenden historischen Epochen hier auch betrachtet. Im Anschluss werden die damit verbundenen Fragen bezüglich der Einheitlichkeit, des / der Verfasser und der Entstehungszeit des Buches diskutiert.

1.1.2.1 Wegführung und Exil

In Jerusalem installierte Ägypten erst den Vasallenkönig Jehoahas (609), dann seinen Bruder Jehojakim (608–598). Doch 605 v.Chr., nach der Niederlage der ägyptischen Armee bei Karchemis durch Babylon unter Nabopolassar (626 –604; Jer 46:12), wurde Juda Babylon untergeordnet. Jehojakim versuchte, diese Tatsache zu ignorieren (2 Kön 23:34–24:5), doch sein Nachfolger Jehojachin (597) musste sich wieder Babylon unter Nebukadnezar ergeben (604–562), was die erste Deportation 597 v.Chr. und die Zerstörung des Tempels (2 Kön 24:6–16) nach sich zog. Zedekiah (597–586) wurde als König für die im Land Verbliebenen eingesetzt. Er wagte die Rebellion, die 587 v.Chr.

---

[1] Die Jahreszahlen der Regierungszeiten wurden Coogan (2006:328, 351, 360, 402, 431) entnommen. Die Zeitspannen beziehen sich auf Regierungszeiten, nicht auf Lebenszeiten. Andere Forscher schlagen andere Datierungen vor, doch hier ist nicht der Raum, dies zu diskutieren.

[2] Siehe: 1.1.1 Verfasser des Buches – der Prophet Jesaja.

[3] Siehe: 1.1.3 Diskussion der Einheitlichkeit.

zum Fall und zur Zerstörung Jerusalems und zur zweiten Deportation führte, fünf Jahre später folgte eine dritte (Jer 52:28–30). Ein großer Teil des Volkes blieb noch immer im Land zurück, nämlich die Armen, die nichts besaßen (Jer 39:10). Der zerstörte Tempel wurde immer noch als der rechtmäßige Ort der Anbetung Jahwes betrachtet (Jer 41:5). Im Gegensatz zu Samaria besiedelten keine anderen Völker das Gebiet von Juda und sicherlich bestanden Kontakte zwischen dem Volk im Exil und denjenigen, die zurückgeblieben waren. Die Exilanten bewahrten ihre Einheit und Identität, wahrscheinlich besonders durch die Beachtung des Sabbats und der Beschneidung und durch die Einrichtung der Ältesten Judas (Hes 8:1).

1.1.2.2 Rückführung ins Land

Kyros (559–530), König von Persien, unterwarf die Meder 550 v.Chr., Kleinasien 546 v.Chr. und Babylon 539 v.Chr. Das Edikt des Kyros erlaubte den Exilanten 538 v.Chr. die Rückkehr (Jes 52:11–12; Esra 1:2–4). Eine erste Rückkehrwelle fand im gleichen Jahr unter Serubbabel statt (Esra 1:5). Dieser legte das Fundament für die Wiedererbauung des Tempels (Esra 1:5). Die schwierige wirtschaftliche Situation (Hag 1:5–11), aber auch die Indifferenz der Bevölkerung (Hag 1:4), verzögerten die Fertigstellung. Durch den Einsatz von Haggai und Sacharia wurde der Tempelbau 520 v.Chr. wieder aufgenommen und 515 v.Chr. konnte der Tempel eingeweiht werden (Es 6:15). Spannungen entstanden zwischen den Rückkehrern und den „Leuten des Landes" (Esra 4:4), womit wahrscheinlich die im Land Zurückgebliebenen gemeint waren, die fremde Elemente aufgenommen und eine starke politische Position bezogen hatten (Esra 4:5, Jes 57:1). Es gab zwei weitere Wellen von Rückkehrern, zuerst unter Esra (458) und dann unter Nehemia (445). Durch den Einfluss der drei Propheten Haggai, Sacharia und Maleachi richteten die Menschen ihren Blick wieder mehr auf die Zukunft und auf die verheißene Erlösung, den Wert der richtigen Religionsausübung und die Notwendigkeit, gerecht miteinander umzugehen.

1.1.3 Diskussion der Einheitlichkeit

In der Beschreibung der Literar-, Form- und Redaktionskritik wurden vorwiegend Argumente dargestellt, welche die Einheitlichkeit des Jesajabuches im Sinne eines einzelnen Verfassers ablehnen. Diese werden in der folgenden Diskussion nicht im Detail wiederholt; Verweise sollen genügen, während Gegenargumente vermehrt zum Zuge kommen. Auch Argumente aus der Literar- und Formkritik werden erneut aufgenommen, da sie auch heute noch die Diskussion prägen und die Arbeit mit den Methoden der Redaktionskritik ohne die vorangegangenen Epochen der Literar- und Formkritik nicht denkbar wäre.

1.1.3.1 Prophetie

Im Jesajabuch wird Bezug auf Tatsachen genommen, die sich deutlich später als das 8. Jh., die Lebenszeit des Jesaja, abspielten. Childs (2001:3–4) schreibt, dies könne nicht einfach dadurch erklärt werden, dass Jesaja in die Zukunft gesehen habe. Coogan (2006) bezeichnet den Fall Jerusalems (Jes 40–55), den Aufstieg zur Macht des persischen Königs Kyros (Jes 44:28; 45:1) und seinen Sieg über Babylon (Jes 48:14) als Ereignisse, die eindeutig nach ihrem Eintreffen beschrieben worden seien. Er fährt fort:

> This critical judgement does not allow for the possibility that the prophets could, under divine inspiration, know of events in the distant future … it should be said that the rise of a king in Persia who would conquer Babylon would have made little sense to an eighth-century Judean audience, for whom Persia was unknown and Babylon no threat at all. (Coogan 2006:331)

Bezeichnenderweise beginnt die Ablehnung der Einheitlichkeit des Buches nicht lange nach dem Beginn der geistesgeschichtlichen Aufklärung und der damit einhergehenden Ablehnung des Supranaturalismus. Eine weitere Anfrage an die Prophetien ist laut Motyer (1999:29–30): wenn es denn möglich gewesen sei, die Zukunft vorauszusagen – wozu sei es gut gewesen, das Volk auf einen Zeitpunkt weit in der Zukunft zu vertrösten?

Motyer selbst widerspricht diesem Argument: Es stelle eine Karikatur des Jesaja dar, wenn ihm unterstellt werde, er habe nur billig auf die Zukunft vertröstet. Motyer zitiert Wright, der schreibt: „Jede Prophetie ist früher als das, was sie voraussagt und aber zeitgleich oder später als das, was sie annimmt." Motyer kommentiert, dies bedeute einfach, dass jede Prophetie in ihrer Zeit verwurzelt sei – und genau das treffe auf Jesaja zu. Während seiner gesamten Lebens- und Wirkungszeit waren die politischen Kraftgleichgewichte sehr fragil und das Exil hing als Drohung über den Köpfen der Menschen.

Laut Archer (1987:221) sei es im gesamtbiblischen Kontext nicht ungewöhnlich, dass eine Prophetie mit einem konkreten Namen versehen werde. Als Beispiele nennt er den Propheten aus Juda, der den Namen König Josias vorausgesagt hatte – drei Jahrhunderte bevor Josia das goldene Kalb und den Götzentempel zerstörte, den Jerobeam errichtet hatte (1 Kön 13:2); Micha nennt Bethlehem als den Geburtsort des kommenden Messias sieben Jahrhunderte vor dem Ereignis (Mi 5:2). Im Neuen Testament wird erzählt, dass Saulus Hananias in einer Vision sah und vor der eigentlichen Begegnung seinen Namen erfuhr (Apg 9:12). Die Nennung des Namens „Kyros" könne auch nicht als spätere Einfügung erklärt werden, weil damit die parallele Struktur von Jesaja 44:26–28 zerstört werde.

Das gottlose Leben des Volkes unter König Manasse verlangte eine Reaktion Gottes. Die Deportation Judas könnte laut Archer (1987:223–224) lediglich als Schicksalsschlag gedeutet werden, wie er auch anderen Völkern widerfuhr. Auch wenn die Deportation als Strafe Gottes angesehen werde, hebe das Israel und seinen Gott noch nicht aus den anderen Völkern hervor, denn auch heidnische Religionsphilosophen interpretierten solche Ereignisse ähnlich: die babylonische Chronik erklärt die Unterwerfung Babylons durch Kyros mit dem Ärger Marduks über die Stadt, und König Mescha von Moab begründet die Unterwerfung Moabs durch Israel mit dem Zorn Kemoschs auf seine Anhänger. Erst die exakte Prophetie bezeugt Gottes Herrschaft über die geschichtlichen Ereignisse: Jahwe unterscheidet sich von allen anderen Göttern, denn er sagt in seiner Souveränität und Gerechtigkeit das Strafgericht und die folgende Erlösung lange Zeit vor ihrem tatsächlichen Eintreten voraus.

Der Umgang mit Prophetie spiegelt das Gottesbild des Exegeten wider; Prophetie kann letztlich nicht belegt oder widerlegt werden. Bei der Einstellung zur Prophetie handelt es sich um eine grundsätzliche Annahme, welche die

1.1 Einleitungsfragen

Bearbeitung aller folgenden Punkte beeinflusst. Wer vorausschauende Prophetie für unmöglich hält, für den ist die Abfassung des gesamten Jesajabuches durch den Propheten Jesaja im 8. Jh. v.Chr. unmöglich. Der Umkehrschluss darf aber nicht gezogen werden: Auch wer vorausschauende Prophetie für denkbar befindet, muss nicht zwingend von der Abfassung durch Jesaja alleine überzeugt sein.

1.1.3.2 Theologie

Exegeten stellen eine unterschiedliche Theologie sowohl innerhalb der Teile Jesaja I, II und III, wie auch in der Gegenüberstellung derselben, fest. Eißfeldt[4] unterscheidet in Jesaja I sehr differenziert zwischen echten und unechten Jesajaworten. Die Androhungen von Strafe und Gericht spricht er meist Jesaja selbst zu, während Worte des Heils und der Gnade später ergänzt worden seien. Gemäß Brueggemann (2003:164) hebt sich innerhalb von Jesaja I besonders Jesaja 24–27 hervor: Dieser Teil werde im Allgemeinen als die jüngste Tradierung angesehen, enthalte keine Hinweise auf einen historischen Kontext und eine mögliche Datierung. Hier finden sich allumfassende Ansprüche Jahwes bezüglich seiner Souveränität in Gericht und Gnade.

Fohrer ist der Meinung, die „eigenartige theologische Gedankenwelt" in Jesaja II weiche von Jesaja I völlig ab. Gemäß Brueggemann bewegt sich Jesaja II mehr in Richtung Monotheismus und laut Archer (1987:237–238) sagen Kritiker, Jesaja II betone die Souveränität Gottes eingehender als Jesaja I, außerdem sei der leidende Gottesknecht ein Thema, das lediglich in Jesaja II vorkomme.

Laut Koole (1997:20) ist auch der theologische Schwerpunkt von Jesaja II und III unterschiedlich: Jesaja III handle von „Gesetz und Gerechtigkeit", es ermutige nicht nur im Hinblick auf das zukünftige Heil, von Gott geschenkt, sondern betone auch die Verantwortung des Menschen. Die beiden Teile zitierten sich ständig gegenseitig, wobei der zitierte Text im Vergleich zum ursprünglichen jeweils eine etwas geänderte theologische Bedeutung annehme.

Archer vertritt die Meinung, die Verschiebung des theologischen Schwerpunktes sei durch die Situation unter dem gottlosen König Manasse ausreichend erklärbar. Jede in Jesaja II verkündete Lehre finde sich auch in Jesaja I. Die Betonung der Souveränität Jahwes sei besonders unter den abgöttischen Praktiken des Manasse nötig gewesen. Die Unabwendbarkeit des Gerichts bringe die Lehre der stellvertretenden Sühne mit sich, ohne die es keine Hoffnung auf ein geistliches Überleben geben könne, deshalb die Lehre vom leidenden Gottesknecht.[5] Motyer (1999:32f.) führt aus, dass alle sechs theologischen Themen aus Kapitel 1–39 auch in Kapitel 40–55 wieder erscheinen: Gott als Herr der Geschichte (Jes 10:5–15), Gottes Souveränität über Götzen (Jes 2:12–20), der Rest (Jes 8:11–20), die Versöhnung zwischen Gott und Sünder durch ein Sühnopfer (Jes 6:7), die Wiederherstellung Zions (Jes 1:26–27) und der davidische Messias (Jes 9:1–7). Die ersten drei Themen

---

4 Anmerkung der Herausgeber: Eine ausführlichere Diskussion dieser Fragen findet sich in den Kapiteln über Formkritik und Redaktionskritik in Simone Becks theologischer Masterarbeit.

5 Es gibt sowohl von konservativer als auch von kritischer Seite verschiedene Theorien, wen der Gottesknecht verkörpert. Darauf soll hier nicht eingegangen werden.

werden in Jesaja 40–48 behandelt; Jesaja 53:1–12 sei die Erfüllung von Jesaja 6:6–7 (Versöhnung durch ein Sühneopfer); Jerusalem sei ein zentraler Gedanke durch das ganze weitere Buch hinweg; und Jesaja 55:3–4 enthalte die Enthüllung des Knechtes innerhalb des davidischen Bundes. Walvoord und Zuck (1998:7) denken, die Annahme, Jesaja 40–55 sei während oder nach der Zeit des Kyros geschrieben, beraube diesen Teil des Buches seines theologischen Wertes und mache es beinahe bedeutungslos.

Motyer (1999:33) zeichnet ein Bild des Jesaja zur Zeit König Manasses in Jerusalem: Jesaja habe, aufgezeichnet in Kapitel 1–39, Hoffnung und Herrlichkeit gepredigt (Jes 1:26–27; 4:4–6), doch auch Verlust und Katastrophe (Jes 5:24–30; 7:17–25). Nun müsse er sich fragen lassen, wie diese beiden Richtungen miteinander zu vereinbaren seien, besonders nach der klaren Ankündigung des Exils gegenüber König Hiskia (Jes 39:3–7). Es liege nun nahe, dass die Kapitel 40–55 die Antwort auf diese Frage darstellten. Alles was er sage, sei relevant für seine Zeitgenossen, ohne einen spezifischen Zeitrahmen vorzugeben. Es sei wichtig zu sehen, dass in Jesajas Vision nicht der Knecht, sondern Kyros das Volk zurückbringe: Die Erlösung sei politisch, nicht geistlich. Auch das Volk, das zurückkommt sei noch immer gottlos und ohne Frieden mit Gott (Jes 48:22). Deshalb geschehe die Darstellung der Zurückgekommenen (Jes 56–66) noch mit Worten ähnlich denen in der Zeit vor dem Exil. Auch die Führung des Volkes habe sich nicht maßgeblich geändert. Jesajas vorexilische Botschaften passten auch zu dem Volk nach dem Exil.

Unterschiedliche theologische Schwerpunkte können Einheitlichkeit letztendlich weder beweisen noch widerlegen: Ein und derselbe Verfasser kann über verschiedene Themen schreiben, wie auch eigene Themen weiterentwickeln, besonders in sich wandelnden Zeiten; genauso kann ein zweiter Verfasser die theologischen Gedanken eines vorhergehenden aufnehmen und weiterentwickeln. Lediglich klare Widersprüche wären ein eindeutiger Hinweis auf unterschiedliche Verfasser. Diese liegen nicht vor.

1.1.3.3 Historischer und lokaler Hintergrund

Brueggemann (2003:164–165) entdeckt verschiedene historische Hintergründe innerhalb von Jesaja I: Er ordnet die Weissagungen gegen die Völker (Jes 13–23) generell einer späteren Zeit zu als der des historischen Propheten. Den Abschnitt gegen Babylon (Jes 13–14) hält er für den wichtigsten; Babylon habe aber im 8. Jh. v.Chr. nicht am Horizont des Propheten Jesaja sein können. Die Kapitel bildeten eine Parallele zu einem späteren Teil des Buches. Genauso versteht er die Vorhersage der Wiederherstellung Jerusalems in Jesaja 34–35 als eine Parallele zur Freude über die Heimkehr Israels in Jesaja II. Es bestehe auch eine Verbindung zwischen den Ereignissen von 701 und denen von 587: Jesaja habe gezeigt, dass die Erlösung Judas 701 von den Assyrern ein Geschenk Jahwes gewesen sei, nun strahle das Vertrauen des Propheten auf die schwierigere Situation im Jahre 587 aus. Des Weiteren geht Brueggemann (2003:167–168) von einer langen historischen Zäsur aus zwischen Jesaja 39:5–8, das die Deportation nach Babylon erwarte, und Jesaja 40:1–11, das die Rückkehr von Babylon erhoffe.

Die historische Situation war laut Coogan (2006:408) zur Zeit des Jesaja I, als Assyrien der Hauptfeind gewesen war, völlig anders als zur Zeit des Jesaja II, als die Bedrohung von Babylon ausging.

1.1 Einleitungsfragen

Babylon habe Assyrien im späten 7. Jh. v.Chr. als dominierende Macht im Nahen Osten abgelöst. Jesaja II enthält gemäß Fohrer und Sellin (1979:410) Angaben, die auf eine Abfassung während der Exilszeit schließen lassen: Jerusalem und der Tempel seien zerstört (Jes 44:26–28), das Volk weile in Babylon (Jes 43:14), Babylon werde mit dem Untergang bedroht (Jes 48:14) und Kyros sei auf dem Siegeszug (Jes 45:1–3).

Den historischen Hintergrund von Jesaja III sieht Brueggemann (2003:170) in der Zeit nach der Rückkehr, als die Gemeinschaft Fragen des sozialen Lebens und der religiösen Praxis bearbeiten musste. So datiert er den Teil zwischen den Bau des zweiten Tempels (520–516), also der Zeit Haggais und Sacharjas einerseits und der Zeit Esras und Nehemias (nach 450) andererseits. Laut Coogan ist zur Zeit des Jesaja III der Tempel wieder erbaut (Jes 56:7) oder zumindest in Arbeit (Jes 66:1) und es wurde dort angebetet (Jes 66:3–4). Der Hintergrund sei also Juda, nicht Babylon. Koole (1997:4) macht darauf aufmerksam, dass in Jesaja III keine Rede von den Mischehen sei; das mache eine Datierung in die postexilische Zeit schwierig. Er hält die Parallelen zwischen Nehemia 10:31, 13:15–22 und Jesaja 56:2ff, 66:23 (die Einhaltung des Sabbats), zwischen Esra 7:27 und Jesaja 60:7, 9, 13 (die Herrlichkeit des Tempels) und zwischen Sacharja 7 und Jesaja 58 (das Fasten) nicht für ausreichend, um ein postexilisches Entstehen zu beweisen. Die Ähnlichkeiten resultieren gemäß Koole aus einer postexilischen Redaktion des Jesaja-Materials. Motyer (1999:31–32) relativiert die Annahme, dass Jesaja II in Babylon entstanden sein müsse. Die Orientierung richte sich zwar nach Babylon aus (43:14; 47:1; 48:14 und 20), doch das setze keinen babylonischen Ursprung und Wohnort des Propheten voraus. Aussagen über Babylon sind allgemein gehalten, sie sind nicht so detailliert, wie es von einem Augenzeugen zu erwarten wäre. Dagegen ist der palästinensische Hintergrund noch präsent: die Herstellung eines Götzen zum Götzendienst (46:14) war in Babylon nicht möglich. Die Bäume sind die von Palästina, die Öle die von Westasien (41:19; 55:13). Die Landschaft und das Klima setzen einen westlichen Hintergrund voraus: es ist von Bergen, Wäldern, Seen, Schnee und Regen die Rede – nicht von Bewässerung. Die Bäume, die erwähnt werden, sind Zedern, Kiefern, Eichen und Fichten (Jes 41:19; 44:14), nämlich die Bäume Palästinas.

Harrison (1970:778) weist darauf hin, dass auch in Jesaja II die Festung Zion und die Städte von Juda noch existieren (Jes 40:9; 62:6) und in Jesaja III werden die Stadtmauern in einem Kontext des Wohlstandes beschrieben (Jes 62:6). Beides lässt sich nicht mit der Zeit des Exils oder kurz danach vereinbaren. Andererseits betrachtet der Prophet die Gefangenschaft vorrausschauend als eine gegenwärtige Tatsache bereits in Jesaja 1:7–9, 5:13 und 14:1–4. Durch die spezifische Verurteilung des Götzendienstes in Jesaja II und III wird deutlich, dass dies ein gegenwärtiges Problem gewesen sein muss. Es handelt sich um den heidnischen Kult auf den Opferhöhen (Jes 57:7; 65:2–4), laut Archer (1987:231) aber nicht um Opferkult in Babylon, das Flachland ist. Götzendienst wurde besonders unter König Manasse praktiziert. Die Juden, die zwischen 536 und 450 wieder ins Land zurückkehrten, brachten keinen Götzendienst mit sich. Dies zeigen die nachexilischen Propheten (Haggai, Sacharja und Maleachi) und Geschichtsschreiber (Esra und Nehemia). Das Volk sündigte zwar noch immer gegen seinen Gott, doch der Götzendienst und das Götzenopfer der vorexilischen Zeit waren ausgestorben. Einen wirklichen Versuch, den Götzendienst in Israel wieder einzuführen, machte erste Antiochus Epiphanes im 2. Jh. v.Chr. Für

Webb (1996:37) beantwortet sich die Frage, warum Jesaja II und III im Vergleich zu Jesaja I auffallend wenig historische Einzelheiten beinhalten (mit Ausnahme der Nennung von Kyros), mit der Annahme, dass Jesaja von einer zukünftigen Zeit spreche, die ihm nur in groben Strichen gezeigt worden sei.

1.1.3.4 Zusammenführung

Laut Eißfeldt sei es denkbar, dass „40–55 und 56–66 als anonyme Prophetien hinter Jes 1–39 auf derselben Buchrolle zu stehen gekommen und dass dann allmählich diese anonymen Teile dem zuletzt genannten Propheten, also Jesaja, zugeschrieben worden sind".

Wahrscheinlicher aber sei die Annahme, dass die drei Teile vereint worden seien, „weil stilistische und sachliche Ähnlichkeiten die Herleitung von demselben Verfasser nahe legten". Das Pathos heroischen Gottvertrauens habe Deuterojesaja mit Jesaja gemeinsam, bis in den Sprachgebrauch hinein sei dies festzustellen. Laut Fohrer und Sellin (1979:411) wurden die Schriften aufgrund der gleichen eschatologischen Grundhaltung zusammengefügt. Außerdem habe Jesaja später als der Prophet schlechthin gegolten, so sei der Anschluss Deuterojesajas an Jesaja einer offiziellen Anerkennung gleichgekommen. Laut Eißfeldt seien die Kapitel 36–39 aus dem Wunsch heraus ergänzt worden, alles über Jesaja in einem Buch zu haben. Brueggemann betont:

> The artistic achievement of the final form of the text is not only literary, however, for the twinning of chapters 1–39 and chapter 40–55 constitutes a core Isaianic assertion concerning inescapable judgment reliably followed by generous restoration. Thus the two themes together constitute both Israel's lived memory and Israel's defining theological conviction. The shape of the book of Isaiah ... is a theological shaping. (Brueggemann 2003:170)

Heute wird laut Beuken (2003:28) allgemein nicht mehr davon ausgegangen, die drei Teile seien isoliert voneinander entstanden. Jeder Teil habe für sich einen komplizierten Entwicklungsprozess mitgemacht, und man müsse zudem mit einem nicht weniger bedeutsamen Redaktionsprozess rechnen, der die Teile aufeinander abgestimmt habe. Zenger (1995:315) stellt sich diesen von Anfang an mit einem engen Anschluss von Jesaja 40ff. an Jesaja 1–39 in der Entstehungsphase vor. Jesaja II und III haben nie selbständig bestanden, sondern seien als Fortschreibung von Jesaja I entstanden, das sie voraussetzen.

Die gleichen Argumente, die für die Zusammenführung angeführt werden, können auch für eine einheitliche Entstehung angeführt werden. Sie wirken hier konstruiert.

1.1.3.5 Fazit

Die Manuskripte des Jesajabuches sind zuerst ein historisches Dokument, das mit seinem inneren Zeugnis und in seiner vorliegenden Form akzeptiert werden muss, bis zwingende Argumente gegen seine Einheitlichkeit und Authentizität vorgelegt werden. Selbst Zenger (1995:314) räumt ein, dass die Beweislast bei dem liege, der Texte dem Propheten abspreche. Weder die Theologie, noch der Stil, noch die Themen von Jesaja I, II und III oder innerhalb derselben sind so unterschiedlich oder gar widersprüchlich, dass verschiedene

1.1 Einleitungsfragen

Autoren angenommen werden müssten. Es spricht nichts gegen Palästina als historischen Hintergrund und nichts gegen eine vorexilische historische Situation des gesamten Buches. Es ist widersprüchlich, dass dieselben Themen, die zuvor für eine Teilung des Werkes herhalten mussten, nämlich Stil, Theologie und historischer Hintergrund im Jesajabuch, nun als Gründe für die Zusammenführung der Teile auf derselben Rolle gelten. Das Arrangement des historischen Einschubes in der Gesamtkomposition und der Zeitraum, der für die Verbreitung eines Buches bis zu seiner allgemeinen Anerkennung als autoritativ nötig ist, sprechen für eine frühe Fertigstellung des Gesamtwerkes, nämlich vor dem Exil. Die Unwahrscheinlichkeit der Anonymität eines Deutero- und Tritojesajas und die Verweise im Neuen Testament auf Jesaja weisen auf die Abfassung des ganzen Buches durch den Propheten Jesaja selbst hin. Deshalb ist es folgerichtig, den Propheten Jesaja aus dem 8. Jh. v. Chr. als alleinigen Verfasser des Jesajabuches anzunehmen. Bedenklich scheint auch, dass die kritische Richtung seit über zwei Jahrhunderten intensiver Jesaja-Forschung nicht annähernd zu einem einheitlichen Ergebnis bezüglich der Entstehung des Jesajabuches gekommen ist. Wichtig ist ein erneuter Blick auf das Thema „Prophetie": Dreytza schreibt folgendes bezüglich alttestamentlicher Geschichtsberichte, doch derselbe Grundsatz gilt auch für die Prophetie:

> Es gibt letzte philosophische und theologische Voraussetzungen, die ein Historiker mitbringt, wenn er an die Geschichten des AT herangeht. Diese sind in seinem Weltbild, im Glauben, in weltanschaulichen Prämissen u.a.m. verwurzelt. Sie bestimmen das Urteil ‚historisch möglich', ‚historisch unwahrscheinlich' usw. mit. Es gehört zur Wissenschaftlichkeit, sich über diese letzten Voraussetzungen Rechenschaft zu geben. Es wäre kurzsichtig, eine eingeschränkte, die Analogie verabsolutierende Wirklichkeitssicht mit der Wissenschaft zu verwechseln. Auch ein Historiker muss mit unableitbarem und analogielosem Geschehen rechnen. (Dreytza, Hilbrands, and Schmid 2002:129)

Das trifft auch in Bezug auf die Prophetie zu. So ist J.A. Alexander zuzustimmen, der schreibt:

> Wer einen bestimmten Jesaja-Abschnitt ablehnt, weil er konkrete Vorhersagen enthält über zukünftige Ereignisse, die ein Mensch normalerweise nicht vorhersagen kann, weil sie zu weit in der Zukunft liegen, wird seine Ablehnung mit bestimmten Beweisen begründen wollen, die auf Sprache, Stil und Idiom eines Abschnittes, seinen historischen oder archäologischen Anhaltspunkten, seinem rhetorischen Charakter, seiner moralischen Färbung oder auf seiner religiösen Einstellung beruhen. Auf die Entdeckung und Darstellung solcher Beweise muss die zuvor aufgestellte Behauptung, die er zu begründen suchte, zwangsläufig einen die Tatsachen entstellenden Einfluss haben. (zitiert in Archer 1987:220)

1.2 Abgrenzung der Perikope

1.2.1 Inhaltliche Abgrenzung

1.2.1.1 Abgrenzung nach vorne

Die vorangehende Perikope (Jes 40:1–11) leitet Jesaja II ein; in ihrem Mittelpunkt steht die tröstende und zuwendende Seite des Charakters Gottes. Sie endet mit der Ankündigung seiner Ankunft, er wird sein Volk weiden wie ein Hirte seine Herde. In der zu besprechenden Perikope wird Gottes Charakter unter einem anderen Aspekt dargestellt: Gott ist der unfassbar und unvergleichlich Große und Majestätische, in Bezug auf die Schöpfung und auf den Menschen. Er ist ein Gott, der sich zwar denen zuwendet, die auf ihn hoffen, der aufgrund seiner Größe und Überlegenheit aber auch fern scheint. Eine andere Seite des Charakters Gottes als in der vorangehenden Perikope steht im Mittelpunkt. Die Perikope ist vor Vers 12 nach vorne abgegrenzt.

1.2.1.2 Abgrenzung nach hinten

Die vorliegende Perikope stellt Gott als den unendlich Großen dar; sie endet damit, dass er seine Kraft weitergibt. Der nachfolgende Vers leitet durch den Wechsel der Angeredeten eine neue Perikope ein: in 40:31 sind es die auf Gott Hoffenden, in 41:1 die Inseln und Völker, die Gott mit seinem Schwert zerstört. Die strafende und vergeltende Seite des Charakters Gottes ist sichtbar.

1.2.2 Grammatische Abgrenzung

1.2.2.1 Abgrenzung nach vorne

Die Perikope beginnt mit dem Fragewort מִי; es bezieht sich auf vier Fragen mit ihren Verben im Perfekt. Im letzten Vers der vorangehenden Perikope steht eine Reihe von Aussagen, die sich alle auf die Zukunft beziehen, sie stehen im Imperfekt. In Vers 12 beginnt ein neuer Gedankengang.

1.2.2.2 Abgrenzung nach hinten

In den letzten drei Versen der Perikope stehen 12 Verben im Imperfekt; sie beschreiben, wie Gott Kraft verleiht und welche Auswirkungen das hat. Die nachfolgende Perikope beginnt mit dem Wort הַחֲרִישׁוּ „sei ruhig", ein Imperativ an die Völker. Der Adressat wechselt von Juda auf seine Nachbarn. Die Reihe der Versprechen ist zum Ende gekommen, ein neuer Gedankengang beginnt.

1.2.3 Einheit der Perikope

Die meisten Exegeten sehen die Perikope als eine in sich geschlossene Einheit. Das liegt im Verhältnis der einzelnen Teile zueinander begründet. Die einleitenden rhetorischen Fragen kommen in den Versen 27 bis 31 zu ihrem Ziel; ihre Bedeutung ist erst verständlich, wenn man sie von der Antwort am Ende der Perikope her versteht. Dem in Vers 27 aufgeworfenen Vorwurf, dass

Gott nicht eingreife, liegt die Frage zugrunde, ob Gott nicht helfen kann oder nicht helfen will. Ersteres wird in den Versen 12–17 (im Blick auf die Natur und die Völker), 18–24 (im Blick auf die Machthaber) und 25–26 (im Blick auf die Gestirne) widerlegt; zweiteres wird in den Versen 28–31 (im Blick auf die Kraft, die er schenkt) widerlegt. Auch die Gliederung zeigt, dass die Perikope eine Einheit mit einem logisch aufgebauten Gedankengang ist.[6]

1.3 Kontext

1.3.1 Enger Kontext

1.3.1.1 Vorangehender und nachfolgender Kontext

Jesaja 40:1–11	Drei Stimmen des Trostes
Jesaja 40:12–31	Trost aus Gottes Charakter
12–24	weil er der Schöpfer ist
25–31	weil er sein Volk nicht vergisst
Jesaja 41:1–7	Trost aus der Geschichte
1–4	weil er die Herrscher beherrscht
5–7	weil er den Götzendienst beherrscht
Jesaja 41:8–20	Drei Bilder des Trostes

1.3.2 Weiter Kontext

Jesaja 40–55	Gott tröstet sein Volk

1.3.2.1 Vorangehender Kontext

Jesaja 40:1–11	Gott tröstet sein Volk

1.3.2.2 Nachfolgender Kontext

Jesaja 41:1–29	Gott behütet und sorgt für sein Volk
Jesaja 42:1–9	Gott sendet seinen Knecht in die Welt
Jesaja 42:10–25	Gott befreit sein Volk
Jesaja 43:1–13	Gott erlöst sein Volk, das zeugt für ihn
Jesaja 43:14–28	Gott vergibt seinem Volk
Jesaja 44:1–23	Gott ist erhaben über die Götzen
Jesaja 44:24–45:8	Gott macht Kyros zu seinem Werkzeug
Jesaja 45:9–13	Gott ist seinen Geschöpfen keine Rechenschaft schuldig
Jesaja 45:14–25	Alle Welt soll sich Gott zuwenden
Jesaja 46:1–13	Gott ist mit niemandem zu vergleichen

---

6 Anmerkung der Herausgeber: Ausführlichere Diskussionen (z.B. zur Gliederung der Perikope oder Wortstudien zu Schlüsselbegriffen der Perikope) finden sich in Simone Becks Masterarbeit, konnten aber in diesem Kapitel nicht berücksichtigt werden.

Jesaja 47:1–15	Gottes Gericht über Babylon
Jesaja 48:1–11	Gott nimmt Israel an, obwohl es sich von ihm abwendet
Jesaja 48:12–22	Gott belohnt die Gehorsamen
Jesaja 49:1–6	Gott verherrlicht sich durch seinen Knecht
Jesaja 49:7–26	Gott vergisst sein Volk nicht
Jesaja 50:1–3	Gott und sein Volk sind durch Sünde getrennt
Jesaja 50:4–11	Gott steht seinem Knecht bei im Leiden
Jesaja 51:1–8	Gottes Gerechtigkeit bleibt ewig
Jesaja 51:9–16	Gott tröstet und befreit sein Volk
Jesaja 51:17–52:6	Gott kümmert sich um sein erniedrigtes Volk
Jesaja 52:7–12	Gottes erlöst sein Volk, das ist Grund zum Jubel
Jesaja 52:13–53:12	Gottes Knecht leidet stellvertretend
Jesaja 54:1–17	Gott verspricht seinem Volk die Beständigkeit seiner Gnade
Jesaja 55:1–13	*Bündelung der Themen*: Einladung zu Gottes ewigem Bund

1.3.2.3 Anmerkung

Die Perikope steht fast am Anfang von Jesaja II. Dieser Teil beschreibt die liebende und fürsorgliche Seite von Gottes Charakter facettenreich. Der Schwerpunkt liegt auf dem Trost für Israel nach der verdientermaßen empfangenen Strafe. Gott in seiner Souveränität erlöst sein Volk, er vergibt ihm und befreit es. Gott ist unvergleichlich, er ist erhaben über die Götter und benutzt die weltlichen Machthaber als seine Werkzeuge. Deshalb müssen sich alle Völker ihm zuwenden. Gott vergibt seinem Volk und heilt es von ihrer Sünde durch seinen Knecht. Durch ihn verspricht er die Beständigkeit seiner Gnade und seinen ewigen Bund. Innerhalb dieses Themenkomplexes spielt die vorliegende Perikope eine zentrale Rolle: Gott stellt sich seinem Volk erneut vor; mit seinem ganzen Wesen und Sein, das er in der Perikope darstellt, bürgt er für die Wahrheit und Beständigkeit aller anschließend folgenden Verheißungen. Gott demonstriert seinen Charakter bildhaft, nämlich seine Größe und Majestät, die erhaben ist über die Schöpfung, über die Götter, über die Machthaber der Welt, über das Universum. Gott stärkt das Vertrauen seines Volkes, indem er zeigt, wie groß und mächtig ihr Gott ist, der sie befreien und trösten wird, der sich ihnen persönlich zuwendet. Die Größe und Majestät Gottes ist Garant dafür, dass er die Macht hat, seine Verheißungen tatsächlich auszuführen.

1.3.3 Kontext im Buch Jesaja

1.3.3.1 Vorangehender Kontext

Jesaja 1–39: Gottes Gericht
- Jesaja 1–5 Gericht über Juda
- Jesaja 6–9 Jesajas Wirken in der Anfangszeit
- Jesaja 10–12 Ein Rest wird gerettet
- Jesaja 13–25 Gericht über die Völker und die Welt
- Jesaja 25–27 Dank für die Erlösung
- Jesaja 28–35 Gottes Handeln mit Israel, Ägypten und Assyrien
- Jesaja 36–39 Geschichtlicher Bericht

Jesaja 40–55: Gottes Trost für sein Volk
- Jesaja 40:1–11 Gott tröstet sein Volk

1.3.3.2 Nachfolgender Kontext

- Jesaja 40–55 Gottes Trost für sein Volk
- Jesaja 56–66 Das kommende Heil

1.3.4 Arbeitsübersetzung im Überblick

Vers 12
Wer misst das Wasser mit seiner hohlen Hand und bestimmt mit seiner Spanne das Maß des Himmels und erfasst den Staub der Erde in einem Messbecher und wiegt die Berge mit einer Waage und die Hügel mit zwei Waagschalen?

Vers 13
Wer bestimmt Jahwes Geist und ist sein Ratgeber, der ihn belehrt?

Vers 14
Mit wem berät er sich und wer belehrt ihn und lehrt ihn den Pfad des Rechts und lehrt ihn Wissen und belehrt ihn über den Weg der vollen Einsicht?

Vers 15
Siehe, die Völker sind wie ein Tropfen aus dem Schöpfeimer und wie Staub auf zwei Waagschalen werden sie geachtet. Siehe, er hebt die fernen Länder auf wie Staub.

Vers 16
Und der Libanon ist nicht genug um ein Feuer anzuzünden und seine Tiere genügen nicht als Brandopfer.

Vers 17
Alle Völker sind vor ihm wie nichts, sie werden für nichtig und nichts geachtet vor ihm.

Vers 18
Und mit wem wollt ihr Gott vergleichen? Und mit welchem Abbild wollt ihr ihn gleichstellen?

Vers 19
Das Gottesbild – der Handwerker gießt es und der Goldschmied überzieht es mit Gold und stattet es mit silbernen Ketten aus.

Vers 20
Der Arme wählt einen Baum, der nicht verfault, als Beitrag. Er sucht sich einen weisen Handwerker, um das Gottesbild aufzustellen, dass es nicht wackelt.

Vers 21
Wisst ihr nicht? Hört ihr nicht? Hat er es euch nicht von Anfang an verkündigt? Habt ihr es nicht verstanden von der Gründung der Erde?

Vers 22
Er thront über dem Kreis der Erde und ihre Bewohner sind wie Heuschrecken. Er spannt den Himmel aus wie feinen Stoff und er breitet ihn aus wie ein Zelt, um zu wohnen.

Vers 23
Er macht die Würdenträger zu nichts und er macht die Richter der Erde zu nichts.

Vers 24
Ja, sie werden nicht gepflanzt. Ja, sie werden nicht gesät. Ja, ihr Schoßreis ist nicht in der Erde verwurzelt. Er bläst auch noch über sie und sie werden trocken und der Sturm trägt sie fort wie ein Strohhalm.

Vers 25
Und mit wem vergleicht ihr mich und (wem) bin ich gleich?, sagt der Heilige.

Vers 26
Hebt eure Augen nach oben und seht: Wer hat dies geschaffen? Er führt das Heer des Himmels abgezählt heraus. Er ruft sie alle beim Namen. Wegen seiner großen Allgewalt und seiner starken Kraft fehlt keiner.

Vers 27
Warum sagst du, Jakob, und sprichst du, Israel: „Mein Weg ist vor Jahwe verborgen und mein Recht entzieht sich meinem Gott"?

Vers 28
Weißt du nicht? Hast du auch nicht gehört? Gott ist ewig. Jahwe hat die Enden der Erde erschaffen. Er wird nicht müde. Und er wird nicht matt. Seine Einsicht ist unerforschlich.

Vers 29
Er gibt den Müden Kraft und er vermehrt die Stärke derer, die ohne Kraft sind.

Vers 30
Und Knaben werden müde und matt und junge Männer straucheln ganz sicher.

Vers 31
Und die, die auf Jahwe harren, gewinnen neue Kraft. Sie fliegen auf mit Flügeln wie Adler. Sie laufen und werden nicht matt. Sie gehen und werden nicht müde.

1.4 Analyse der Poesie in Jesaja 40:12–31

1.4.1 Parallelismus in Jesaja 40:12–31

Es finden sich zahlreiche Bikola (Parallelismus mit zwei Stichoi), aber auch Trikola (Parallelismus mit drei Stichoi), Tetrakola (Parallelismus mit vier Stichoi) und Pentakola (Parallelismus mit fünf Stichoi). Es handelt sich immer um semantischen Parallelismus, teilweise unterstützt durch phonologische Merkmale und Wortketten, die sich auch über mehrere Parallelismen erstrecken. Grammatisch sind die Parallelismen entweder symmetrisch oder chiastisch angeordnet. Im nächsten Punkt erscheinen die Parallelismen tabellarisch übersichtlich dargestellt.[7]

1.4.2 Metrum oder Rhythmus in Jesaja 40:12–31

Hier soll die Frage der Existenz von Metrum bzw. von rhytmischen Mustern in der Perikope geklärt werden. Die folgenden Zahlen geben die betonten Silben innerhalb eines Stiches an. Sie wurden gemäß des Ley-Sievers-Budde-Akzentsystems gezählt. Bestand Spielraum für Interpretation, wurde er jeweils so genutzt, dass sich eine größere Regelmäßigkeit ergab.

---

[7] Siehe auch Petersen and Richards (1992:50, 60); Dreytza, Hilbrands, and Schmid (2002:71–72); hier sei auf seine übersichtliche Auflistung der Stilfiguren in der hebräischen Poesie hingewiesen.

I   V. 12: 3-3-3-3-2
    V. 13: 3-3
    V. 14: 2-1-2-2-3
    V. 15: 3-3; 4
    V. 16: 3-3
    V. 17: 3-3
II V. 18: 3-3
    V. 19: Prosa
    V. 20: Prosa
III V. 21: 2-2-4-3
    V. 22: 3-2-3-3
    V. 23: 3-3
    V. 24: 2-2-4; Prosa
IV V. 25: 2-1; Prosa
    V. 26: Prosa
V   V. 27: 3-2; 3-3
    V. 28: 2-2; 2-2; 1-1; 3
    V. 29: 3-3
    V. 30: 3-3
    V. 31: 3-3-3-3

Ein Metrum, das über 97% Regelmäßigkeit (gemäß Vance) aufwiese, ist eindeutig nicht vorhanden. Es kann auch nur sehr bedingt von Rhythmus gesprochen werden. Immer wieder erscheinen kurze rhythmische Muster, die längsten erstrecken sich über die Verse 16–18 und 29–31.

1.4.3 Stil

In der Perikope findet sich ein Reichtum an Stilfiguren. Folgende wurden in der vorliegenden Perikope verwendet:

Anthropomorphismus
Die Stilfigur verwendet menschliche Attribute in der Rede über Gott. Gemäß Schirrmacher (1997:16) wird Gottes Wollen und Empfinden mit Hilfe für Menschen gebräuchlicher Ausdrücke beschrieben. Laut Caird (1980:174) ist der Anthropomorphismus die gebräuchlichste Form des Vergleichs, da der menschliche Körper, seine Sinne, Gefühle und Gedanken dem Menschen am nächsten seien; es sei ein kognitives Prinzip, vom Bekannten auf das Unbekannte zu schließen. Zudem enthielten Anthropomorphismen eine lebhafte Aussagekraft und appellierten stark an die menschliche Vorstellungskraft. Da der Mensch als Ebenbild Gottes geschaffen wurde, ist es folgerichtig, Attribute des Menschen als Annäherung und Umschreibung für den unbeschreibbaren Gott zu verwenden, jedoch ohne Implikation der menschlichen Begrenzungen. Ein Anthropomorphismus wird dreimal in Vers 22 und zweimal in Vers 26 gebraucht.

Hypokatastasis
Diese Stilfigur drückt laut Bulliger (2003:744) eine implizierte Ähnlichkeit oder Repräsentation aus ohne ausdrückliche Nennung des Vergleichspunktes.

1.4 Analyse der Poesie in Jesaja 40:12–31

Deshalb fordere diese Stilfigur die Aufmerksamkeit des Lesers mehr als andere Stilfiguren heraus, involviere ihn stark und habe eine intensive Aussagekraft. Die Hypokatastasis wird zweimal (mit jeweils drei Verben) in Vers 24 verwendet und einmal (auch mit drei Verben) in Vers 31.

Merismus
Laut Bühlmann und Scherer (1994:84) beschreibt diese Stilfigur die Gesamtheit eines Sachverhaltes durch zwei oder mehrere ihrer wesentlichen, oft polaren Teile. Ein Merismus wird in Vers 12 verwendet.

Metonymie und Antonymie
Diese Stilfigur besteht laut Bulliger (2003:538–539), wenn ein Substantiv durch ein anderes ersetzt wird, mit dem es in einer besonderen Beziehung steht. Am gebräuchlichsten sind die Metonymie der Ursache (die Ursache steht für die Auswirkung), der Auswirkung (die Auswirkung steht für die Ursache), des Subjekts (das Subjekt steht für das Objekt, z.B. der Besitzer für den Besitz) und des Adjunkts (das Objekt steht für das Subjekt, z.B. der Besitz für den Besitzer). Die Stilfigur lädt den Leser zum Nachdenken ein, denn er muss die Beziehung der Metonymie nachvollziehen. Eine Metonymie des Subjekts wird zweimal in Vers 30 gebraucht. Die Antonymie arbeitet in gleicher Weise mit Wortersatz, das Prinzip liegt aber nicht in der Kontinuität, sondern in der Diskontinuität, dem Gegensatz; eine Antonymie findet sich in Vers 22.

Simile
Diese Stilfigur bezeichnet einen direkten Vergleich, gekennzeichnet durch die Präposition כ; laut Bulliger (2003:726f.) bezeichnet sie immer einen Vergleich aufgrund einer Ähnlichkeit. Sie diene dazu eindeutige, klare, sogar harte Aussagen zu treffen, die keiner weiteren Erklärung bedürften. Bühlmann und Scherer (1994:70) fügen hinzu, dass bei der Simile das Bild und das Verglichene nicht miteinander verschmelzen, sondern dass zwischen den beiden Komponenten nur eine teilweise Ähnlichkeit bestehe. In Vers 15 werden zwei Simile gebraucht, eine weitere in Vers 22.

Synekdoche
Laut Schirrmacher (1997:76) steht in dieser Stilfigur ein Teil für das Ganze oder das Ganze für einen Teil. Im ersten Fall wird ein wichtiger Teil für das Ganze gesetzt, im zweiten Fall wird ein übergeordneter Begriff benutzt, wenn ein untergeordneter Begriff gemeint ist. Eine Besonderheit stellt laut Caird (1980:135) dabei die Eponymie dar, hier steht der Name eines Vorfahren für ein ganzes Volk. Eine Synekdoche kommt in den Versen 16 und 27 (Eponymie) vor.

Die Perikope besteht aus fünf Strophen, jede Strophe beginnt mit einer Reihe von rhetorischen Fragen. Es schließt sich eine Folge von Aussagesätzen an, die bedingt auf die Fragen antworten, sie aber immer in irgendeiner Form kommentieren. Inhaltlich haben die Strophen unterschiedliche Bedeutungsschwerpunkte, nämlich folgende: Gott ist größer als die Schöpfung, größer als die Götzen, größer als die Fürsten, größer als das Universum und größer als die Kraftlosigkeit. Die Strophen sind intern und übergreifend mit Leitmotiven (Bühlmann and Scherer 1994:24, 39) durchzogen, das ist die freie Wiederholung eines Wortes oder einer semantischen oder grammatischen Wortgruppe, die die Thematik eines Textes bestimmt.

Folgerungen
Die ganze Perikope stellt eine Bewegung von Gott zum Menschen dar. Darauf weist bereits die erste Pentakola (Vers 12) mit ihrer Katabasis hin, in welcher die Objekte mehr und mehr in menschliche Nähe rücken und doch gleichzeitig ganz die Schöpfermacht Gottes ausdrücken. Während die einleitende Katabasis Gottes Größe und Kraft im Blick hat, zeigt die abschließende Katabasis, wie die Größe und Kraft Gottes im Leben des gläubigen Menschen wirkt. In der Perikope findet ein ständiger Wechsel statt: die Stilfiguren sprechen von Gott (V. 12: Messen der Schöpfung; V. 13/14: Ratgeber für Gott?; V. 16: Opfer für Gott?; V. 22: Ausspannen des Himmels; V. 26: Herausführen der Sterne) und von den Menschen (V. 15: Völker wie Tropfen und Staub; V. 22: Menschen wie Heuschrecken; V. 24: Fürsten verwehen wie Spreu; V. 31: Kraft wie Adler). Die Bezüge auf Gott sind zu Beginn dichter, während die in Bezug auf den Menschen zum Ende hin dichter werden. Schließlich überschneiden sich die beiden Pole in den Versen 29 bis 31: der unbegreiflich große Gott gibt seine Kraft an die Menschen weiter. Ein Abstieg scheint der Thematik der Größe Gottes diametral zu widersprechen, eher wäre ein Klimax zu erwarten. Doch darin zeigt sich der Charakter Gottes: seine wahre Größe besteht nicht darin, dass er alleine groß ist, sondern dass er von seiner Kraft und Größe an den Menschen weitergibt, dass er sich selbst klein macht in seiner Größe.

Die sorgfältig komponierten Parallelismen vermitteln eine ausdrucksstarke Intensität und Dringlichkeit: Der Schöpfergott wendet sich dem Menschen zu, er muss nur auf ihn hoffen und warten. Die Vergleiche und Bilder wirken eindringlicher und bleiben besser im Gedächtnis haften, als es für explizite Aussagen in Prosa je möglich wäre. Die Wiederholungen und Leitmotive verleihen den Aussagen großen Nachdruck. Das Gedicht bezieht sich auf die konkrete historische Situation des Volkes Israel unter seinem gottlosen König Manasse, zwar bedrängt von seinen übermächtigen Nachbarvölkern, doch gleichzeitig ermutigt, auf seinen macht- und kraftvollen Gott zu schauen. Gleichzeitig weisen die Aussagen des Gedichts darüber hinaus und der Gläubige darf sie zu allen Zeiten für sich in Anspruch nehmen. Für diese Doppeldeutigkeit ist Poesie besonders geeignet. Poesie vermittelt dem Leser Zeitlosigkeit und Allgemeingültigkeit ihrer Aussagen.

1.5 Diskussion offener Fragen

1.5.1 Wie lautet die Antwort auf die Fragen in Vers 12?

Eine Fragereihe leitet die Perikope ein: „Wer misst das Wasser mit seiner hohlen Hand und bestimmt mit der Spanne das Maß des Himmels und erfasst den Staub der Erde in einem Messbecher und wiegt die Berge mit einer Waage und die Hügel mit zwei Waagschalen?"[8] Die Antwort lautet entweder „Gott" oder „niemand". Laut Childs (2001:309) ist die intendierte Antwort „niemand". Auch Westermann (1970:44) schreibt: „Die Antwort (niemand!) ist so evident, dass sie nicht ausgesprochen zu werden braucht." Elliger (1978:47) führt aus,

---

[8] Siehe: 1.3.4 Arbeitsübersetzung im Überblick.

1.5 Diskussion offener Fragen

die Antwort sei „niemand", er begründet: „Nicht die Schöpfertätigkeit Jahwes wird beschrieben und gefeiert, sondern zum Staunen und Nachdenken über die in der fertigen Schöpfung offenbare Macht und Weisheit des Schöpfers wird aufgefordert." Er argumentiert weiter, kein Mensch sei imstande, die in der Schöpfung sichtbare Größe und Herrlichkeit mit seinen eigenen kümmerlichen Möglichkeiten zu erfassen und zu begreifen. Dieser Meinung ist auch Botterweck et al. (1984:455), räumt aber ein, dass „Jahwe allein" auch möglich, allerdings kühner sei. Auf der anderen Seite lautet die intendierte Antwort gemäß Goldingay „Jahwe". Er fügt hinzu, dass die Antwort heutzutage „wir" heißen müsse. Auch gemäß Delitzsch ([1897] 1984:418) ist von Jahwe die Rede, genauso wie in den ähnlichen Fragen in Sprüche 30:4. Die Fragen redeten anthropomorph über Gott und wollten zu Bewusstsein bringen, dass nur Jahwe den Bestandteilen des Kosmos ihr quantitatives Maß und ihre Gestalt gebe. Koole (1997:88ff.) zeigt, inwiefern das Verb תכן „messen" einen Hinweis auf die Antwort gibt: Das Wort beziehe sich auch an anderen Stellen auf die Schöpfungstätigkeit: während Gott das Wasser (Hiob 28:25) und die Erde (Ps 75:4) schuf, maß er sie. Die Fragereihen in den Versen 13–14, 18 und 25 (nach einem Ratgeber und einem Vergleich für Gott) müssen eindeutig mit „niemand" beantwortet werden. Doch die Antwort zur letzten מי-Frage in Vers 26 „Wer hat dies alles geschaffen?" ist zweifelsohne „Jahwe", so bilden die Verse 12 und 26 ein Inclusio für die anderen Fragereihen. Durch die Verknüpfung von Vers 12 und 26 wird außerdem darauf hingewiesen, dass auch Vers 12 von der Schöpfung spricht. Entgegen Ellinger ist es nicht möglich, die Schöpfertätigkeit Gottes und die daraus resultierende Schöpfung zu trennen. Das Ziel von Vers 12 (und der ganzen Perikope) ist nicht, von der Großartigkeit der Schöpfung zu erzählen, sondern von der Großartigkeit Gottes. Gott bildet das Zentrum aller Fragen in dieser Perikope, sei es explizit in der Frage (V. 13–14, 18, 25) oder implizit in der Antwort (V. 12, 26). Deshalb lautet die intendierte Antwort der Fragen in Vers 12 „Jahwe".

1.5.2 Die Bedeutung von איש עצתו in Vers 13

Vers 13 lautet : מִי־תִכֵּן אֶת־רוּחַ יְהוָה וְאִישׁ עֲצָתוֹ יוֹדִיעֶנּוּ und wird meist übersetzt im Sinne von: „Wer stellt Jahwes Geist zurecht und (ist) sein Ratgeber, der ihn belehrt?"[9] איש עצתו im zweiten Teilsatz, „sein Ratgeber", ist in dieser Übersetzung Prädikatsnominativ zu „wer", יודיענו „belehren" schließt sich als Relativsatz an, sein Objektsuffix bezieht sich auf Jahwe zurück: „der ihn (Jahwe) belehrt." Luther übersetzt ähnlich: „... und welcher Ratgeber unterweist ihn?" Laut Koole (1997:92–93) ist איש עצתו eine Apposition zu מי und sollte mit „als sein Ratgeber" übersetzt werden. So übersetzt die NIV: „... or instructed him as his counsellor?" Das unterschiedliche grammatische Verständnis bewirkt keinen Unterschied in der Bedeutung. Koole ist der Meinung, die Erwähnung eines Ratgebers beziehe sich auf die Berater, die jeder irdische König habe. Auf dem babylonischen Hintergrund könne es auch eine Anspielung auf die Götter sein, die sich gegenseitig bei Entscheidungen beraten. Goldingay (2005:41) weist darauf hin, dass in der babylonischen Religion beschrieben werde, wie Marduk Eas Ratschlag brauche und erhalte. Auch laut Oswalt (1998:60) wird hier auf das himmlische Pantheon angespielt, wo einer der Götter eine

---

9 Siehe: 1.3.4 Arbeitsübersetzung im Überblick.

Rolle übernehme, die dem irdischen Ratgeber an einem Königshof entspreche. Elliger (1978:52) allerdings weist darauf hin, dass das Verb עצה (das איש עצתו „Ratgeber" zugrunde liegt) im zweiten Teil von Jesaja nie „beraten" bedeute, sondern sich auf einen gefassten Plan, eine getroffene Entscheidung beziehe. Im Relativsatz יודיענו sei deshalb Jahwe das Subjekt, das Suffix beziehe sich auf איש „Mann" als indirektes Objekt zurück, עצתו „sein Plan" sei das direkte Objekt.

Somit ergäbe sich die Bedeutung: „Wer ist der Mann, dem er seinen Plan mitteilt?" Elliger weist zudem darauf hin, dass der altorientalische Herrscher seine Absichten dem Ratsmann mitgeteilt, dass aber keiner seinen Herrn bestimmt habe. Als Beispiel nennt er die vorangehende Perikope Jesaja 40:1–8: dort sei es Aufgabe der Ratgeber, Gottes souveräne Beschlüsse bekannt zu machen oder zu verwirklichen, nicht aber Rat zu geben oder selbst einen Plan zu entwickeln. Auch Kyros, der mit demselben Begriff bezeichnet werde (Jes 46:11), sei nicht derjenige, der Gott berate, sondern den Gott für seinen Plan gebrauche. So sieht es auch Childs: Gott teile zwar Jesaja seinen Heilsplan mit (Jes 46:11), es trete jedoch nie ein Ratgeber Gottes in Erscheinung. Doch genau das ist die Botschaft der Übersetzung „... der ihn berät": Gott braucht keinen Berater. Die Antwort auf die vorangehende und die nachfolgenden Fragen in den Versen 13 und 14 ist „niemand". Wird hier aber die Bedeutung „... dem er seinen Plan mitteilt" angenommen, ist die Antwort „niemand" nicht möglich, da Gott sehr wohl zu verschiedenen Zeiten und in verschiedenen Situationen Menschen, wie den Propheten, seinen Plan zumindest teilweise mitteilt. So ist es folgerichtig איש עצתו יודיענו grammatisch so zu verstehen wie zu Beginn dargestellt und mit „Wer ist der Ratgeber, der ihn belehrt?" zu übersetzen – mit ironischem Unterton. Die Anspielung auf das babylonische Pantheon liegt nahe.

1.5.3 Die Bedeutung von מסכן in Vers 20

Der Begriff מסכן erlaubt laut Koole (1997:105–106) vier verschiedene Bedeutungen: Die erste Möglichkeit ist „arm", so ist das Wort auch in Deuteronomium 8:9 gebraucht; daraus könne sich die Bedeutung ergeben: „Wer zu arm ist wählt ein Opfer ..." Das ist die übliche Übersetzung. „Der Arme" lässt verschiedene Variationen zu: bei Schlachter steht: „Wer aber arm ist ...", in der Hoffnung für alle ist zu lesen: „Wem eine solche Götterstatue zu teuer ist ...", und die NKJV schreibt: „Whoever is too impoverished for such a contribution ...". McKenna (1994:413) übersetzt: „Whoever is too impoverished ..."; Calvin (1996:223) übersetzt: „The poor chooseth for his offering ..."; Delitzsch ([1897] 1984:421) schreibt: „Der Verarmte an Weihgaben ..."; Schneider (1990:28 und 35) übersetzt: „Wer zu arm ist für solche eine Gabe ...", er erläutert, diese Übersetzung vertiefe die Ironie der Aussage: Die Götter spiegeln die gesellschaftliche Schicht ihrer Anbeter wider – der Gott ist vom Reichtum seines Herstellers abhängig anstatt Reichtum an seine Nachfolger zu verschenken. Oswalt (1998:64) weist die verbreitete Übersetzung „arm" zurück: Der Kontrast zwischen dem Reichen und dem Armen funktioniere nicht, da Holz, das nicht fault, sehr teuer und ein guter Handwerker zur Bearbeitung nötig sei. Die zweite Bedeutungsmöglichkeit ist „vertraut sein", das ergebe das Subjekt „wer erfahren ist". Watts (1987:87)

1.5 Diskussion offener Fragen

plädiert für diese Bedeutung, nämlich im intensivierenden Piel; als Partizip sei die Bedeutung dann „the expert in such offerings".

Als dritte Bedeutung steht „formen / bilden" zur Diskussion, das ist eine Ableitung vom ugaritischen *skn*; die Bedeutung des Satzes sei dann „derjenige, der ein Götzenbild gemacht hat ..." Und schließlich bildet „Baum / Holz" die vierte Möglichkeit. Die LXX übersetzt folgendermaßen: ξύλον γὰρ ἄσηπτον ἐκλέγεται τέκτων, „der Handwerker sucht Holz aus, das nicht verfault".

Hieronymus übersetzt mit „Maulbeerbaum", der Satz heißt dann: „Als ein Geschenk wählt er den Maulbeerbaum." Auch Childs (2001:310) übersetzt „Maulbeer-Holz", Goldingay (2005:50) übersetzt mit „SissooHolz", allerdings ohne Begründung. Die Herausgeber der BHS bieten in ihrem textkritischen Apparat „morus (genus ligni)" mit der Bedeutung „Maulbeerbaum (Holzart)". Auch Oswalt entscheidet sich für Sissoo-Holz und bezieht sich auf eine assyrische Inschrift, auf die er nicht weiter eingeht. Er ist der Meinung, die Verse 19 und 20 sprächen vom gleichen Götzen, nämlich Vers 19 von seiner Herstellung und Vers 20 von seiner Aufstellung. Koole kombiniert die Interpretationen „Maulbeerbaum" und „hohe Position" für תרומה „Beitrag" und übersetzt „Maulbeer-Holz als Erhöhung" als Ausruf am Satzanfang. So sei auch der Parallelismus zu Vers 19 gewahrt, der mit dem Ausruf „das Gottesbild!" beginne. Das Subjekt des Verses sei somit ein unpersönliches.

Elliger (1978:62) will diese Entscheidung gar nicht treffen, er ist aufgrund einer fehlenden Hebung im Metrum der Meinung, dass die Zeile nur die notdürftig zurechtgestutzten Trümmer eines zuvor umfangreicheren Textes beinhalte. Die Bedeutung sei nicht mehr zu rekonstruieren. Er nennt den Text hoffnungslos und alle Versuche der Auslegung erzwungen. Wie jedoch gezeigt wurde, bleibt eine Argumentation mit dem Metrum sehr vage.[10] Letztlich ist keine Lösung überzeugend, doch inhaltlich scheint „der Arme" am naheliegendsten. So wird der Begriff auch in Deuteronomium 8:9 gebraucht: „... ein Land, wo du Brot genug zu essen hast, wo dir nichts mangelt." מסכנת, das von der hier gebrauchten Verbwurzel abgeleitete Substantiv, wird hier mit „Mangel" übersetzt. Außerdem funktioniert der Gegensatz arm-reich, obwohl Holz, das nicht fault, teuer ist; denn Holz gilt noch immer als weniger kostbares Material als Edelmetalle.

1.5.4 Die Bedeutung der Negation in Vers 24

Vers 24 lautet:

אַף בַּל־נִטָּעוּ אַף בַּל־זֹרָעוּ אַף בַּל־שֹׁרֵשׁ בָּאָרֶץ גִּזְעָם וְגַם־נָשַׁף בָּהֶם וַיִּבָשׁוּ
וּסְעָרָה כַּקַּשׁ תִּשָּׂאֵם:

In jedem der drei Stichoi steht בַּל die Negation in poetischen Texten. Goldingay (2005:57) übersetzt: „They are really not planted ...", und Calvin (1996:229): „It is as if they had not been planted ..." Die Interjektion אַף leitet jeden der drei Stichoi ein, es unterstreicht die Tatsächlichkeit und Gewissheit des Gesagten („ja") Gesenius (1962:57), es bedeutet meist „auch / sogar / noch". Wenn es als Interrogativpartikel interpretiert wird, entstehen rhetorische negierte Fragen: So übersetzt Koole (1997:112): „Wurden sie nicht gepflanzt? Wurden

---

10 Anmerkung der Herausgeber: Siehe die ausführlicheren Erläuterungen zu „Metrum oder Rhythmus" in Simone Becks Masterarbeit.

sie nicht gesät?" בַּל kann gemäß Koole auch „noch nicht / kaum" bedeuten, somit laute der Satz, nicht als Frage, sondern als Aussage: „Sie wurden gerade erst gepflanzt ..." Auch McKenna (1994:413) übersetzt entsprechend: „Scarcely shall they be planted ..." Die Mehrzahl der Übersetzungen lautet entsprechend, nämlich Luther und Schlachter: „Kaum sind sie gepflanzt ...", ähnlich lauten englische Übersetzungen, nämlich die NIV: „No sooner are they planted ...", die NKJV: „Scarcely shall they be planted ..." und die NASB: „Scarcely have they been planted ...", diese fügt in der Fußnote hinzu: „*Or*: Not even". Der Parikel גַּם im folgenden Satz könne gemäß Koole auch adversativ gebraucht werden; das wirkt sich auch auf die Übersetzung der drei Stichoi aus, die dann lauten: „Obwohl sie gerade erst gepflanzt wurden ... Und trotzdem ..." Die letztgenannte Übersetzung scheint am elegantesten. Die Bedeutung ändert sich kaum durch die verschiedenen grammatischen Varianten: Es geht immer darum, dass die Pflanzen keine Chance haben, sich in der Erde zu verwurzeln, bevor der Wind über sie bläst, doch die Gedankenfolge wirkt logischer mit der Übersetzung „kaum". In jedem Fall wird der unendliche Gegensatz dargestellt zwischen dem Gott, der alle Macht in der Hand hält und den Machthabern, die selbst versuchen, ihre Macht zu sichern.

1.5.5 Der Vergleich mit dem Adler in Vers 31

Die ersten beiden Stichoi von Vers 31 lauten:

וְקוֹיֵ יְהוָה יַחֲלִיפוּ כֹחַ יַעֲלוּ אֵבֶר כַּנְּשָׁרִים

Das Verb עלה „auffahren" bezieht sich in Vers 31 auf den Gläubigen, der mit dem Adler verglichen wird, angezeigt durch die Präposition כ. Die Präposition zeigt Ähnlichkeit, bzw. Gleichheit, an, als Adverb ist es Gleichheit der Art und Weise (Joüon and Muraoka 1991:490). Das Verb kann im Qal mit „auffliegen" übersetzt werden oder im Hiphil mit „wachsen lassen". Aus der Bedeutung „auffliegen" folgt: „... dass sie auffahren mit Flügeln wie Adler ...", wie bei Luther. „Flügel" werden dann als adverbiale Ergänzung, nämlich instrumental, verstanden. Merwe et al. (1999:245) nennt eine mögliche Sinnrichtung für ein Adjunkt „means / method", in diese Kategorie passt אבר. Auch mit Joüon (1991:459) kann diese Kategorisierung belegt werden, er bezeichnet sie als attributiven Akkusativ (obwohl er ihr Vorkommen grundsätzlich in Frage stellt). Schlachter übersetzt ebenso wie Luther und englische Übersetzungen lauten entsprechend, nämlich die NIV „they will soar on wings like eagles" und NKJV „they shall mount up with wings like eagles".

Ist die Bedeutung „wachsen", wie in Jesaja 53:2, dann sind die Flügel das Objekt und es entsteht „ihnen wachsen Flügel wie Adler". Dafür spricht, dass im hebräischen Text die Präposition כ „wie" vor „Adler" steht, jedoch keine Präposition vor „Flügel"; bei der Übersetzung mit „wachsen" ist es entsprechend. Laut Koole (1997:127) sei diese Bedeutung wahrscheinlich, denn die neuen Flügel korrespondierten mit der neuen Kraft. Auch Goldingay (2005:72) übersetzt: „... grow pinions like eagles". Elliger (1978:101) plädiert ebenso für „wachsen lassen", er schreibt, dass die auf Jahwe Hoffenden Schwingen wie Adler bildeten. Er betont, dass sich der Vergleich des Gläubigen mit dem Adler nicht auf das Wachsenlassen, sondern auf die Schwingen beziehe; er übersetzt dann: „aufsteigen mit Flügeln". So führt seine Interpretation letztendlich über das Wachsen der Flügel hinaus zum Bild des Adlerfluges und dieselbe Bedeutung entsteht wie z.B. bei der Übersetzung Luthers. Oswalt (1998:74)

1.5 Diskussion offener Fragen

vermutet, die Aussage reflektiere die alte Tradition, dass Adlern für hundert Jahre alle zehn Jahre neue Federn wüchsen.

Er räumt allerdings ein, dass das Verb nie an anderer Stelle für das Wachsen von Federn gebraucht werde, sondern lediglich für das Wachsen von Pflanzen. Außerdem beziehe sich das Substantiv „Flügel" nie nur auf Federn, sondern immer auf gefederte Flügel. Er vertritt schließlich die Meinung, dass sich die Aussage auf das Aufheben der Flügel eines Adlers beziehe und übersetzt: „... they will stretch out their wings as the eagles." Delitzsch ([1897] 1984:426) argumentiert ähnlich: wenn hier auf die Mauser des Adlers und das Wachstum neuer Federn Bezug genommen werde, dann hätte נוצה „Feder" anstatt אבר „Flügel" gebraucht werden müssen. So übersetzt er: „... heben empor die Schwingen Adlern gleich."

Die Argumentation ist überzeugend, dass das Verb nur für das Wachsen von Pflanzen gebraucht wird und zudem wachsen dem Adler keine neuen Flügel, sondern neue Federn. So wirken alle Kombinationen mit „wachsen" konstruiert. Delitzschs Übersetzung gibt wohl am klarsten wieder, was wörtlich gemeint ist. Trotzdem kann freier übersetzt werden: „... sie fliegen auf mit Flügeln wie Adler", oder gar „... wie mit Adlerflügeln", denn dieses Bild steht im Hintergrppund. Zudem korrespondiert in der Tetrakola „fliegen" mit den Verben der Bewegung „laufen" und „gehen".

1.5.6 Das Problem der Müdigkeit von Gläubigen in Vers 31

Vers 31 wirkt sehr optimistisch: wer auf Gott hofft, dem geht die Energie nicht aus. Er erhält neue Kraft, er fliegt wie ein Adler, er rennt, er geht ohne müde zu werden. Doch spricht die Bibel auch von Menschen, wie vom Propheten Elia und selbst vom Gottesknecht, die müde geworden sind. Dies scheint ein Widerspruch zu sein. Die Schöpfungsordnung besagt, dass der Mensch einen Rhythmus von Arbeit und Ruhe braucht: jeder wird müde durch Anstrengung und regeneriert sich wieder durch Ruhe. Diese Ordnung erscheint bereits exemplarisch im Schöpfungsbericht: Gott arbeitet sechs Tage lang und ruht am siebten Tag. Sogar der Ungläubige erhält neue Kraft durch Ruhephasen – und auch diese Kraft kommt von Gott, da er ein Geschöpf Gottes ist und Lebenskraft ausschließlich als Gabe Gottes zu denken ist. Doch auch der Gläubige kommt ans Ende seiner Kraft und wird müde auf seinem Lebensweg. Er erlebt Krankheit, Erschöpfung, Depression und, ein moderner Begriff, „burn out"; er gerät in Täler, die tiefer sind als vorübergehende Kraftlosigkeit. Elliger schreibt:

> Während die nur von ihren natürlichen Kräften Zehrenden schließlich zu Boden gehen, schwingen sich die wie mit wunderbar gewachsenen Flügeln mit der Kraft der Hoffnung auf Jahwe Begabten empor, dass sie kühn wie die Adler die schwierigsten Hindernisse im Fluge nehmen und das höchste Ziel ihnen nicht unerreichbar bleibt. (Elliger 1978:101)

Wer das nicht erlebt – hat der sich das selbst zuzuschreiben? Vertraut er zu sehr auf seine eigene Kraft? Hofft er zu wenig auf Jahwe? Diese Antworten wären zu einfach, und die Aussage Elligers scheint unrealistisch in der Vielschichtigkeit der menschlichen Lebenswirklichkeit. Der Schlüssel liegt wahrscheinlich in den Verben הלך „gehen" und רוץ „rennen". Es gibt Zeiten, in denen der Gläubige fliegt oder rennt – aber nicht ununterbrochen. Doch das

Verb „gehen" bezieht sich auf den gesamten Lebensweg des Gläubigen und selbst „rennen" kann dafür stehen. Er bekommt immer wieder neue Kraft, auf seinem Weg weiter zu gehen, sein Leben in Verantwortung vor Gott zu leben. Das Maß an Energie, die Gott dafür schenkt, ist individuell unterschiedlich und der Mensch ist verantwortlich dafür, dass er vernünftig entsprechend der Energiereserven lebt, die ihm geschenkt werden. Immer wieder gibt es Zeiten des außerordentlichen Krafteinsatzes und Gott schenkt besondere Kraft für besondere Aufgaben. Und dann mutet Gott auch dem Gläubigen ausgedehnte Zeiten der Kraftlosigkeit zu. Es gibt jedoch entgegen Elliger keinen qualitativen Unterschied zwischen natürlicher Kraft und übernatürlicher Kraft, denn alle Kraft kommt von Gott. Trotzdem verleiht die Hoffnung auf Gott und sein Eingreifen immer wieder neue Lebensenergie und -freude. Der Begriff כֹּחַ „Kraft" steht mitnichten nur für außerordentliche Kraft, sondern für die ganz normale, alltägliche Lebenskraft. Was der Mensch hoffentlich im Alltag erlebt, ist einfach genügend Kraft auf seinem Weg weiterzugehen und so zu leben, wie es Gott gefällt – im sinnvollen Rhythmus von Arbeit und Ruhe.

1.6 Betrachtung der einzelnen Verse

1.6.1 Jesaja 40:12–14   I Größer als die Schöpfung; a) Rhetorische Fragen

Die Perikope beginnt mit einer Fragereihe nach dem, der die Elemente der Schöpfung messen kann. Das Interrogativpronomen ist מִי „wer"; gemäß Goldingay (2005:35) leitet es häufig rhetorische Fragen ein. Die Verben beschreiben technische Vorgänge. Messen und Wiegen bedeutet, eine Maßeinheit mit einer zu messenden Länge, Größe, Schwere o.ä. zu vergleichen. Maßeinheit und Gemessenes müssen in Beziehung zueinander stehen. Das ist hier nicht der Fall. Die Maßeinheiten sind zu klein für das, was gemessen wird. Im dritten Stich wird der Staub der Erde mit einem Messbecher gemessen. „Erde" korrespondiert hier mit „Wasser" und „Himmel", während „Staub" mit den folgenden „Bergen" und „Hügeln" korrespondiert. Im vierten und fünften Stich werden die Berge und Hügel mit einer Waage gemessen. Delitzsch ([1897] 1984:418) erklärt die beiden genannten Typen von Waagen: פֶּלֶס ist eine Schnellwaage; sie besteht aus einem ungleicharmigen Waagbalken, der in die Höhe schnellt, wenn er entlastet wird. מֹאזְנַיִם ist eine aus zwei Waagschalen bestehende Krämerwaage.

In allen fünf Fragen scheint es absurd, dass verschwindend kleine Maße für unerfassbare Größen gebraucht werden. Es ist intendiert, dass die Maßeinheiten unrealistisch sind und dem zu messenden Objekt nicht entsprechen. Das bedeutet, die Aufgabe ist aus menschlicher Perspektive unvorstellbar. Die gebrauchten Verben des Messens und Wägens passen in die Welt des Handwerkers, doch die Aufgabe ist zu groß. Webb (1996:165) fügt hinzu, dass Gott das Universum so mühelos erschaffe wie ein begabter Handwerker, der ein Modell auf seiner Werkbank konstruierte. Goldingay erklärt, die fünf zu messenden Objekte verwiesen auf die drei Stockwerke der Erde (Wasser, Himmel und Erde) und auf die Säulen, die Himmel und Erde tragen (Berge und Hügel). Somit sei alles eingeschlossen, was existiere. Motyer (1999:246) ergänzt, dies entspreche dem hebräischen Idiom, das Ganzheit durch Kontrast ausdrückt.

1.6 Betrachtung der einzelnen Verse

Die Antwort auf die fünf Fragen lautet „Jahwe".[11] Der jüdische Leser soll es lernen für die Zeit im babylonischen Exil und der Konfrontation mit der babylonischen Religion. Zwar preist laut Goldingay (2005:35–36) Enuma Elish den Gott Marduk als Schöpfer und beschreibt ihn als den, der die Wasser des Meeres abmesse; aber nicht Marduk, sondern Jahwe ist der Schöpfergott, mit seiner Größe und Majestät garantiert er die Stabilität des Kosmos. Die Beschreibung der Größe Gottes passt in die Zeit und Situation der Leser gut – das sind die Antworten auf Israels Frage in V. 27. Es gab viel, was Jesaja und seine Zeitgenossen entmutigte – und noch mehr, was ihre Nachkommen entmutigen würde, nämlich die Demütigung der Deportation und das Leben in der Fremde.[12] Es ist keine neue Idee, sondern vielmehr das Fundament der jüdischen Religion, dass der Gott Israels der Schöpfer der Erde ist und den Verlauf der Weltgeschichte in seiner Hand hält, aber es fällt nicht leicht, daran zu glauben, wenn Gefahr durch die politischen Nachbarn droht und die Heimat in Ruinen liegt. Der Verfasser kleidet die uralte Wahrheit in eine lebendige, bildhafte Sprache, damit sie die Benommenheit derer durchdringt, die fast die Hoffnung aufgegeben haben, und damit sie es wieder neu glauben und sich daran festhalten können. Hier findet sich ein Hinweis auf natürliche Offenbarung (Röm 1:20): „Denn Gottes unsichtbares Wesen, das ist seine ewige Kraft und Gottheit, wird seit der Schöpfung der Welt ersehen aus seinen Werken, wenn man sie wahrnimmt." Nicht nur Gottes Macht, sondern auch etwas von Gottes Charakter und Zuwendung zum Menschen wird an der Größe und Weite der Schöpfung deutlich.

Die Verse 13 und 14 führen die Fragereihe von Vers 12 fort. Die Antwort zu den Fragen muss nun „niemand" sein. In der Logik der Gedankenfolge verbirgt sich die Frage: wenn der Menschen nicht einmal die sichtbare Welt messen kann, wie kann er dann Gottes Größe ermessen? Im ersten Stich steht „Geist" naheliegenderweise als Synonym für das Sein, den Charakter, das Wesen Gottes. Gæbelein (1986:245) allerdings hält es für möglich, dass der Begriff auf den Schöpfungsbericht anspiele: „... der Geist Gottes schwebte auf dem Wasser" (Gen 1:2), denn der vorige Vers beschreibe Gottes Schöpfungsmacht. Auch Delitzsch ([1897] 1984:418) ist der Meinung, der Verfasser knüpfe an die Schöpfungsgeschichte an und an den Geist, der das Chaos gestaltet habe. Diese Parallele scheint etwas zu weit gefasst, der Begriff רוח „Geist" wird stilistisch gebraucht, er steht für Gott selbst, für sein ureigenes Wesen, einbezogen ist dabei sein Beurteilungs- und Entscheidungsvermögen, das keine Beratung benötigt. Formal besteht die Fortführung von Vers 12 in der Wiederholung des Verbs תכן „messen": Gott misst das Universum, aber niemand kann Gott messen, verstehen, ihm etwas vorschreiben.

Das Wort עצתו „Rat", das dem Begriff „Ratgeber" zugrunde liegt, bezieht sich auf die Beratung selbst, die jemand erfährt und auch auf den Plan, der auf der Basis dieses Rates formuliert wird. Der Plan, um den es Jahwe geht, ist die Zukunft der Nationen und seines Volkes. Es bestehen Parallelen zu irdischen Herrschern, die sich Pläne für die Regierung ihrer Völker erstellen und dafür Beratung brauchen. Doch im Gegensatz zu irdischen Herrschern braucht Jahwe keinen, der ihn berät[13] und seine Pläne werden ausgeführt, kein Gegner kann sich ihm in den Wege stellen. Jesaja 46:11 bezeichnet Kyros mit dem gleichen

---

[11] Siehe: 1.5.1 Wie lautet die Antwort auf die Fragen in Vers 12?
[12] Siehe: 1.1.2 Historische Situation – politisches Umfeld.
[13] Siehe: 1.5.2 Die Bedeutung von איש עצתו in Vers 13.

Begriff – hier findet sich schon eine Einführung des zukünftigen persischen Herrschers, den Gott für die Ausführung seines Plans gebraucht.

Goldingay (2005:41) schreibt, dass die in den Versen 13 und 14 gebrauchten Verben des Lehrens eher zum Bereich der religiösen Bildung, zur Schulbildung und zum täglichen Leben gehörten als zum Königshof, wo der König seine professionellen Ratgeber konsultiere. Dies sei Teil der intendierten Polemik, denn der Verfasser wolle einen absurden Eindruck erwecken, der Wortgebrauch mache die Idee, dass Jahwe Ratgeber brauche, noch lächerlicher. Die Verben des Lehrens und Wissens drücken hier nach Motyer (1999:247) die unbegrenzte und unübertroffene Weisheit Jahwes aus. Gott braucht zwar keinen Ratgeber, keinen, der ihn lehrt und unterrichtet, er teile aber den Menschen seine Heilsabsicht mit – das ist seine freie und souveräne Entscheidung. Das Wort משפט „Recht" im dritten Stich von Vers 14 bezieht sich auf Gottes souveränes Recht und seine Gerechtigkeit. Im Vorausblick auf das Exil ist es wichtig, dass Gott mit vollem Recht und in voller Gerechtigkeit handelt, wenn er sein Volk bestraft. Genauso wird Gott Recht üben, wenn er sein Volk befreit und dessen Feinde bestraft. Laut Elliger ist das Recht hier „die Ordnung und der Lauf der Dinge, die der dazu allein fähige, die Welt regierende Geist kraft eigener Willensentscheidung festsetzt" Elliger (1978:54). Das Recht wird in den folgenden Kapiteln als die Aufgabe des Gottesknechts dargestellt, hier findet sich schon ein erster Hinweis auf ihn. Der Begriff wird mit ארח „Pfad" kombiniert, dies ist laut Elliger ein altes nomadisches Wort: „[D]er Pfad ist die Art und Weise, in der sich der göttliche Wille in der von ihm regierten Welt durchsetzt und zu seinem Ziele kommt." Im fünften Stich korrespondiert דרך תבונות „Weg der Einsicht" mit ארח משפט „Pfad des Rechts". „Einsicht" bedeutet das Verständnis und die Weisheit, mit der Gott die Weltgeschichte regiert. Gottes Herrschaft erstreckt sich auf dem langen Weg von der Schöpfung über die Regierung der Geschichte bis heute. Das sind keine unterschiedlichen Herrschaftsbereiche, weder chronologisch noch qualitativ, sie gehören zusammen. Gott ist gegenwärtig Herr der Schöpfung und Herr der Geschichte, darauf weist die Kombination von Vers 12 mit Vers 13/14 hin. Das Gegenstück zu den Versen 13 und 14 ist Psalm 119:66 mit der Bitte, dass Gott den Menschen lehren möge. Nach Calvin (1996:219) soll der Hörer aus diesen Versen Demut und Gehorsam lernen; das menschliche Verständnis sei im Dunkeln, bis es von Gott erleuchtet werde.

1.6.2 Jesaja 40:15–17   I Größer als die Schöpfung; b) Folgerung

Vers 15 beginnt mit הן und wiederholt die Interjektion in der Mitte des Verses. Der Ausruf gibt hier eine logische Konsequenz wieder, so wie Jesaja 41:24, 29 das Gericht als logische Konsequenz für Götzendienst darstellt. Wenn Gott die Dimensionen der Schöpfung mit seiner Hand und die Berge auf einer Waage misst (Vers 12), dann folgt daraus, dass der Mensch auf solch einer Waage nicht mehr als Staub wiegt. Oswalt (1998:61) übersetzt den Partikel mit „in fact" – „tatsächlich". Elliger (1978:54) übersetzt „die Völker sind doch ..." Beides ist angemessen. Der מר „Tropfen" (ein Hapaxlegomena) vom דלי „Eimer" (sonst nur in Num 24:7) im ersten Stich bezieht sich laut Koole (1997:95) auf den Tropfen, der unbeachtet vom Eimer fällt, wenn er vom Brunnen hochgezogen wird. Der Tropfen korrespondiert mit dem gesamten Wasser der Erde, das Jahwe mit seiner hohlen Hand misst (Vers 12).

1.6 Betrachtung der einzelnen Verse

Das Verb שחק, das dem im zweiten Stich gebrauchten Substantiv zugrunde liegt, bedeutet „pulverisieren"; für das Substantiv folgt die Bedeutung „Staubschicht". Die gefürchteten Weltmächte können in der Weltgeschichte genauso wenig ausrichten, wie Staub die Waage bewegen kann. Motyer (1999:247) versteht das Bild etwas anders: wenn ein Apotheker eine Zutat für ein Medikament akkurat abmessen will, bläst oder wischt er vorher den Staub von den Waagschalen. Genauso bedeutungslos wie dieser Staub sind die Völker. Das Verb חשב „für etwas halten" bezieht sich auf beide Stichoi und steht – anders als gewöhnlich – am Ende. Das verstärkt das Gewicht der beiden Vergleiche. Dem Verb נטל „hochheben" im dritten Stich wird meist „er" als impliziertes Subjekt und „ferne Länder" als Objekt zugeordnet. Der Übersetzungsvorschlag von Gesenius (1962:501) lautet: „Insellander wiegen nicht mehr wie ein Stäubchen." Delitzsch ([1897] 1984:420) aber übersetzt mit „emporschweben", die Inseln werden dann zum Subjekt. Sie sind vor Gott wie ein Stäubchen, das schon durch einen geringen Luftzug nach oben schwebt. Die Übersetzung mit „hochheben" müsse „die Antwort auf die Frage: wieso und wozu? schuldig bleiben". Dieses Verständnis ist besonders im Kontext der Gewichtslosigkeit von Staub naheliegend. Koole (1997:96) denkt, dass mit איים „Inseln / ferne Länder" die Küste des Mittelmeeres und das am denkbar weitesten entfernte Land gemeint sei – aber nicht die Region als solche, sondern ihre Bewohner, parallel zu den Völkern, die auch aus Menschen bestehen. Der Begriff „ferne Länder" führt den Kreis der Völker bis in die weiteste Ferne vollständig vor Augen. Diese Völker stellten für Israel eine Bedrohung dar – doch vor Gott sind sie nichtig. Der Vers ist ein Trost für Israel, das unter dem Druck Assyriens leidet und dem die Wegführung nach Babylon ins Exil bevorsteht. Er bedeutet nicht, dass Jahwe sich nicht um die Völker kümmere, oder dass sie ihm nicht wichtig seien – diese Frage steht hier nicht zur Diskussion. Es geht um Gottes Größe und Majestät über Menschen und Völker, sodass die Nationen das tun müssen, was Gott für sie plant (Jes 10:5–6).

Der Libanon im ersten Stich von Vers 16 war sprichwörtlich bekannt für seinen reichen Waldbestand, besonders für die sogenannte „Libanon Zeder". Laut Schneider (1990:34) waren die Bäume wegen ihrer gewaltigen Höhe und ihres riesigen Umfangs weithin bekannt und begehrt. Vers 16 illustriert Vers 15: unter all den Völkern ist sogar der Libanon mit all seinen Bäumen nichtig. Sein Holz reicht als Brennmaterial für Gottes Altar nicht aus. בער bedeutet „brennen", kann aber in der Terminologie des Opfers auch bedeuten „ein Feuer am Brennen halten", bzw. im Piel „das Anzünden eines Feuers". Hier steht das Verb für das Feuer selbst. Auch die wilden Tiere des Libanons im zweiten Stich sind nicht ausreichend für dieses Opfer. Der Begriff עולה „Brandopfer" beschreibt ein Opfer, das vollständig verbrannt und Jahwe gegeben wird; kein Teil bleibt für den Menschen zum Verzehr. Frey malt dem Leser das Bild der Bikola vor Augen:

> ... ein Riesenopferaltar; darauf aufgeschichtet der ganze Hochwald mit seinen Riesenmasten, der die Abhänge des Libanongebirges deckt; und darauf alles Wild, das in seinen Forsten wimmelt, als Brandopfer geschlachtet. Für Menschengedanken eine unvorstellbare Opferglut! Gott – wird davon gar nicht erreicht. Frey (1938:28)

Der Text stellt nebenbei den Opferkult in Frage, indem er zeigt, dass kein Opfer ausreichend sein kann. Hier wird nicht (wie z.B. in Mi 6:6ff.) das übertriebene Opfer der Gleichgültigkeit gegenüber Gottes Geboten und dem Fokus auf den eigenen Vorteil gegenüber gestellt. Hier wird Gottes Größe beschrieben: die Schöpfung entstand durch Gott und gehört Gott – er braucht das Opfer von Menschen nicht. Kein Opfer kann den Abgrund zwischen Gott und Mensch überbrücken. Motyer (1999:247) sagt, der Vers stelle das Ende aller „do-it-yourself Mentalität" bezüglich des Heils dar: jede Anstrengung, Gott zu unserem Vorteil zu manövrieren sei unzureichend. Das steht gemäß Koole (1997:98) im Gegensatz zur mesopotamischen Theologie, denn dort brauchten die Gottheiten Menschen, die ihr Überleben durch Opfer sicherten – im Gegenzug war die Gottheit verpflichtet, dem Menschen Gutes zu tun. Jahwe hat es nicht nötig, sich auf solch einen Handel einzulassen.

In Vers 17 kommt der Verfasser wieder zur Aussage von Vers 15 zurück, er sagt es nun nicht mehr mit einem Bild, sondern hart und klar: die Völker sind nichts. Durch die Kombination der drei vernichtenden Begriffe אין „Nichtvorhandensein", אפס „Ende" und תהו „Öde" in den beiden Stichoi wird die absolute Nichtigkeit und Wertlosigkeit der Feinde Israels deutlich. Die Präposition כ vor אין hat laut Goldingay nicht die Bedeutung des Vergleichs, sondern der Definition oder Identität. Die Völker sind nicht lediglich „wie nichts", sondern sie sind selbst per Definition „gar nichts". Die Präposition מן „weg von" vor אפס kann laut Koole (1997:99) entweder partitiv „als nichtig betrachtet" oder komparativ „weniger als nichts", das noch stärker wirke, verstanden werden. Laut Waltke und O'Connor (1990:265) sei das Adjektiv (hier ein Adverb), von dem מן abhänge, ausgelassen, es müsse durch den Kontext verstanden werden. Oswalt (1998:57) fügt noch den Ursprung „vom Nichts kommend" hinzu. Delitzsch ([1897] 1984:420) vertritt eine partitive Bedeutung und übersetzt „der Nichtigkeit und Leere angehörig". Koole hält wegen des angedeuteten Vergleichs im vorangehenden Vers und durch die Häufung der drei negativen Begriffe die komparative Bedeutung für angemessen. Auch Calvin (1996:221) plädiert dafür: die Nationen seien nichts im Vergleich mit der Majestät Gottes. Da die gesamte Perikope von Vergleichen lebt, ist diese Interpretation naheliegend.

Laut Goldingay (2005:43) verstärkt die Präposition נגד „vor (ihm)" die Negation und zeige erneut, dass es hier nicht um den intrinsischen Wert der Nationen gehe, sondern um ihren Status gegenüber Jahwe. Daher ist die Übersetzung „in seinen Augen" geeignet. Auch diese Präposition drückt laut Watts (1987:87) einen Vergleich aus: verglichen mit Gott ist es fast so, als existierten die Nationen gar nicht. Das ist die Basis des ersten der drei täglichen Danksprüche der Juden: „Danke, oh Herr, unser Gott, König der Welt, der mich nicht als Heide geschaffen hat." Das bedeutet nicht, dass die Menschheit dem Schöpfer gleichgültig sei; im Gegenteil, Gott hat sie als Krone der Schöpfung, als sein Ebenbild geschaffen und als Mit-Regenten der Welt eingesetzt (Psalm 8). Auch Elliger weist darauf hin, dass

> die Völker noch etwas bedeuten. Aber sie sind eben nur wie Himmel, Erde, Meer usw. Teile der Schöpfung und müssen die Funktion erfüllen, die der Schöpfer Jahwe ihnen in seinem Weltenplan zugedacht hat und die sein Geist ihnen im Laufe der Geschichte immer von neuem zudenkt. (Elliger 1978:55–56)

Während Israel sich gegenüber den Völkern wertlos fühlt, sind es die Völker, die nichtig sind vor Gott. Israel darf seine Hoffnung nicht auf die

1.6 Betrachtung der einzelnen Verse

es umgebenden Völker setzen, sondern auf seinen Gott alleine, den Schöpfer der Welt.

1.6.3 Jesaja 40:18 II Größer als die Götter; a) Rhetorische Fragen

Vers 18 nimmt die Fragereihen der Verse 12–14 und den Opferkult von Vers 16 auf. Gemäß Oswalt (1998:58) führt das ו am Anfang des Verses eine Apodosis ein und wird mit „so / also" übersetzt. Die Fragen sprechen den Leser direkt an. Wenn er aufgefordert wird, Jahwe zu vergleichen, dann muss er zugeben, dass er keinen findet, der Gott in Erscheinung oder Charakter ähnlich sein könnte. Botterweck et al. (1984:272) halten die Fragen aber nicht lediglich für rhetorisch, da es offensichtlich unter den angeredeten Exilanten Israeliten gegeben habe, die Vergleiche zwischen Jahwe und den siegreich scheinenden Fremdgöttern anstellten. Auch bei einer früheren Datierung des Textes liegt es nahe, dass Menschen Vergleiche zwischen ihrem eigenen Gott und den Göttern ihrer benachbarten, erfolgreichen Weltmächte angestellt haben.

Goldingay (2005:47) weist darauf hin, dass der Verfasser im ersten Stich אל „Gott" anstelle von Jahwe benutzt. Er ist der Meinung, dass dieser Begriff eine monotheistische Konnotation impliziere – mehr als Jahwe, der ja der spezifische Name für den Gott eines spezifischen Volkes sei. Oswalt (1998:62) schreibt, dass der gebräuchlichste Begriff für Gott אלוהים sei, er beinhalte allgemein die Charakteristika von Göttlichkeit, während אל auch für den höchsten Gott im kanaanäischen Pantheon benutzt werde. Somit drücke der Verfasser die absolute Überlegenheit seines Gottes aus. Diese Diskussion ergibt sich, wenn angenommen wird, dass Jahwe der Schöpfergott und der einzige lebendige Gott ist.

Der zweite Stich geht über den ersten hinaus, weil er vom allgemeinen Vergleich nun zum Vergleich mit einem Bild übergeht. Das Wort דמות „Ebenbild", das sich vom Verb דמה „vergleichen" im ersten Stich ableitet, führt mit einem Wortspiel die Polemik über Götzenbilder ein (Vers 19/20). Elliger (1978:71) allerdings ist der Meinung, hier sei kein Bild im eigentlichen Sinne gemeint, sondern „ein Abstraktum, das mit dem Verbum zusammen bedeutet ‚einen Vergleich anstellen'", denn das Verb ערך „zurichten / gleichstellen" werde nirgendwo im AT für das Aufstellen eines Götterbildes gebraucht. Es habe laut Koole (1997:101) die Konnotation des Kultes und könne sich auf die Vorbereitung eines Altars beziehen. Der Begriff „Bild" spricht allgemein von der Ähnlichkeit des Aussehens, sowohl im Sinne von plastischen Bildern, als auch von falschen Vorstellungen. Da aber die folgenden Verse die Herstellung von Bildern beschreiben, liegt es nahe, den Begriff schon hier so zu verstehen. Bilder führen zu dem Irrglauben, Menschen könnten Gott kontrollieren und beherrschen, indem er zu einem Teil des sichtbaren Kosmos wird. Allerdings ist die einzige Basis, auf der etwas über Gott gesagt werden kann, die Analogie zur menschlichen Erfahrung oder die Negation. Weil der Mensch als Bild Gottes geschaffen ist, sind menschliche Vergleiche für einen nicht-menschlichen Gott durchaus angebracht, Watts (1987:91) schreibt, dass die Bibel selbst in anthropomorphen Ausdrücken über Gott spreche. Der Mensch suche nach etwas innerhalb seiner Erfahrung, um über die Dinge nachdenken zu können, die außerhalb seiner Erfahrung lägen. Falsch werde es erst, wenn der Mensch annimmt, er habe Gottes Denken verstanden und könne Gott beraten und ihn korrigieren. Das sei genauso Abgötterei wie die Herstellung von Bildern.

Calvin (1996:222) geht davon aus, dass der Vers im Hinblick auf die Zukunft des Volkes geschrieben worden sei: im zukünftigen Exil würde das Volk mit schlechten Vorbildern konfrontiert werden, dann sollten sie sich nicht dem Gedanken hingeben, dass falsche Götter Sicherheit und Wohlstand schaffen würden; dann sollten sie daran festhalten, dass die Majestät des wahren Gottes unvergleichlich sei.

1.6.4 Jesaja 40:19-20   II Größer als die Götter; b) Folgerungen

Die Verse 19 und 20 beschreiben die praktische Herstellung eines Götzen. Die Begriffe פסל „Gottesbild" und חרש „Handwerker" erscheinen sowohl in Vers 19 als auch in Vers 20 – das Gottesbild ist eindeutig das Produkt menschlicher Arbeit. Dazwischen folgt eine Aufzählung der Materialien, die benutzt werden: Gold, Silber, Holz. Im ersten Teilsatz von Vers 19 fügt die Frontalstellung des Wortes פסל „Gottesbild" der Aussage einen ironischen Unterton bei. Der Leser hat noch die vorangehende Frage nach dem Vergleich mit Gott im Ohr. Er erhält nun die Antwort im Sinne von „etwa ein Gottesbild??". Dafür spricht auch die Annahme Elligers (1978:74), der Artikel habe einen deiktischen Einschlag, die Bedeutung „So ein Götterbild ..." ergibt sich. Schlachter übersetzt geschickt: „Das Götzenbild? Das hat der Künstler gegossen ..."

Das Verb רקע „ausbreiten" im zweiten Teilsatz erscheint im Schöpfungsbericht als Substantiv, das trägt zur Polemik bei. Während auf dem Götzen Gold ausgebreitet wird, breitet Gott den Himmel aus (Gen 1:7). Das Subjekt ist ein Partizip von צרף „schmelzen" und es ist die Berufsbezeichnung desjenigen, der sich mit Edelmetallen handwerklich beschäftigt. Elliger (1978:75) weist darauf hin, dass es Götterfiguren gegeben habe, deren aus Bronze bestehender Kern ganz oder teilweise mit Gold- oder Silberfolie belegt gewesen sei. Sie stammten zwar aus dem zweiten Jahrtausend, doch wahrscheinlich habe sich die Technik nicht verändert.

Die Bedeutung von רתקות (Hapaxlegomena) im dritten Teilsatz ist ungewiss: das zugrunde liegende Verb wird auch in Nahum 3:10 und Prediger 12:6 im Sinne von „anketten" gebraucht, doch der Text ist schwach belegt. In 1. Könige 6:21 bedeutet das Substantiv wahrscheinlich „Ketten". Meist wird der Begriff auch hier mit „Ketten" übersetzt, doch der Zusammenhang mit dem Götzenbild ist nicht eindeutig. Vielleicht wurden sie um das Götzenbild gelegt, um es zu befestigen oder zu schmücken. Goldingay (2005:50) vermutet letzteres. Watts (1987:87) hält „Befestigung" für eine bessere Übersetzung als „Ketten". Laut Koole (1997:102) könnte der Begriff „Klammer" bedeuten und von der Befestigung des Götzenbildes auf einem Podest zeugen – doch für diese Übersetzung gäbe es mehr archäologische als lexikalische Belege. Obwohl „Ketten" nicht eindeutig ist, ist es dennoch besser belegt als andere Vermutungen. Die Tempus-Folge Perfekt – Imperfekt – Partizip gibt dem Leser laut Oswalt (1998:64) das Gefühl ein Zeuge des Vorgangs zu sein: der Götze wurde hergestellt und nun sehen wir zu, wie er mit Gold überzogen und mit Silberketten versehen wird. Und dies soll nun der Schöpfer des Universums sein?

Über המסכן „der Arme", das den ersten Teilsatz von Vers 20 einleitet,[14] schreibt Brandenburg (1961:9) ironisch: „Von der Kaufkraft des Bestellers

---

[14] Siehe: 1.5.3 Die Bedeutung von מסכן in Vers 20.

1.6 Betrachtung der einzelnen Verse

hängt es ab, ob sein Gott aus Metall oder Holz ist. Aber bitte: Holz, das ja nicht fault! Wie peinlich wäre es für einen Gott, wenn er allmählich in Fäulnis überginge!" תרומה „Beitrag" bedeute gewöhnlich „Opfer", in anderen alttestamentlichen Texten sei immer ein spezifisches Opfer gemeint. In 2. Samuel 1:21 könne sich das Wort aber auch auf eine hohe Position beziehen. Laut Elliger (1978:79–80) sei es die von der Gottheit selbst angeordnete, für den Kult erhobene Abgabe, komme also einer Steuer gleich, und sei somit nicht die Stiftung eines Gottesbildes. Als Beleg führt er Maleachi 3:8 an, wo über den Betrug des Zehnten Klage geführt werde. Es könne sich nur um eine regulierte, keine freiwillige Leistung handeln. Elliger ist der Meinung, dass das Holz, das nicht fault, zu einem Podest für das Gottesbild diene. Somit ginge es in den Versen 19 und 20 um die Herstellung von nur einem Gottesbild, nicht um die Unterscheidung zwischen metallenen und hölzernen Gottesbildern. Die Grundlage für seine Theorie bildet das Verständnis von הון „fest machen", das sei die Grundbedeutung der Wurzel und ihr Normalgebrauch, daraus ergebe sich „dauernd unbeweglich hinstellen / sichern", auch der konsekutive Relativsatz „so dass es nicht wackelt" weise darauf hin. Somit sei der Holzfachmann, also der dritte involvierte Handwerker, kein Bildschnitzer, sondern ein Zimmermeister, der für die silber- und goldgeschmückte Bronzefigur einen Sockel aus Holz anfertige, der seine Standfestigkeit garantiere. Elliger allerdings legt sich nicht fest, was das erste Wort im Vers bedeutet, er hält den Text für korrumpiert; bedeutet es „der Arme", wird ein Gegensatz zwischen Vers 19 und Vers 20 geschaffen und es handelt sich um die Herstellung von zwei unterschiedlichen Göttern. Die Bedeutung der beiden Verben „sichern" und „wackeln" entspricht durchaus der Interpretation Elligers.

Der Vers beschreibt die Sorge, dass der Gottheit ein Unglück widerfahren könnte. Die Verben בחר „wählen" und בקש „suchen" stehen für die Sorge und die daraus resultierende Sorgfalt; sie bilden ein Inclusio für die negierten Verben רקב „verfaulen" und מוט „wackeln", die das gefürchtete Unglück beschreiben. Laut Koole (1997:104) ist die Ironie von בחר folgende: Die Erlösung Israels beginnt damit, dass Gott sein Volk erwählt hat (Jes 41:8–9), Israel ist das auserwählte Volk Gottes (Jes 45:4). Wenn auch Menschen denken, sie wählten sich ihren Gott, so ist das tatsächlich unmöglich. Die Vorsorge wegen des Unglücks ist durchaus berechtigt: gemäß Goldingay (2005:50) weisen mesopotamische Texte auf Götterbilder hin, die von ihrem Podest gefallen sind. Doch der wahre Gott verleiht Sicherheit – für die Welt (Ps 93:1), für sein Volk (Ps 46:5), für die Gläubigen (Ps 15:5). Er stellt sicher, dass die Welt nicht wackelt – und hier stellt ein Mensch sicher, dass sein Gott nicht wackelt und stürzt, wie es dem Gott Dagon widerfuhr (1 Sam 5,1–4). Die fehleranfällige Technik der Götzenhersteller steht im Gegensatz zu Gottes großzügiger Schöpfung (Vers 12). Zwar machte das religiöse Denken einen Unterschied zwischen einem Gott und seiner bildlichen Repräsentation, doch allgemein wurde angenommen, dass der Gott im Bild präsent ist. Auch Elliger (1978:73–74) merkt an, dass in den Versen 19 und 20 von Bildern anstatt von den Göttern selbst die Rede sei, weist aber darauf hin, dass Bild und Sache nicht getrennt, sondern als Einheit verstanden worden seien. Vor dem jüdischen Hintergrund der Bildlosigkeit des Kultes und der Unabbildbarkeit Gottes demonstriert der Verfasser die Inferiorität der fremden Götter am Beispiel ihrer Bilder und ihrer banalen Entstehung. Ein geschaffenes Gottesbild kann den Schöpfergott nicht repräsentieren. Westermann schreibt treffend:

Das Erstaunliche an dieser Schilderung der Herstellung eines Götterbildes ist, dass der sie Schildernde sich mit der fast photographischen Exaktheit der Wiedergabe des Vorgangs begnügt, ohne auch nur einen Satz der Kritik oder des direkten Spottes hinzuzufügen. Die Schilderung, so dachte er offenbar, kann völlig für sich selbst sprechen. Es ist nichts hinzuzufügen. Allein aus der Betonung der Haltbarkeit und Standfestigkeit (nicht wackelt) ist ein feiner indirekter Spott zu hören. (Westermann 1970:47)

1.6.5 Jesaja 40:21 III Größer als die Machthaber; a) Rhetorische Fragen

Die vier Ja-/Nein-Fragen in Vers 21 beginnen alle mit הלוא als Einleitung. Die Fragen erwarten eine positive Antwort: Israel müsste eigentlich wissen, müsste eigentlich gehört haben. Immer wieder muss Israel sich den Vorwurf gefallen lassen, dass es ihm an Wissen und am Zuhören mangelt. Die Menschen weigern sich, Gottes Führung in der Geschichte und in ihrem Leben zu verstehen (Jes 48:4–5). Der Inhalt dessen, was Israel wissen, was es gehört haben sollte, wird noch nicht gesagt. Die vier Fragen sind chiastisch angeordnet: ידע „wissen" im ersten Stich korrespondiert mit בין „verstehen" im vierten, und שמע „hören" im zweiten Stich mit נגד „verkünden" im dritten. Die Verben des Wissens und Verstehens erinnern an einen Schulkontext. Die Leser erscheinen wie eine Klasse, die von ihrem Lehrer an ihre Lektion erinnert wird. Doch hier geht es nicht um mangelndes Wissen, sondern um mangelndes Vertrauen.

נגד hat die Bedeutung der Verkündigung des Heils. Die Präpositionalphrase „von Anfang an" bezieht sich entweder auf den Beginn der Weltgeschichte (Spr 8:23) oder auf den Beginn der Geschichte Gottes mit seinem Volk; auf zweiteres weist die Ergänzung לכם „euch" hin. Schneider (1990:36) ist der Meinung, der Anfang sei die Erlösung aus Ägypten, denn dieses Ereignis werde vom Volk Gottes konstant im Gottesdienst gefeiert. Calvin (1996:225) denkt, es sei sowohl die Belehrung seit der Kindheit gemeint, als auch die Zeit der Vorväter (besonders Abraham und Mose). Gott, der sich den Vätern offenbart habe, sei immer noch der gleiche. Da im folgenden Stich parallel von der Gründung der Erde gesprochen wird, ist mit „Anfang" wohl die Schöpfung gemeint – denn auch die Schöpfung erzählt von Gottes Wesen (Röm 1:20).

Das Verb בין „verstehen" mit der Grundbedeutung „unterscheiden / beurteilen können", betont, dass zum Hören das Verstehen kommen muss. Das ist nicht nur ein intellektueller, sondern auch ein gefühls- und willensgesteuerter Vorgang. Die Präpositionalphrase kann temporal „seit der Gründung ...", oder instrumental „durch die Gründung der Erde" verstanden werden, oder als Ergänzung des Inhalts „wie die Erde gegründet wurde", so bezöge sie sich inhaltlich auf alle vier Verben. Dies knüpft zwar gut an die Beschreibung der Größe und Majestät des Schöpfers und der Schöpfung in Vers 12 an, doch scheint es zu kurz gegriffen; eine instrumentale Bedeutung ist wahrscheinlicher. Auch Oswalt (1998:66) schreibt, dass das Nachdenken über die Schöpfung zu einem Schöpfer jenseits der Schöpfung führen müsse; der Kosmos könne nicht selbst für seine Existenz verantwortlich sein. Auf diese Weise sei schon Aristoteles zum „unbewegten Beweger" gelangt. Watts (1987:92) wirft die Frage auf, ob der Begriff als territoriales Gebiet verstanden werden müsse oder im Sinne der ganzen Erde. Der Hinweis im Kontext auf Nationen und Herrscher (Verse 15,

1.6 Betrachtung der einzelnen Verse

17, 22, 23) spreche für das erste, der auf Sterne und Himmel (Verse 22, 26) fürs zweite. Das instrumentale Verständnis der Präpositionalphrase bedingt, dass die ganze Erde gemeint ist.

Die beiden letzten Verben stehen im Gegensatz zu den beiden ersten im Perfekt. Der Imperfekt wirkt laut Oswalt (1998:66) intensivierend: es ist möglich zu wissen – und doch nicht zu wissen, zu hören – und doch nicht zu hören. So übersetzt er eindringlich: „Will you not know? Can you not hear?" Gemäß Koole (1997:107) weist der Tempuswechsel zum Perfekt darauf hin, dass das Volk Israel dieses Wissen vor langer Zeit hätte erwerben können, aber mit der Aufgabe des alten Glaubens Schuld auf sich geladen habe. Laut Elliger (1978:81) ist der Tempuswechsel dadurch begründet, dass zuerst an die eigene, gegenwärtige Erfahrung der Hörer angeknüpft und dann an die von den Vätern überkommene Tradition appelliert werde. Doch es gebe keinen Unterschied in der Qualität der Gotteserkenntnis: sie sei zwar Tradition, aber keine tote, sondern eine lebendige und werde von jeder Generation neu erlebt.

1.6.6 Jesaja 40:22–24   III Größer als die Machthaber; b) Folgerungen

Die drei Partizipien mit Artikel in den Versen 22 und 23, הישׁב „der Sitzende", הנוטה „der Ausspannende" und הנותן „der Gebende", beziehen sich auf Gott. Sie weisen laut Goldingay (2005:53) darauf hin, dass Gott nicht lediglich der deistische Uhrmacher sei, der den Kosmos ursprünglich in Bewegung gesetzt habe, sondern der heute aktive und souveräne Herrscher.

Der Ausdruck חוג הארץ „Kreis der Erde" in Vers 22 ist typisch für die Theologie der Schöpfung. Im biblischen Denken bezieht er sich auf die entfernten Horizonte, die bildhaft das Ende der Erde darstellen. Das verdeutlicht Jahwes absolute Überlegenheit über die Schöpfung. Das Verb ישׁב wird hier dreifach gebraucht. Zuerst bezieht es sich als Partizip und Subjekt auf Gott, der über der Erde thront. Gott ist König und Richter, er herrscht souverän über diese Welt. Die Betonung liegt auf Jahwes Größe: im Vergleich zu ihm sind die Bewohner (dasselbe Verb, auch ein Partizip) der Erde wie ein Schwarm Heuschrecken. Der Vergleich entspricht der Selbstbezeichnung der Spione, die das vor ihnen liegende Land auskundschafteten: „Wir sind wie Heuschrecken" (Num 13:33). Menschen haben letztlich keine Autorität auf der Erde, trotz ihrer Hybris. Gott aber thront über der Erde. Das betont die Distanz des Menschen zu Gott. Gott ist immer der andere, der Fremde, weil er so ganz anders ist als die Menschen, der Unbegreifliche. Das Verb נטה „ausspannen" im dritten Stich wird spezifisch für das Ausspannen eines Zeltes gebraucht (Gen 12:8), so auch für das Zelt des Himmels (Jes 42:5). Das Substantiv דק bezieht sich auf etwas Feines und Dünnes und spielt hier auf die Transparenz der Luft an. Das zugrunde liegende Verb bedeutet gemäß Oswalt (1998:65) „fein zermahlen". Laut Koole (1997:109) könne der Begriff aber auch mit אהל „Zelt" im vierten Stich kombiniert werden. Er plädiert für die Interpretation „himmlisches Zelt", das wie das Zelt der Begegnung vorzustellen sei: von außen sehe es aus wie ein dunkles Nomadenzelt, doch im Inneren verberge es wertvollen Stoff. Dies scheint etwas weit gegriffen. Hier erscheint das Verb ישׁב zum dritten Mal, nun im Infinitiv, es bezieht sich auf denjenigen oder diejenigen, die unter dem Himmelszelt wohnen. Das könnte laut Koole (1997:109–110) Gott selbst sein, denn gemäß des Alten Testaments ist er derjenige, der im Himmel wohnt und während der Wüstenwanderung wohnte er in einem Zelt. Doch gemäß Calvin

(1996:227) besage der Vers, dass der Ort unter dem Zelt den Menschen von Gott zum Bewohnen gegeben sei. Das korrespondiert auch mit dem zweiten Stich, der die Menschen als Bewohner der Erde nennt, somit befinden sie sich unter dem himmlischen Zelt. Jedenfalls ist es für Gott so einfach, den Himmel auszuspannen, wie es für einen Menschen ist, einen Stoff auszubreiten.

Vers 23 beschreibt nun, wie Gott in den Lauf der Welt eingreift. Er befreit Menschen von denen, die unrechtmäßig über sie herrschen und Macht ausüben, nämlich von den רוזנים „Wichtigen" im ersten Stich und von den שפטי ארץ „Richtern der Erde" im zweiten Stich. Der erste Begriff hat die Konnotation der Würde und der Autorität, er erscheint gewöhnlich parallel zu „Könige". Der zweite Begriff bezieht sich nicht nur auf Richter im engeren Sinne, sondern auf diejenigen, die dafür verantwortlich sind, das Volk zu führen und gerechte Bedingungen im Leben der Gemeinschaft herzustellen (wie im Buch der Richter). Beide Begriffe beschreiben ursprünglich die Macht und Stärke eines Königs. Da die Richter der Erde bei ihrer Aufgabe, Recht und Ordnung herzustellen, versagen, löscht Jahwe sie aus, um dann selbst Recht zu schaffen. Er macht sie zu nichts, zu אין und תהו (siehe Vers 17). Das Verb נתן „geben" im ersten Stich wird gemäß Oswalt (1998:67) gebraucht, wenn jemand zu einer offiziellen Position auserwählt wird. Hier wird ironisch impliziert: Diese wichtigen Leute, die jemand für eine wichtige Aufgabe auserwählt hat, sind in der Realität zur Nichtigkeit erwählt worden, verglichen mit der Autorität und Wichtigkeit Gottes. Das parallel gebrauchte Verb עשה „(zu etwas) machen" im zweiten Stich steht im Perfekt: schon immer hat Gott die Wichtigen der Welt zu Nichts gemacht und er wird das auch in Zukunft tun, das ist eine allgemeingültige Tatsache. So würde es auch der gegenwärtige Herrscher Nebukadnezar erfahren müssen: verglichen mit der Macht Gottes und in der Hand Gottes ist er so insignifikant, dass er einem Nichts gleichkommt. Gemäß Goldingay (2005:57) wurden Königtum und Machthaber im Mittleren Osten als die Fundamente der Erde betrachtet, als die Prinzipien der Weltordnung. Doch hier wird das Gegenteil beschrieben: die Personifizierung der Ordnung und Macht wird zur Personifizierung der Nichtigkeit.

Wie in Vers 24 vergleicht die Bibel Menschen immer wieder mit Pflanzen (Hos 2:25); der Traubenstock und der Feigenbaum sind Bilder der davidischen Königslinie (Jes 11:1); Jonas Sorge um seine Pflanze wird mit Gottes Sorge um Ninive verglichen (Jona 4:9–11). Hier illustriert das Bild der Pflanzen was unter „zu Nichts machen" (Vers 23) zu verstehen ist: die Machthaber werden „gepflanzt", „gesät" und „schlagen Wurzeln" – oder eben auch nicht. Im ersten Stich beschreibt נטה „pflanzen", wie die Wurzeln einer Pflanze ins Erdreich gepflanzt werden. Im zweiten Stich besagt זרע „säen", dass Saatgut auf die Erde geworfen wird. Im dritten Stich bezieht sich שרש „Wurzeln schlagen" laut Koole (1997:111–112) auf die Methode, den Schößling eines Baumes, z.B. eines Olivenbaums, zusammen mit einem Teil der Wurzel an einen anderen Ort zu verpflanzen, damit der neue Baum leicht eigene, neue Wurzeln entwickelt. Es geht um drei verschiedene Methoden, wie pflanzliches Leben entsteht. Die beiden ersten so begonnenen Sätze sind kurz und prägnant, der dritte ist etwas länger, dies gibt der Aussage ein schnelles Tempo, das den Leser fast außer Atem kommen lässt: Menschen erscheinen gerade erst auf der Bildfläche, und schon sind sie wieder verschwunden. Die Negation בל wird hier angemessen mit „kaum" übersetzt: „kaum sind sie gepflanzt …"[15]

---

[15] Siehe: 1.5.4 Die Bedeutung der Negation in Vers 24.

1.6 Betrachtung der einzelnen Verse

Der Gedankengang der zweiten Vershälfte ist folgender: Wenn der Wind auf die Pflanzen weht, dann vertrocknen sie und werden weggeweht wie wertloses, nichtiges Spreu – es ist so, als seien die Machthaber nie vorhanden gewesen. Spreu symbolisiert bei Jesaja das Schicksal der Nationen (Jes 29:5). Der Satz wird mit גם „auch" eingeleitet, so entsteht besonderer Nachdruck. Oswalt (1998:67) schreibt wie in der Targume die Bedeutung des Bildes interpretiert wird: „Though they increase, though they multiply, though their children grow up in the land, yet will he send his anger against them." In der Vergangenheit wurde Israel immer wieder von seinen Nachbarn bedroht und erlebte dann, wie Jahwe die Macht der Feinde brach. Daran soll es auch während der Bedrohung durch Assyrien denken – und in der Zukunft, scheinbar verloren in der Hand der Babylonier. Die Weltmächte sind kaum gepflanzt, kaum wachsen sie auf, da zerstört Gott sie schon wieder.

1.6.7 Jesaja 40:25   IV Größer als das Universum; a) Rhetorische Fragen

In Vers 25 greift der Verfasser die Frage nach dem Vergleich zwischen Jahwe und den Göttern von den Versen 18–20 wieder auf. Das ו zu Beginn des ersten Stiches führt eine Apodosis ein und wird mit „so / somit" übersetzt. Von Vers 18 wird im ersten Stich das Verb דמה „gleichen" übernommen, parallel wird im zweiten Stich שוה „gleich sein" / „auf dem gleichen Level sein" gebraucht. Ein bedeutender Unterschied zu Vers 18 ist, dass in Vers 25 Gott selbst in der ersten Person spricht. Das Wort קדוש, die Selbstbezeichnung Gottes im Nachsatz, unterstreicht, dass kein Mensch, kein Gott und kein Gottesbild die Antwort auf diese Frage darstellen kann. Das Fehlen eines Artikels zeigt gemäß Oswalt (1998:68), dass es sich um einen Namen, nicht lediglich um eine Beschreibung handle. Goldingay (2005:59) weist darauf hin, dass hier die Anbetung der Seraphime aufgenommen werde, die Jahwe mit „Heilig, heilig, heilig" (Jes 6) anrufen. Der „Heilige" weist auf seine Einzigartigkeit hin, seine göttliche Natur, das, was den geschaffenen Menschen vom ungeschaffenen Gott unterscheidet. Motyer (1999:250) schreibt, es scheine, als könne das Alte Testament nicht über den Schöpfer nachdenken, ohne sich dann seiner Heiligkeit und Herrschaft über die Welt zuzuwenden. Israel könne sich auf Gottes souveräne Fürsorge und Weisheit verlassen, doch es sei immer die Souveränität des Heiligen und deshalb ziehe ihre Schuld und ihr Vergleichen mit anderen Göttern seinen heiligen Zorn nach sich. Der Titel ist somit gleichzeitig ein Vorwurf: der Heilige hat ein Volk erwählt und geheiligt, aber es verhält sich weder wie ein geheiligtes Volk, noch betet es seinen heiligen Gott an.

1.6.8 Jesaja 40:26   IV Größer als das Universum; b) Folgerungen

Vers 26 gibt eine bildhafte Antwort auf die Fragen in Vers 25. Von der Herausforderung zum Vergleich geht der Verfasser weiter zu einem Vergleichspunkt (parallel zu Vers 18 mit 19/20). Der Leser soll seine Augen heben und sehen. Die Verben נשא „heben" und ראה „sehen" im ersten und zweiten Teilsatz bilden auch an anderen Stellen eine Einheit (Gen 13:10; Jes 49:18). Die Aufforderung die Augen zu heben impliziert, dass jemand bisher etwas zu wenig Beachtung geschenkt hat, das volle Aufmerksamkeit erfordert.

„Sehen" bedeutet, dass etwas erst mit den bloßen Augen betrachtet – und dann absorbiert wird. Erst wurde der Leser indirekt zum Hören aufgefordert (Vers 21), nun zum Sehen.

Im dritten Teilsatz wird dem Leser die Frage nach dem Schöpfer gestellt. Die Antwort zur Frage muss „Jahwe" lauten, während die Antwort in Vers 25 „niemand" war. Dies kehrt die Reihenfolge der Verse 12 und 13/14 um – dort war die richtige Antwort erst „Jahwe", dann „niemand". In Vers 26 geht es nicht in erster Linie um die Identität des Schöpfers – Jahwe oder Marduk, sondern es geht um die Weisheit und Macht, mit der Gott seine Schöpfung hervorgebracht hat und erhält, dieselbe Weisheit und Macht, die auch in Vers 12 illustriert wird. Das Verb ברא bezieht sich ausschließlich auf Gott und beschreibt seine souveräne schöpferische Tätigkeit in der Vergangenheit, in der Gegenwart und in der Zukunft; somit schließt die Frage die Antwort schon mit ein. Die Gestirne bleiben zunächst implizit, wie in Genesis 1, sie werden mit אלה „diese" eingeführt; erst im vierten Teilsatz bezeichnet der Verfasser die Himmelskörper als צבא „Heer des Himmels". Das schmälert ihre Bedeutung und widerspricht ihrer Überschätzung im Denken der anderen Völker. Das kanaanäische Denken betrachtete die Sterne als sichtbare Repräsentation Gottes, dies zeigt sich an den Berichten, wie die Israeliten in der Vergangenheit der Versuchung erlagen, das Heer des Himmels anzubeten (2 Kön 17:16). Aus dem Spott in Jes 47 wird deutlich, dass Israel gegenwärtig mit der Anbetung der Himmelskörper konfrontiert war. Die Babylonier verehren die Sonne als Gott Shamash, auch Mond und Sterne gelten als mystisch und göttlich, damit sollte Israel in Zukunft konfrontiert werden. Das Verb יצא „herausführen" hat einen Beiklang des Militärs: wie ein General seine Armee, so setzt Jahwe die Himmelskörper in Bewegung. Das Wort beschreibt hier den Auf- und Untergang von Sonne, Mond und Sternen wie das Aufmarschieren einer Armee. Auch der Begriff במספר „abgezählt", oder nach Elliger (1978:89) auch „vollzählig", hat die Konnotation des Militärs: der General mustert seine Truppen – alle, die aufgerufen werden, müssen erscheinen. במספר צבא meint die volle Anzahl aller Himmelskörper, jeden einzelnen.

Im fünften Teilsatz kann das Verb קרא sowohl „rufen", als auch „nennen" bedeuten. „Nennen" drückt Autorität aus, wie sie Eltern über ihre Kinder haben; der Begriff hat eine Konnotation der Beziehung und der Verantwortung. Da ein Name hier fehlt, ist die Bedeutung „rufen" wahrscheinlicher. Laut Elliger wird hier auf dem Hintergrund des Militärs ein „Befehls- und Gehorsamsverhältnis" ausgedrückt, ähnlich dem von Kyros zu Jahwe, den er bei Namen ruft (Jes 41:25). Wenn jemand bei seinem Namen gerufen wird, bedeutet dies, dass er in seiner Individualität gemeint ist. Oswalt (1998:70) schreibt, dass die Kenntnis des Namens eines Menschen in der alten Welt die Kenntnis seiner Natur und somit Macht über ihn bedeutet habe. Frey (1938:33) ist der Meinung, der Ausdruck „mit Namen rufen" bedeute hier: „ins Dasein rufen" / „Leben geben". Das ist zu weit gegriffen. Die Präposition מן im letzten Teilsatz kann laut Koole (1997:116) unterschiedlich verstanden werden: wenn רב אונים „große Allgewalt" und אמיץ כח „starke Kraft" Bezeichnungen für die Himmelskörper sind, dann hat die Präposition ihre übliche Bedeutung: „Von den vielen Vermögenden und denen mit starker Kraft fehlt keiner." Die Präposition kann auch bedeuten, dass kein Stern hinter Jahwe und seiner Kraft zurückbleibt. Zuletzt, und das reiht sich natürlich in das Verständnis des Textes ein, kann sie kausale Bedeutung haben: „Wegen seiner großen Kraft ... fehlt

1.6 Betrachtung der einzelnen Verse

keiner." Das lässt das Augenmerk allein auf Gottes Größe und Macht ruhen. אִישׁ „Mensch" kombiniert mit der Negation bedeutet hier „keiner" und bezieht sich auf die Gestirne. Das ist ungewöhnlich, da der Begriff fast ausschließlich für Menschen gebraucht wird. Wahrscheinlich liegt der Gebrauch im Bild der Armee aus dem vorangehenden Satz begründet. Der Vers verdeutlicht, dass nicht die Sterne, interpretiert durch die Astrologie, die Rahmenbedingungen für das Leben vorgeben, sondern dass der Mensch in ihrer Bewunderung auf die Herrschaft Gottes hingewiesen wird. Das Bild sagt: Gott ist nicht Teil des Kosmos und der Kosmos ist nicht Teil von Gott. Gott ist transzendente Macht – und zugleich Persönlichkeit. So führt Calvin (1996:232) aus, der Mensch sei darauf angelegt, die Sterne zu betrachten und auf den Schöpfer zu schließen. Es gehöre zur Gottlosigkeit des Menschen, das nicht zu akzeptieren, was ihm offensichtlich vorgelegt sei.

1.6.9 Jesaja 40:27–28a   V Größer als die Kraftlosigkeit; a) Rhetorische Fragen

Der Vers bildet das Zentrum der Perikope,[16] die facettenreich anhand verschiedener Themen Gottes Größe und Majestät vor Augen führt, und so zeigt, dass Israels Klage, Gott könne oder wolle sich nicht um seinen Weg kümmern, gegenstandslos ist.

Gott ist sowohl willig als auch fähig sein Volk zu retten. Das Interrogativpronomen לָמָּה „was" (Elliger 1978:96) bezieht sich auf beide Stichoi der ersten Bikola. Das Pronomen leitet oft einen Tadel oder eine Klage ein (Ps 44:25). Die Leser werden mit „Jakob" im ersten und mit „Israel" im zweiten Stich angesprochen. Die beiden Bezeichnungen erscheinen oft parallel. Dahinter steht laut Elliger die Vorstellung von der korporativen Persönlichkeit, die den Stammvater mit allen nachfolgenden Generationen als Einheit sehe. Die Anrede mit dem Doppelnamen spielt auf die Namensänderung des Patriarchen an (Gen 32:22ff.): das Volk wird an die Erwählung seiner Vorfahren, an die geschenkten Verheißungen, an den Bund, den Gott mit ihm geschlossen hat, erinnert. Trotz der Schuld, die das Volk auf sich geladen hat, und der bevorstehenden Strafe ist Israel-Jakob immer noch Gottes Volk, seine Schöpfung.

דֶּרֶךְ im ersten Stich der zweiten Bikola bedeutet die Lebenssituation, in der sich Gottes Volk befindet. Israels Weg scheint von Gott unbeachtet und ihm unbekannt zu sein – Gott kümmert sich nicht darum, dass sein Volk von seinen Feinden bedroht wird. Gemäß Schneider (1990:39) wird „Weg" immer wieder im Alten Testament für den im Hebräischen nicht vorhandenen Begriff „Geschichte" gebraucht. Das Wort hat aber auch die Konnotation von „Bewegung / Fortschritt / Zukunft". Israel ist also auf einem Weg – und Gott nimmt keine Notiz davon, dass es keinen Ausweg sieht. Bitterkeit und Unglaube entstehen. Der Begriff hat eine weitere Bedeutungstiefe: Jesaja gebraucht ihn für den Weg, auf dem die Erlösten geführt werden (Jes 8:23; 42:16); Gott kennt nicht nur die sündigen Wege des Volkes (Jes 8:11), sondern auch die hoffnungsvollen Wege, die er für es geplant hat. Parallel dazu wird מִשְׁפָּט im zweiten Stich gebraucht. Das intensiviert den Parallelismus: von der persönlichen Erfahrung (Weg), geht der Gedankengang nun zur moralischen Auswertung (Recht). Der Begriff beschreibt Gottes Charakter: er wird nichts

---
[16] Siehe: 1.2.3 Einheit der Perikope.

tun, das nicht dem Recht, der Gerechtigkeit und der Wahrheit entspricht. Wenn das Volk sagt, sein Recht gehe an seinem Gott vorbei, dann wirft es Gott vor, er würde entweder nicht wissen oder sich nicht kümmern um das, was Israels Recht sei. Das Suffix der ersten Person singular an „Recht" („mein Recht") gibt der Aussage einen fordernden Unterton. Es impliziert, dass Israel selbst bestimmen könne, was sein Recht vor Gott sei, was es von Gott erwarten könne. Die Präposition מן (anstatt על) vor „Gott" hat laut Elliger die Konnotation „als gehe es nicht vorn an Jahwe vorbei, sondern hinter seinem Rücken, so dass er es nicht sieht" Elliger (1978:97). Das dazu gehörende Verb עבר hat sowohl die Bedeutung „vorüber gehen", als auch „keine Notiz von etwas nehmen" (1 Kön 22:24). Derjenige, der sich selbst als der Richter vorstellt, kümmert sich offenbar nicht um das Recht seines Volkes. Zusammen mit אלהי „mein Gott" (auch hier Suffix 1.P. sing.) wird die Anklage Israels fast ironisch: was für ein „mein Gott" ist das, der mir nicht zu meinem Recht verhilft? Doch gemäß Oswalt (1998:72) impliziert das Suffix auch das Bündnisverhältnis zwischen Gott und seinem Volk. Trotzdem wird Gott angeklagt, weil er von seinem Volk abwesend sei. Der Kontext der Perikope verdeutlicht, dass die Anklage absurd ist: nicht Gott hat sich von seinem Volk abgewandt, das Gegenteil war der Fall. Laut Webb (1996:165) schwingt hier die archetypische Lüge mit, der Zweifel an Gott, der zuerst von der Schlange im Paradies ausgesprochen wurde (Gen 3:4–5): Ist Gottes Wort zuverlässig? Trotzdem ist eine solche Klage gegenüber Gott zulässig, das zeigen die Parallelen mit den Klagepsalmen und dem Klagelied. Die Frage mit dem Unterton des Tadels wird in Vers 28a fortgesetzt. Der Verfasser benutzt erneut die Verben ידע „wissen" und שמע „hören" parallel in den beiden Stichoi der Bikola; die Fragen sind ähnlich formuliert wie in Vers 21, doch nun im Perfekt, denn Information war schon lange erhältlich. Das Verb „hören" erklärt, wie das „wissen" hätte erreicht werden sollen. Die implizierte Antwort ist hier: natürlich hat das Volk Gottes gehört und es weiß auch, doch sie haben es nicht verstanden und es sich nicht zu Herzen genommen, deshalb fehlen die in Vers 21 gebrauchten Verben נגד „verkünden" und בין „verstehen".

1.6.10 Jesaja 40:28b–31 V Größer als die Kraftlosigkeit; b) Folgerungen

Als Reaktion auf den Zweifel und die Klage in Vers 27 wird Gottes Wesen erneut beschrieben. Die Antwort lautet im ersten Stich der zweiten Bikola des Verses: Jahwe ist עולם „ewig". Das ist nicht nur ein temporaler Ausdruck, sondern bedeutet auch, dass Gott souverän ist über die Welt und die Geschichte, von Anfang bis Ende. Er ist der alte Gott, der für immer bestehen wird.

Dies wird im zweiten Stich weiter erläutert: Gott ist nicht nur Gott seines Volkes, sondern der קצות הארץ „Enden der Erde", des Ortes, von dem Gott die Völker sammeln wird. Gott steht also nicht nur über der Zeit, sondern auch über dem Raum. Gemeint sind hier die Ränder des geographischen und politischen Horizontes Israels. Darüber hinaus sind die Ränder der Erde gemeint und alles, was sie umschließen. Die Nennung der Ränder stellt dar, dass auf der ganzen Erde kein Raum frei bleibt, an dem Gott nicht seine Herrschaft durchsetzt. Dies ist ein Trost für die kommende Zeit des Exils: für das Volk Gottes ist Jerusalem der Mittelpunkt der Welt, doch Gott hat auch die Enden der Erde im Blick und übt dort seine Herrschaft aus. Die Schöpfungstätigkeit,

1.6 Betrachtung der einzelnen Verse

die sich zuvor auf die Himmelskörper bezog, fokussiert sich nun auf die Erde. Der Verfasser denkt weniger an die ursprüngliche Schöpfung der Erde als an ihre konstante Erhaltung bis heute. Gott, der Schöpfer, kann tun, was immer er will – scheinbare Hinauszögerung der Hilfe bedeutet nicht, dass er nicht helfen wollte oder könne. Doch Gott selbst ist nicht Teil der Schöpfung. Um Gott zu erkennen, ist die Schöpfung nicht genug, der Mensch braucht Offenbarung (Jes 55:6–11).

Die Verben יעף „müde" und יגע „matt", die parallel in der folgenden Bikola gebraucht werden, sind sehr ähnlich in ihrer Bedeutung und stehen auch an anderen Stellen parallel (Jer 51:58). Koole (1997:123) schlägt vor, das erste bedeute Kraftverlust aufgrund ungenügender Nahrung (1 Sam 14:28) und das zweite aufgrund großer Anstrengung (Jes 47:12). Sie zeigen, dass die Energie des Menschen begrenzt ist. Die Negationen vor beiden Verben weisen deutlich auf Gottes Allmacht hin: Gott wird nicht müde und muss nicht ausruhen. Weinfeld, zitiert in Goldingay (2005:71), versteht den Vers als Polemik gegenüber dem Schöpfungsbericht in Genesis, wo berichtet wird, dass Gott am siebten Tag ruhte (Gen 2:2). Er räumt aber ein, dass der Vers einen polemischen Kontrast zu den kanaanäischen Göttern darstellen könnte, die müde wurden. Hier wird lediglich ein Faktum konstatiert, ohne jegliche Polemik. Zudem lässt sich eine Anspielung auf die feindlich gesinnten Nachbarvölker Israels erkennen, die schließlich auch müde werden. Der Nachsatz drückt grammatisch negativ („seine Einsicht ist nicht erforschbar") einen positiven Gedanken aus: es ist dumm, das zu limitieren, was Gott tun kann. Gottes Weisheit, sein Verständnis mit dem er die Welt regiert, kennt keine Grenzen. Doch weil der Mensch Grenzen kennt, kann er über Gottes Größe nur in der Negation denken.

Vers 29 ist das Gegenstück zu den Versen 15–17 und 23–24: die Mächtigen verlieren ihre Macht, doch die Müden werden mit Kraft ausgestattet. Verglichen mit der Kraft Gottes, ist der Mensch kraftlos. Gott ermüdet nicht – der Mensch wird müde. Gott hat רב אונים „viel Kraft" (Vers 27) – der Mensch hat אין אונים „keine Kraft". Doch Gott gibt von seiner Kraft weiter. Das Verb נתן „geben" im ersten Stich erscheint als Partizip: die Gabe von Kraft ist kein einmaliger Akt, sondern eine Charakteristik Gottes. Anstatt sich über Gottes Abwesenheit zu beklagen, gibt es allen Grund, sich über seine Gegenwart zu freuen. Die Verse schauen schon voraus auf Israels Kraft- und Machtlosigkeit im Exil. Gott ist ein großer und ein großzügiger Gott, darauf weist das Verb רבה „vermehren" im zweiten Stich hin. Der Verfasser bezieht sich vielleicht auf die Geschichte Jakobs bei Peniel (Gen 32:24ff.), der in seiner Kraftlosigkeit neue Kraft erhielt. Genauso wird es seinen Nachkommen gehen, wenn sie sich auf ihren Gott berufen. Doch gemäß Calvin (1996:237) muss der, der von Gott neue Kraft erhalten will, seine eigene Schwäche und Kraftlosigkeit zugeben; er zitiert Paulus: Ich will „mich am allerliebsten rühmen meiner Schwachheit" (2 Kor 12:9).

Die Begriffe נערים und בחורים „junge Männer" im ersten und zweiten Stich von Vers 30 beziehen sich auf das Alter; junge Männer sind der Inbegriff von Kraft (Spr 20:29). Der erste Begriff meint junge Männer allgemein, der zweite wird laut Oswalt (1998:71) eher für Männer gebraucht, die speziell für den militärischen Dienst ausgewählt und ausgebildet wurden (Ri 20:15). Ihre Frontalstellung betont die Begriffe und die Konjunktion ו zu Beginn des Verses verleiht der Aussage laut Oswalt (1998:74) zusätzlichen Nachdruck: „sogar Knaben …" Die Kraftlosen von Vers 29, die neue Kraft erhalten, korrespondieren mit den kräftigen jungen Männern, die kraftlos werden, wenn die Beziehung zu einer transzendenten Kraftquelle fehlt. Die normale menschliche Situation von Macht und Ohnmacht, Stolz und Demütigung, Trost und Not erfährt eine Umkehrung, wenn Gott eingreift und jedem seinen Platz zuweist und seine Kraft so verteilt, wie er es will. Dies wird deutlich durch die Wiederholung der Verben יעף „müde werden" und יגע „erschöpft werden" aus Vers 28 im ersten Stich; sie treffen nicht auf Gott, wohl aber auf Menschen zu, sogar auf junge Männer. Es ist nicht nur eine Möglichkeit, sondern der Lauf der Welt, dass sie stolpern, das wird durch die figura ethymologica von כשל im zweiten Stich ausgedrückt, „sie stolpern ganz sicher".

Vers 31 bildet den Höhepunkt der Perikope. Die Konjunktion ו zu Beginn des Verses ist laut Oswalt (1998:73) adversativ und formt einen Kontrast zwischen den jungen Männern von Vers 30 und denen, die auf Gott warten. Childs (2001:311) betont: Gottes Unvergleichbarkeit und Allmacht ist nicht ein theoretisches Thema, das hier abgehandelt wird, sondern Gott kommt damit seinem Volk zu Hilfe. Der Vers schließt nach dem Einschub von Vers 30 direkt an Vers 29 an. Das grammatische Subjekt ist der Mensch, der mit dem Partizip von קוה „warten" im ersten Stich der Tetrakola bezeichnet ist. Gemeint ist hier ein aktives und gespanntes Warten, ja „erwarten" und „hoffen". Diejenigen, die warten, bekommen neue Kraft, denn das Bewusstsein, dass Gott die Klage gehört hat und darauf antworten und eingreifen wird, gibt neue Kraft mit den Anforderungen des gegenwärtigen Lebens fertig zu werden. Der Fokus ist nicht auf dem menschlichen Warten, sondern auf dem göttlichen Handeln. Wie Gott eingreifen wird, ist noch unbekannt, doch der Wartende hält an der Erwartung des Eingreifens fest mit der Kraft, die Gott bis dahin gibt. Das Wort impliziert eine völlige Abhängigkeit von Gott, denn der Mensch muss Gott über die Art und Weise der Hilfe entscheiden lassen. Es ist das Eingeständnis, dass es keine andere Hilfe gibt, weder innerhalb noch außerhalb des Menschen. Laut Koole (1997:126) bedeutet das Verb חלף „etwas an die Stelle von etwas anderem stellen" oder, nach Goldingay (2005:74), etwas Altes aufgeben und etwas Neues erhalten. Es habe einen tieferen Bedeutungsgehalt als die bloße „Erneuerung" von Kraft, es impliziere den Anschluss an eine neue Kraftquelle. Doch der Hiphil deute darauf hin, dass das Volk selbst aktiv sein müsse, nämlich einen Neubeginn starten und Gottes Versprechen in Anspruch nehmen, um so Gottes Kraft zu erhalten. Der zweite Stich gebraucht das Bild des נשר „Adler" oder „Gänsegeier". Der Adler, der in diesem Kontext näher liegt, wird bewundert für seinen hohen Flug und für sein Tempo (Hi 39:27ff.). Der Vergleich liegt im Auffliegen des Adlers.[17] Watts (1987:96) ergänzt, dass der kraftvolle Flug des Adlers nicht durch die Kraft seiner Flügel bedingt sei, sondern durch die Windströmungen, die den Adler mit seinen Flügeln trügen.

Im dritten und vierten Stich werden die Verben יעף und יגע aus den Versen 28 und 30 aufgenommen. Diejenigen, die auf Gott hoffen, werden im Gegensatz zu den jungen Männern nicht müde. Der Gott, der selbst nicht müde wird, teilt seine Kraft mit seinem Volk. Das Verb רוץ „rennen" im dritten Stich entstand wahrscheinlich aus dem Vergleich mit den jungen Männern, es erinnert an einen Wettläufer. Das Verb הלך „gehen" im vierten Stich wirkt weniger kraftvoll, es erinnert an das Marschieren eines Soldaten. Duhm, zitiert in Elliger (1978:102), ist der Meinung, dass das Verb „das vorhergehende Bild

---

[17] Siehe: 1.5.5 Der Vergleich mit dem Adler in Vers 31.

entschieden schädigt", doch Elliger selbst widerspricht dem, weil sich Bilder in der hebräischen Poesie oft stoßen. „Gehen" beschreibe die realistische Verlangsamung vom Höhepunkt zur Ausdauer – nicht nur der Start, sondern auch das Ziel sei wichtig. Das Verb impliziert eine Richtung, nicht ziellose Bewegung. Jemand, der sich seines Weges sicher ist, kann auch langsam und ausdauernd gehen, er muss nicht sinnlos hetzen. Motyer (1999:251) erklärt den Gebrauch der Verben folgendermaßen: mit „rennen" seien die anstrengenden Herausforderungen des Lebens gemeint, „gehen" beziehe sich auf das tägliche Leben mit seiner Arbeit und Mühe. Der Allmächtige Gott gibt seinem Volk Kraft, im mühsamen Alltag auf seinem Weg weiter zu gehen und er geht ihm selbst voraus. Gæbelein (1986:246) sieht eine dreifache Abstufung: das größte Ausmaß an Gnade werde nicht gebraucht für das seltene Fliegen oder das gelegentliche Rennen, sondern für das konstante Gehen. Die Zusage ist eine Ermutigung für den gläubigen Rest im Volk, die Vertreibung ins Exil und die spätere Rückführung durchzustehen und dabei den Blick und die Hoffnung auf Gott nicht zu verlieren. Laut Calvin (1996:240) sei es zwar realistisch, dass Gläubige entmutigt und müde werden, doch sie erhalten langfristig neue Kraft von Gott. Er zieht eine Parallele zu Paulus:

> Wir sind von allen Seiten bedrängt, aber wir ängstigen uns nicht. Uns ist bange, aber wir verzagen nicht. Wir leiden Verfolgung, aber wir werden nicht verlassen. Wir werden unterdrückt, aber wir kommen nicht um. (2 Kor 4:8–9)

1.7 Inhaltliche Übersetzung

1.7.1 Jesaja 40:12–17   I Größer als die Schöpfung

Wer misst das Wasser mit seiner hohlen Hand,
Und bestimmt mit seiner Spanne die Weite des Himmels?
Wer misst den Staub der Erde in einem Messbecher,
Und wiegt mit einer Waage die Berge,
Und die Hügel mit Waagschalen?

Wer ermisst das Wesen Jahwes,
Und welcher Ratgeber belehrt ihn?
Mit wem hat er sich beraten,
Und wer unterrichtet ihn?
Wer weist ihm den Pfad der Gerechtigkeit,
Und wer lehrt ihn Wissen,
Und wer zeigt ihm den Weg der vollkommenen Weisheit?

Die Völker sind doch wie ein Tropfen, der vom Eimer fällt.
Sie sind so unbedeutend wie ein Staubkorn auf einer Waagschale.
Die fernen Länder schweben doch nach oben wie Staubflocken.
Selbst die Bäume des Libanons genügen nicht für ein Feuer auf dem Altar.
Und seine Tiere reichen nicht aus für ein Brandopfer.

Alle Völker sind Gott gegenüber so, als existierten sie nicht.
Im Vergleich zu ihm zählen sie weniger als nichts.

1.7.2 Jesaja 40:18–20   II Größer als die Götter

Also, mit wem vergleicht ihr Gott?
Und welches Bild ist ihm gleich?

Etwa ein Götterbild? Das gießt doch der Handwerker! Der Goldschmied überzieht es mit Gold und versieht es mit silbernen Ketten. Wer nicht viel geben kann, der wählt Holz, das nicht verfault. Er sucht sich einen begabten Handwerker, der stellt das Götterbild so auf, dass es nicht wackelt.

1.7.3 Jesaja 40:21–24   III Größer als die Machthaber

Wisst ihr es denn nicht?
Hört ihr es denn nicht?
Wurde es euch nicht von Anfang an bekannt gemacht?
Könnt ihr es nicht verstehen, wenn ihr die Schöpfung betrachtet?

Gott thront über der Erde von Horizont zu Horizont.
Und ihre Bewohner sind wie Heuschrecken.
Er breitet den Himmel aus wie ein feines Tuch.
Er spannt ihn aus wie ein Zelt, damit die Menschen darunter wohnen.

Er gibt die Machthaber der Nichtigkeit preis.
Er macht die Herrscher der Welt zunichte.

Gerade erst wurden sie gepflanzt.
Gerade erst wurden sie gesät.
Ihr Schössling ist gerade erst in der Erde verwurzelt.
Und trotzdem lässt Gott Wind über sie blasen, so trocknen sie aus und der Sturm trägt sie fort wie Spreu.

1.7.4 Jesaja 40:25–26   IV Größer als das Universum

„Mit wem vergleicht ihr mich,
Und wer steht auf gleicher Stufe mit mir?" fragt der heilige Gott.

Seht nach oben und schaut hin: Wer hat das alles erschaffen? Gott lässt das Heer der Sterne aufmarschieren. Jeden Stern ruft er beim Namen. Wegen Gottes umfassender Macht und großen Kraft fehlt keiner.

1.7.5 Jesaja 40:27–31   V Größer als die Kraftlosigkeit

Warum sagt ihr vom Volk Jakobs –
Warum klagt ihr Leute Israels:
„Jahwe kümmert sich nicht darum, auf welchem Weg wir gehen.
Unser Gott nimmt keine Notiz davon, wenn wir nicht zu unserem Recht kommen."?

Wisst ihr es denn nicht?
Habt ihr es denn nicht gehört?

Gott war schon immer und wird ewig sein.
Vom einen zum anderen Ende der Erde hat Jahwe alles erschaffen.
Er wird nicht müde.
Er wird nicht erschöpft.
Gottes Weisheit kennt keine Grenzen.

Gott schenkt den Müden immer wieder neue Lebenskraft.
Er erneuert die Stärke der Kraftlosen.

Selbst Knaben werden müde und erschöpft,
Und starke junge Männer stolpern ganz sicher.

Denjenigen jedoch, die ihre Hoffnung auf Jahwe richten, schenkt er neue Kraft.
Sie fliegen aufwärts mit Flügeln wie Adler.
Sie rennen und werden nicht erschöpft.
Sie gehen und werden nicht müde.

1.8 Anwendung

Gott wendet sich uns, den Kraftlosen, heute persönlich zu und schenkt uns seine Kraft, wenn wir unsere Hoffnung auf ihn setzen. Dafür bürgt Gott selbst mit seiner Größe.

Diese Größe zeigt sich folgendermaßen: Wenn wir die Schöpfung betrachten, dann bezeugt sie Gott: die Unendlichkeit des Wassers, die Weite des Himmels, die Formation der Erde bis an die Horizonte demonstrieren Gottes Majestät, mit der er seine Schöpfung nicht nur erschaffen hat, sondern auch erhält. Es ist heilsam für uns, immer wieder in die Natur zu gehen und uns durch sie bewusst Gottes Größe vor Augen führen zu lassen. Mit der gleichen Größe und Macht wendet er sich uns zu und steht zu uns. Wir sind versucht, oft unbewusst und besonders in schwierigen Lebenssituationen, Gott vorzuschreiben, was er für uns tun soll, ihn manipulieren zu wollen, ihn auf unsere Seite zu ziehen, eine Gegenleistung für unseren Arbeit und Dienst zu erpressen. Dabei nehmen wir uns selbst viel zu wichtig. Doch Gott ist souverän und immer größer als unsere Gedanken und Gefühle. Wir können vor Gott nur kapitulieren und uns ihm ganz anvertrauen. Wenn wir realistisch sind, dann sehen wir, wie unbedeutend wir sind im Vergleich zu Gottes Größe. Auch die Sorgen und Fragen, die uns beschäftigen, sind vor Gott unbedeutend – nicht im Sinne, dass sie ihm egal wären, sondern dass es für ihn einfach ist, Gutes daraus entstehen zu lassen.

Gott ist nicht nur größer als die anderen Götter – viel mehr: kein Gott existiert außer dem einen lebendigen Gott. Trotzdem machen wir uns Götter in unserem Alltag: das, woran wir unser Herz hängen, wird zu unserem Gott. Sei das nun Reichtum und Besitz, Erfolg und Ansehen, die eigene Kraft und Intelligenz oder Beliebtheit – was für manche unwichtig ist, mag für andere den Rang eines Gottes einnehmen. Früher oder später kommen wir dann unweigerlich an unsere Grenzen und erfahren schmerzhaft, wie Gott größer ist als das, was wir uns selbst als Götter zusammenbasteln. Dann es ist befreiend zu erleben, wie viel größer Gott ist als unsere Götter. Wir können uns auf den wahren lebendigen Gott verlassen, wir dürfen mit kraftlosen und leeren Händen vor ihm stehen.

Wir fühlen uns ausgeliefert: dem Lauf der Welt, den Machthabern, denen, die Entscheidungen treffen, die uns betreffen, und wir haben keinen Einfluss darauf. Wir fühlen uns wie ein Rädchen im großen Getriebe, aus dem wir kaum ausbrechen können. Gott sieht das alles aus einer weiteren Perspektive: Diejenigen, die Macht haben, sind ihm gegenüber wie Heuschrecken. Wiederum hilft uns ein Blick auf die Schöpfung, um eine neue Perspektive zu gewinnen: Derjenige, der alles geschaffen hat, bestimmt heute den Lauf der Welt, nicht die scheinbaren Machthaber. Das gibt Gelassenheit, wenn wir die Welt mit ihren täglichen Schreckensnachrichten, mit ihren zahlreichen globalen Ungerechtigkeiten in Politik und Wirtschaft betrachten, und es befreit uns, Verantwortung in unserer eigenen Lebensumwelt wahrzunehmen.

Der Blick auf das Universum, besonders auf die Vielzahl der Sterne, die in einer klaren Nacht zu sehen sind, weist auf die Größe dessen hin, der den Lauf der Gestirne bestimmt. Wir Menschen sehen uns in der richtigen Perspektive, wenn wir den Nachthimmel mit seinen Sternen betrachten. Gleichzeitig verleiht es uns Zuversicht zu wissen, dass es einen gibt, der selbst den fernsten Stern in seiner Hand hat und das Universum zusammenhält. Gott ist es, der nicht nur die Bahn jedes einzelnen Sterns, sondern auch den Lebensweg jedes einzelnen Menschen kennt und sich darum kümmert.

Der Gott, der größer ist als die Schöpfung, als die Götter, als die Machthaber, als das Universum, der ist auch größer als unsere Kraftlosigkeit. Wir leiden an unserer Begrenztheit, an unserer Ohnmacht. Wir beginnen Aufgaben mit Vision und mit Enthusiasmus, bis sie langsam verpuffen – und zurück bleiben Müdigkeit, Kraftlosigkeit und Ohnmacht. Wir werden desillusioniert und frustriert. Gott hat versprochen, uns an seiner Kraft teilhaben zu lassen. Jegliche Kraft kommt von Gott, ob das ein Mensch anerkennt oder nicht. Auch derjenige, der bewusst mit Gott lebt, kennt Müdigkeit und Kraftlosigkeit. Gott hat für uns einen Rhythmus von Arbeit und Ruhe eingerichtet und jeder benötigt Zeiten der Regeneration. Gott hat uns versprochen, genügend Kraft zum Leben zur Verfügung zu stellen, damit wir in Gottes Gegenwart auf unserem Lebensweg weitergehen und ein Leben führen können, das ihm gefällt – manchmal an den Grenzen unserer Kraft. Es ist befreiend, Gott die eigene Unzulänglichkeit und Kraftlosigkeit zu bekennen und ihn bewusst um Lebenskraft für die großen und kleinen Dinge des Alltags zu bitten. Manchmal schenkt Gott Kraft und Energie in Fülle. Manchmal gibt er gerade genug um die Tage mit ihren Anforderungen zu bestehen, gerade genug um den Blick immer wieder zögerlich auf Gott zu richten und an der Hoffnung festzuhalten, dass er irgendwann in einer persönlichen Notlage oder in den Konflikten der Welt eingreifen wird. In all dem ist Gott treu und stellt sich zu uns, wenn wir auf ihn warten und hoffen.

1.9 Zusammenfassung

Wie manifestiert sich die Größe Gottes in Jesaja 40:12–31?

Zu Beginn der ersten Strophe fragt der Verfasser, wer die Maße der Welt, wie Wasser, Himmel, Staub, Hügel und Berge mit viel zu klein anmutenden Maßeinheiten messen könne (Vers 12). Die Fragen sind in einer Katabasis angeordnet, die zu messenden Objekte nähern sich dem Menschen. Darin deutet sich die Bewegung von Gott zum Menschen, die diese Perikope durchzieht,

1.9 Zusammenfassung

bereits an. Die Antwort auf die Fragen muss „Jahwe" lauten, denn er ist der Schöpfer und Erhalter, er ist so viel größer als seine Schöpfung und kann sie mit Leichtigkeit messen.

Wenn der Mensch die Schöpfung nicht messen kann, dann ist er erst recht nicht in der Lage, den Geist Gottes zu ermessen und ihn zu beraten (Verse 13–14). Gott braucht kein Pantheon von Göttern, das ihm Ratschläge gibt, wie es in den Vorstellungen der Nachbarn Israels existiert. Als Folgerung werden die Völker mit einer Simile in ihrer zu vernachlässigenden Winzigkeit gegenüber Gottes Größe beschrieben (Vers 15). Auch die Völker sind Teil der Schöpfung und jedes einzelne muss sich in den Plan einfügen, den Jahwe für es bereithält. Das ist ein Trost für das von seinen Nachbarn bedrohte Volk Gottes, es verdeutlicht die scharfe Trennung zwischen dem Volk des wahren Gottes und den anderen Völkern. Wenn unter den Völkern sogar der Libanon mit seinen weithin berühmten Bäumen und Tieren für ein Opfer unzureichend ist (Vers 16), wie viel mehr dann all die anderen Völker. Das macht auch den Gedanken zunichte, dass der Mensch ein Opfer oder irgendetwas anderes zu seinem Heil beisteuern könnte. So sagt es der Verfasser nun hart und klar: alle Völker sind nichtig vor Gott (Vers 17), es ist so, als existierten sie gar nicht im Vergleich zu seiner Größe, dazu gehören auch die Feinde Israels. Den Völkern wohnt zwar Wert inne als Geschöpfe Gottes, doch sie können nichts ausrichten entgegen dem Willen Gottes. Gott ist so viel größer als seine Schöpfung, größer als die Natur und größer als die Menschen und Völker als Teil der Schöpfung.

Der Verfasser fragt in der zweiten Strophe erneut nach einem Vergleich für Gott, insbesondere nach einem Bild, das ihm standhalten könnte (Vers 18). Vergleiche aus der menschlichen Erfahrung für Gottes Größe sind erlaubt, da der Mensch letztlich nie über seinen eigenen Erfahrungshorizont hinaus denken kann. Doch ist es verboten, Gott etwas gleichzusetzen in Verehrung und Anbetung. Genauso nichtig wie ein Bild für Gott sind auch die Völker, die sich auf ein Gottesbild verlassen – Israel soll wissen, dass sein Gott größer ist.

Als Folgerung beschreibt der Verfasser die Herstellung eines Gottesbildes (Verse 19–20). Das Bild wird mit Sorgfalt und Kunstfertigkeit angefertigt und so befestigt, dass es nicht wackelt. Durch ihre Sachlichkeit wohnt der Beschreibung leise Ironie inne. Die Warnung erinnert an das Gottesbild des Dagon, der in Jahwes Gegenwart zu Boden fiel. Zwar wussten die antiken Völker zu unterscheiden zwischen einem Gott und dem Bild, das ihn repräsentierte, doch gleichzeitig wurde angenommen, dass ein Gott sein Bild bewohne. Offene Verurteilung und die Androhung von Strafe für die Herstellung von toten Götzen sind hier nicht nötig – allein die nüchterne Beschreibung der Anfertigung des Gottesbildes durch den Menschen führt vor Augen, dass ein Götzenbild tot ist und nicht helfen kann. Die Parallelstellen zeigen auf, dass die Anfertigung und Anbetung von Götzenbildern Strafe nach sich zieht. Der Abgrund, der sich zwischen toten Gottesbildern und der Größe des lebendigen Gottes auftut, ist scharf. Gott ist viel größer als alle Vergleiche, als die anderen Götter und ihre Bilder.

In der dritten Strophe muss sich Israel wie eine Schulklasse fragen lassen, ob es denn nicht gehört habe, und nicht wisse (Vers 21) von der Größe Gottes. Die vier Verben bilden einen nachdrücklichen Chiasmus und implizieren durch die Imperfekt-Perfekt-Folge, dass das Wissen schon längst hätte erworben werden können. Dass Israel seinen Gott nicht kennt, liegt nicht an der mangelnden Verkündigung oder der Gelegenheit zum Verständnis, sondern am mangelnden

Vertrauen und Gehorsam. Seit Beginn der Weltgeschichte, abzulesen an der Schöpfung, wendet sich Gott den Gläubigen und seinem Volk zu. Gerade Israel müsste das eigentlich durch seine eigene Geschichte und durch seine Erfahrung mit seinem großen Gott gelernt haben.

Als Folgerung wird wieder explizit gesagt: Gott thront und herrscht über seine Schöpfung (Vers 22), ihm gegenüber sind die Menschen wie Heuschrecken. Während Menschen sich abmühen, Gold über Götzenbildern auszubreiten, breitet der große Gott den Himmel aus. Diejenigen aber, die in der Welt die Macht eines Herrschers, Richters und Gesetzgebers haben, die angeblich die Ordnung der Welt bestimmten, sind nichtig im Vergleich zu Gott (Vers 23). Dies illustriert die folgende Hypokatastasis bildhaft (Vers 24): Die Herrscher sind gerade erst verwurzelt, dann werden sie schon wieder weggeweht vom Wind, den Gott über sie blasen lässt, sie sind wie Spreu – der Innbegriff von Nichtigkeit. Die Parallelstellen verdeutlichen, dass das Bild für Gericht über die Herrscher steht. Das Gericht erfolgt nicht grundsätzlich, weil sie Macht besitzen, sondern weil sie ihre Macht missbrauchen. Gott ist mit seiner Macht, Kraft und Größe den irdischen Machthabern unendlich überlegen. Im Chiasmus der ersten vier Strophen der Perikope korrespondiert die dritte Strophe mit der zweiten Strophe: sowohl die Götter als auch die Machthaber sind diejenigen, die Gott seine Macht streitig machen wollen, die selbst unrechtmäßig nach Macht und Größe streben oder denen sie von Menschen unrechtmäßig zugeschrieben wird.

In der vierten Strophe fragt Gott selbst (Vers 25), wer einem Vergleich mit ihm standhalte. Die Frage aus der zweiten Strophe wird wieder aufgenommen und durch die Wiederholung in ihrer Undenkbarkeit verstärkt. Die Selbstbezeichnung – der Heilige – verdeutlicht die Lächerlichkeit des Vergleichs. Gott ist nicht ohne seine Heiligkeit denkbar und er fordert auch ein heiliges Leben von denen, die zu ihm gehören.

Die Folgerung beinhaltet die Aufforderung, Gottes Schöpfung zu betrachten (Vers 26). Der Betrachter kann von der Schöpfung auf den Schöpfer schließen, von Gottes Werk etwas über seinen Charakter erfahren, nämlich seine Größe und Treue, mit der er die Schöpfung gestaltete und erhält. Wie ein General seine Armee, so beherrscht Gott seine Schöpfung, erkennbar an den Sternen, deren Namen er kennt und deren Bahn über den Himmel er lenkt. Nicht aus dem Lauf der Sterne lässt sich das Schicksal des Menschen ablesen, wie die Nachbarvölker Israels glaubten (besonders das mächtige Babylon), sondern der Gott Israels bestimmt den Lauf der Sterne. Im Chiasmus korrespondiert die vierte mit der ersten Strophe, die auch von der Schöpfung handelt. Gott ist viel größer als das Universum und alles, was er geschaffen hat. Die fünfte Strophe einleitend wird Israel angesprochen (Vers 27), denn es beklagt, dass Gott sich nicht um es kümmere, ihm nicht zu seinem Recht verhelfe, sein Versprechen nicht halte. Es ist die archetypische Lüge, die beim Sündenfall zuerst ausgesprochen wurde: Gott wird der Lüge bezichtigt. Die ersten vier Strophen haben bereits bildhaft und eindrücklich belegt, dass Gott nicht zu klein ist um zu helfen, dass er helfen kann, doch aufgrund seiner Größe scheint er auch fern und unberechenbar. Die Frage, ob Gott helfen will, wird erst in der fünften Strophe beantwortet: Gott will sich in seiner Größe dem Menschen zuwenden, auch wenn er seine Hilfe hinauszögert – sei es aus pädagogischen oder anderen Gründen, für die Gott in seiner Größe und Souveränität vor dem Menschen keine Rechenschaft ablegen muss. Eigentlich müsste das Volk aus seinen zahlreichen Erfahrungen in der Vergangenheit gelernt haben, dass Gott sich um es kümmert (Vers 28a). Diese Aussagen implizieren die aus der dritten Strophe aufgenommenen Fragen durch ihre Wiederholung nachdrücklich.

Die Folgerung ist die erneute Vorstellung von Gottes Charakter (Vers 28b): Gott ist ewig und er herrscht souverän in Ewigkeit. Auch lokal hat er keine Grenzen: er herrscht bis an die Enden der Erde, auch dort, wohin Israel ins Exil gehen wird. Darauf folgen sehr persönliche, sich dem einzelnen Menschen zuwendende Aussagen: Der Mensch wird müde, er braucht Nahrung und Ruhephasen. Doch Gott, der nicht müde wird, gibt dem Menschen von seiner Kraft weiter (Vers 29). Das ist kein einmaliger Akt, sondern beschreibt die Beziehung Gottes zu seiner Schöpfung, insbesondere zum Menschen. Dafür muss der Mensch seine Kraftlosigkeit zugeben. Junge Männer stehen innerhalb der Metonymie für Lebenskraft (Vers 30), doch wenn ihnen eine transzendente Kraftquelle fehlt, dann kommen auch sie an ihre Grenzen, sie werden müde und stolpern – wie viel mehr dann die anderen Menschen! Gott verteilt seine Kraft nicht nach menschlichen Maßstäben sondern entsprechend seines souveränen Willens. Den Höhepunkt (Vers 31) bildet paradoxerweise eine Katabasis mit den Verben „fliegen", „rennen" und „gehen". Es ist eine Hypokatastatis bezüglich eines Lebens, das ausgestattet ist mit Gottes neuer Kraft. Dadurch wird eine Verbindung zur einleitenden Katabasis geschaffen, das bedeutet: Gottes wahre Größe zeigt sich daran, dass er sich klein macht und Menschen an seiner Größe und Kraft teilhaben lässt. Diese Kraft erhält der Mensch, wenn er auf Gott hofft und sein Leben auf ihn ausrichtet. Gemeint ist ein aktives und gespanntes Warten auf Gottes Eingreifen in persönlicher Not und in der Not des gesamten Volkes. Gott gibt in besonderen Situationen besondere Kraft, dass der Mensch auffliegt wie ein Adler, neue Herausforderungen in Angriff nimmt. Er gibt Kraft zum Rennen, um Herausforderungen umzusetzen und zu gestalten. Und er gibt Kraft zum Gehen, also für den alltäglichen Lebensvollzug in Gottes Gegenwart, gemäß dem Willen Gottes. Die fünfte Strophe steht außerhalb des Chiasmus, ist herausgehoben und erhält besondere Aufmerksamkeit. Im Fokus der Perikope steht: Gott ist größer als die Kraftlosigkeit des Menschen, seine Größe besteht darin, dass er von seiner Kraft weitergibt, dass er sich dem Menschen zuwendet. Gottes Größe besteht darin, dass er sich klein macht: dadurch wird der größere Zusammenhang zum Neuen Testament und zur Menschwerdung des Gottessohnes bereits angedeutet.

References

Alter, Robert. 1990. *The art of biblical poetry*. Edinburgh: T&T Clark.
Archer, Gleason L. 1987. *Einleitung in das Alte Testament*. Vol. 1. Bad Liebenzell: Verlag der Liebenzeller Mission.
Beuken, Willem A. M. 2003. *Jesaja 1–12*. Herders Theologischer Kommentar zum Alten Testament. Freiburg: Herder.
Botterweck, G. Johannes, Helmer Ringgren, and Heinz-Joseph Fabry, eds. 1984. *Theologisches Wörterbuch zum Alten Testament*. Stuttgart: Kohlhammer.
Brandenburg, Hans. 1961. *Jesaja. II. Teil: Das Buch von der Erlösung*. Gießen: Brunnen Verlag.

Brueggemann, W. 2003. *An introduction to the Old Testament: The canon and Christian imagination.* Louisville: Westminster John Knox.

Bühlmann, Walter, and Karl Scherer. 1994. *Sprachliche Stilfiguren der Bibel. Von Assonanz bis Zahlenspruch. Ein Nachschlagewerk.* Gießen: Brunnen.

Bullinger, E. W. 2003. *Figures of speech used in the Bible: Explained and illustrated.* Grand Rapids: Baker.

Caird, G. B. 1980. *The language and imagery of the Bible.* London: Duckworth.

Calvin, John. 1996. *Commentary on the book of the prophet Isaiah by John Calvin.* Vol. 3. Grand Rapids: Baker.

Childs, Brevard S. 2001. *Isaiah.* The Old Testament Library. Louisville: Westminster John Knox.

Coogan, Michael D. 2006. *The Old Testament. A historical and literary introduction to the Hebrew scriptures.* Oxford: Oxford University Press.

Delitzsch, F. [1897] 1984. *Jesaja.* Gießen: Brunnen Verlag.

Dreytza, Manfred, Walter Hilbrands, and Hartmut Schmid. 2002. *Das Studium des Alten Testaments: Eine Einführung in die Methoden der Exegese.* Wuppertal: R. Brockhaus Verlag.

Eißfeldt, Otto. 1959. Kanaanäische Religion. In Karl Galling (ed.), *Religion in Geschichte und Gegenwart.* Third edition. Vol. 3. Tübingen: J. C. B. Mohr.

Eißfeldt, Otto. 1964. *Einleitung in das Alte Testament.* Tübingen: J. C. B. Mohr.

Elliger, Karl. 1978. *Biblischer Kommentar Altes Testament. Deuterojesaja 40:1–45:7.* Neukirchen-Vluyn: Neukirchener Verlag des Erziehungsvereins.

Elliger, Karl, and Willhelm Rudolph. 1967/77. *Biblia Hebraica Stuttgartensia (BHS).* Stuttgart: Deutsche Bibelgesellschaft.

Fohrer, Georg, and Ernst Sellin. 1979. *Einleitung in das Alte Testament.* Twelfth, revised and expanded edition. Heidelberg: Quelle and Meyer.

Frey, Hellmuth. 1938. *Das Buch der Weltpolitik Gottes. Kapitel 40–55 des Buches Jesaja.* Stuttgart: Calwer Vereinsbuchhandlung.

Gæbelein, Frank E. 1986. *The expositor's Bible commentary: Isaiah, Jeremiah, Lamentations, Ezekiel.* Vol. 6. Grand Rapids: Zondervan.

Gesenius, Wilhelm. 1962. *Hebräische Grammatik. Völlig umgearbeitet von E. Kautzsch.* Hildesheim: Gert Olms Verlag.

Gesenius, Wilhelm. 1992. *Hebräisches und Aramäisches Handwörterbuch über das Alte Testament.* Berlin: Springer-Verlag.

Goldingay, John. 2005. *The message of Isaiah 40–55: A literary-theological commentary.* New York: T&T Clark.

Harrison, R. K. 1970. *Introduction to the Old Testament.* London: Tyndale.

Joüon, Paul. 1991. *A grammar of Biblical Hebrew: Part Three: Syntax. Paradigms and indices.* Vol. 2. Translated and revised by T. Muraoka. Rome: Editrice Pontificio Istituto Biblico.

Kaiser, Otto. 1969. *Einleitung in das Alte Testament: Eine Einführung in ihre Ergebnisse und Probleme.* Vol. 3. Gütersloh: Verlagshaus Gerd Mohn.

Koole, Jan L. 1997. *Isaiah III: Volume I / Isaiah 40–48.* Historical Commentary on the Old Testament 1. Kampen: Kok Pharos.

References

Luther, Martin. 1985. *Die Bibel.* Revised edition. Stuttgart: Deutsche Bibelgesellschaft.

McKenna, D. L. 1994. Isaiah 40–66. In Lloyd J. Ogilvie (ed.), *The communicator's commentary.* Waco: Word Books.

Merwe, Christo H. J. van der, Jacobus A. Naudé, and Jan H. Kroeze. 1999. *A Biblical Hebrew reference grammar.* Biblical Languages: Hebrew 3. Sheffield: Sheffield Academic.

Motyer, J. Alec. 1999. *Isaiah.* Tyndale Old Testament Commentaries. Leicester: InterVarsity.

NASB. 1995. *New American Standard Bible.* La Habra: The Lockman Foundation. https://www.lockman.org.

NIV. 2011. *Holy Bible, New International Version.* Colorado Springs: Biblica.

NKJV. 1997. *The Nelson Study Bible: New King James Version.* Nashville: Thomas Nelson.

Oswalt, John. N. 1998. *The book of Isaiah: Chapters 40–66.* The New International Commentary on the Old Testament. Grand Rapids: Eerdmans.

Pehlke, Helmut. 2002. *Zur Umwelt des Alten Testaments.* Vol. 1. Holzgerlingen: Hänssler-Verlag.

Petersen, David L., and Kent Harold Richards. 1992. *Interpreting Hebrew poetry: Guides to biblical scholarship.* Minneapolis: Fortress Press.

Schirrmacher, Thomas. 1997. *Die Vielfalt biblischer Sprache.* Biblia et Symbiotica 15. Bonn: Verlag für Kultur und Wissenschaft.

Schlachter, Franz Eugen. 1951. *Altes Testament.* Préverenges: Genfer Bibelgesellschaft.

Schneider, Dieter. 1990. *Der Prophet Jesaja. Kapitel 40–66.* Wuppertaler Studienbibel. Wuppertal und Zürich: R. Brockhaus.

Vance, Donald R. 2001. *The question of meter in Biblical Hebrew poetry.* Studies in Bible and Early Christianity 46. Lewiston, NY: Edwin Mellen.

Waltke, Bruce K., and M. O'Connor. 1990. *An introduction to Biblical Hebrew syntax.* Winona Lake: Eisenbrauns.

Walvoord, John F., and Roy F. Zuck. 1998. *Das Alte Testament erklärt und ausgelegt. Band 3 Jesaja – Maleachi.* Neuhausen-Stuttgart: Hänssler-Verlag.

Watts, John D. W. 1987. *Isaiah 34–66. Word Biblical Commentary 25.* Waco: Word Books.

Webb, Barry G. 1996. The message of Isaiah: On eagles' wings. In *The Bible Speaks Today.* Downers Grove: InterVarsity.

Westermann, Claus. 1970. *Das Buch Jesaja. Kapitel 40–66.* Das Alte Testament. Göttingen: Vandenhoeck & Ruprecht.

Zenger, Erich. 1995. *Einleitung in das Alte Testament.* Stuttgart: Verlag W. Kohlhammer.

2

Backgrounding and Foregrounding, Prominence, and Highlighting in Afghan Wakhi: A Text Discourse Analysis

Simone Beck
SIL Global; Redcliffe College
August 2013

Abstract

This dissertation presents a study of the discourse features foregrounding and backgrounding, prominence, and highlighting as they are used by Afghan Wakhi speakers in the narrative, procedural, behavioural, and expository text genres.

The dissertation first introduces the Afghan Wakhan geographical area and previous research concerning the Wakhi language. Next, it presents the four genres, narrative, procedural, behavioural, and exposition that are examined in this dissertation. In the body of the dissertation, devices used for foregrounding and backgrounding are considered, followed by devices employed for prominence, applied to constituents within a sentence, and highlighting, applied to parts of a story. The narrative genre serves as the model for the use of these devices; the theoretical discussion is, therefore, found within the narrative sections, while in the sections of the other three genres, similarities and differences compared to narratives are pointed out.

Finally, the conclusion summarizes the findings: Wakhi speakers have a multitude of devices at their disposal to express foregrounding and backgrounding, prominence, and highlighting in their speech. According to the research about discourse undertaken so far, these devices do not differ considerably in the four genres examined.

Preface

Discourse without prominence "is like being presented with a piece of black paper and being told, 'This is a picture of black camels crossing black sands at midnight'" (Longacre and Woods 1976:10). This is equally true in considering highlighting, foregrounding, and backgrounding. They all enable the listener to find orientation in a text. This dissertation examines the means to express backgrounding and foregrounding, prominence, and highlighting in Afghan Wakhi. They make a text understandable, and moreover, they make it interesting and exciting!

In this dissertation, the narrative, procedural, behavioral, and expository text genres are considered, and it is illustrated in what ways identical, similar and different devices are employed for discourse purposes. The narrative genre serves as a model for the use of these devices; the theoretical discussion is, therefore, found within the narrative sections, while in the sections of the other three genres, similarities and differences in comparison to narratives are pointed out.

The theoretical framework used is the work of Levinsohn (2023a and 2023b), as laid down in *Self-Instruction Material on Narrative Discourse Analysis* and *Self-Instruction Material on Non-narrative Discourse Analysis*.

For the presented theses, thirty-eight Wakhi texts originating from eighteen speakers, with ages ranging from 17 to 65 years, male and female, from different villages, are examined. The length of the texts ranges between 9 and 205 sentences, between 44 seconds and 12 minutes and 12 seconds long. However, most texts are between three and five minutes. A list of texts included in the corpus and a representative example of each genre are included in the full thesis.

Thanks are due to my supervisors, Dr. Howard Jackson and Dr. Adam Baker, for their assistance, as well as to Erin SanGregory for editing the dissertation for English language use.

2.1 Background information

2.1.1 Geography and population

The Wakhan Corridor is located in Badakhshan province in the northeast of Afghanistan. It stretches between Tajikistan to the north, Pakistan to the south, and it shares a short border with China in the east. The international borders were created in 1877 during the time of the "Great Game"[1] to serve as a buffer zone between the British Empire (India/Pakistan) and the Russian Empire (Rowe 2010:54). The corridor is approximately 300 km long, and between 17 and 30 km wide. The altitude of the valley rises from 2,600 m to 4,500 m.

The Wakhi villages are all located on the banks of the Wakhan River and the Amu Darja between the Pamir and the Hindu Kush mountains. The corridor is inhabited for about two thirds of its length. The Wakhi are agropastoralists, and self-sufficient to a high degree (Kreutzmann 2003:215). The mother tongue of the people is Wakhi.

Wakhi people also live in Pakistan, Tajikistan, and China. The Wakhan in Afghanistan is the original homeland of the Wakhi people and language. From there Wakhi people migrated at different times to their present locations (Kreutzmann 1996). Approximately 17,000 people live in the Wakhan (Duncan and Duncan 2002). The Wakhi population in all four countries numbers about 75,000 (Moseley 2010).

2.1.2 Previous research about the Wakhi language

Wakhi is a southeastern Iranian Pamir language. It is alternatively called Vakhan, Wakhani, Wakhigi (Lewis, Simons, and Fennig 2013), and "Khik" or "Khikwor" by the Wakhi people. Dari – the Afghan variety of Persian – is the

---

[1] The Great Game was a term for the strategic rivalry and conflict between the British Empire and the Russian Empire for supremacy in Central Asia in the time between 1813 and 1907. The term "The Great Game" was introduced into mainstream consciousness by British novelist Rudyard Kipling in his novel *Kim* (1901) (Walberg 2011; Hopkirk 1992).

language of wider communication in northern Afghanistan. Dari and Pashto are the two national languages.

Research about the Wakhi phonology and grammar has a long tradition, considering the remoteness of the area. Shaw (1876) was the first European to examine the Wakhi language in any depth. He published an outline of the grammar, texts, and a vocabulary list. Morgenstierne (1938) published a description of the language, discussing the phonetics and morphology, including vocabulary, and short texts. Later, Lorimer (1958) published a two-volume set including a large amount of material on the phonology, grammar, vocabulary, and some texts. Buddruss (1974) contributed several articles to the knowledge about Wakhi. These linguists predominantly used data originating from Wakhi speakers living in Pakistan.

Russian scholars significantly contributed to the study of Wakhi concerning the variety spoken in Tajikistan. Among them, Grjunberg and Stéblin-Kamensky (1988) published an outline of the Wakhi grammar; Pakhalina (1975) likewise gives a grammar description.

Kieffer (1978) was the first to conduct research in the Afghan Wakhan. He gives a brief introduction to Wakhi; however, he inaccurately predicts the extinction of the Wakhi language in a few years' time.

More recently, Skjaervø (1989) compares phonological and morphological aspects of several modern East Iranian languages, including Wakhi. Payne emphasizes in his article "Pamir Languages" (Payne 1989) that Wakhi is part of the so-called "Pamir Sprachbund". Other languages in Afghanistan are Shughni, Ishkashimi, Sanglechi, and Munji, all spoken in remote parts of Badakhshan province. He holds the opinion that, in spite of their diversity, they share sufficient common features to be called by this name including:

1. Morphological distinctions such as gender, tense, and transitivity.
2. Three verb stems: present, past, and perfect.
3. Verb endings show person and number in the present tense, but agreement particles are movable in the past tense.
4. Demonstrative pronouns show a three-way distinction.
5. The basic word order is subject-object-verb; adjectives and possessive modifiers precede the head, while prepositional phrases and relative clauses follow the head.

The latest linguistic publications about Wakhi are contributed by Reinhold (2006) and Bashir (2009). Reinhold's research concerns the Wakhi variety spoken in Pakistan. She collected and transcribed Wakhi texts, and presented an introduction to Wakhi phonetics. Bashir presents a relatively detailed description of the grammar concerning the varieties spoken in Pakistan and Afghanistan.

No research about discourse analysis of Wakhi has been published so far.

2.2 Four genres

Generally in discourse, four genres can be identified and organized according to the matrix (Levinsohn 2023:11) in table 2.1.

Table 2.1. Four genres of discourse

Organization	+ Agent-oriented	− Agent-oriented
Chronological organisation	Narrative	Procedural
Conceptual/logical organisation	Behavioural	Expository text

Narratives are "a story or a description of a series of events" (Cambridge Dictionaries Online 2011) organized chronologically. In the centre of the text is usually the agent of the story, thus the text is "+ agent-oriented". This dissertation includes folk tales, religious stories, legends, and personal experiences.

Procedurals are "a set of actions which is the official or accepted way of doing something" (Cambridge Dictionaries Online 2011). The speaker relates procedurals in chronological order; therefore it is labelled with "chronological organisation". The focus is not on the person carrying out the procedure; therefore, it is "− agent-oriented". Here cultural procedurals are included, such as the traditions in conducting weddings or deaths rites, as well as daily procedurals, such as food preparation.

Behaviourals centre on a hortatory argument; therefore, they display "conceptual/logical organisation". Since behaviourals encourage people to follow an instruction, they are "+ agent-oriented". Here health themes are included, as well as desired behaviour in professional and family contexts.

Expository texts are "a clear and full explanation of an idea or theory" (Cambridge Dictionaries Online 2011). The speaker argues a point; therefore, the expository text has "conceptual/logical organisation". As an expository text does not address someone in particular, it is "− agent-oriented". Here, expository texts outline religious and professional concepts.

In real life, these four types often mix. In the present corpus, three narratives (B05[2], B06, and B07) are told to encourage the listener to understand and apply the behavioural message. Therefore, they are considered behaviourals rather than narratives. In a procedural about prayer, the speaker includes behavioural elements (P08), but since this is not the main purpose of the text, it is considered a procedural. The "History of Ismaeli Islam" (E01) contains narrative elements, likewise, the expository text about hotsprings (E07).

2.3 Foregrounding and backgrounding

In narratives and procedurals, the foreground material moves the procession of events forward in time and provides the "gist" of the story (Givón 1987:177); background material adds setting, explanation (about participants, culture etc.), and evaluation; it can be collateral (what did not happen), or performative (the author speaks to the audience) (Levinsohn 2023:69) "Background is characterized by a lack of narrative movement, even timelessness" (Haspelmath 2001:562). In expository texts and behaviourals, the orientation is conceptual-logical; therefore the main theses are presented in foreground material.

---

[2] The texts are numbered, beginning with a letter: N for narrative, P for procedural, B for behavioural, and E for expository text.

2.3 Foregrounding and backgrounding

Background material gives supporting arguments and illustrations, often as brief narratives or cultural information.

However, the distinction between foreground and background is not always clear. Texts have several levels of foreground versus background; furthermore, material can be foregrounded or backgrounded with respect to the context. However, background is not equal to being unimportant; background material determines the listeners' perspective on the storyline or on the speaker's claims. Longacre (1996:21) uses the terms "mainline" versus "supportive material".

Wakhi has a multitude of devices at its disposal to mark material as foregrounded or backgrounded, as well as means to promote and demote clauses and sentences. These devices will now be considered. Each of the four genres will be examined in turn. Following the discussion in sections 2.3.1 through 2.3.4 of features marking foregrounding and backgrounding in the four genres, table 2.2 in section 2.3.5 presents a summary, including the number of occurrences of each feature in the various genres.

2.3.1 Narrative

2.3.1.1 The enclitic =ş to foreground background material

The enclitic =ş occurs in material usually considered background, such as reported speech, subordinate clauses, explanations, and perceptions, and promotes it to the foreground on account of its salience for the story. Sentences thus marked tend to raise a question or pose a problem. The enclitic can attach to any constituent of the sentence. However, more research is needed concerning to which constituent the speakers choose to attach it.

In linguistic literature, the enclitic is labelled "particle", "progressive marker", "imperfective marker" or generally ascribed an "unclear TAM (tense, aspect, mood) function" (Backstrom 2009, Grjunberg and Stéblin-Kamensky 1988, Erschler 2010). Bashir calls it an "aspectual clitic", stating that it is used to "express specificity and immediacy, either present relevance or immediate future, and various imperfective meanings" (Bashir 2009:836). Hence, the clitic is glossed *IPFV* (imperfective). According to (Klutz 1999:266), imperfective aspect may be used for foregrounding; it can highlight semantic features if it significantly affects the overall force of the text – as is the case in Wakhi.

Occasionally the clitic is combined with word repetitions. Its frequency in texts varies considerably according to the speaker.

In N08 "Bear Story" s3, explanations concerning the danger of bears are foregrounded, as the narrator would be confronted with such a situation later. The clitic attaches to "old people" in the speech introducer since their experience adds weight to the warning. The bear is left-dislocated (and taken up again as an indirect object pronoun) within the reported speech.

(1) ˈjan də **sɔˈbəqʰ=əʂ**³ **ˈlʊpʰ=əʂ** ˈça-tʰɪ kʰə nɔɣɔrˈdʊm ətʃ
    then in old.time=IPFV big=IPFV say-PST REL bear no
    waχtʰ də mɔlˈtʰəqʰ-ən ja-r qrib mə ˈrəts̩-əv
    time in shotgun-ABL 3SG-DAT close NEG go-2PL
    'Then in old times the big (old people) said: Bears, never go near them (not even) with a shotgun.'

In N01 "King's Daughter" s18, the shepherd relates the king's request for gold to his son. Reported speech, usually in the background, is foregrounded to stress the impossibility to fulfill the request as well as the subsequent importance of gold.

(2) çø ʊtˈrpʰ-ər çan-d e **ˈçan-d=əʂə** kʰ ʉb ɣuˈri tʰeˈlɔ
    own son-DAT say-3SG⁴ INTJ say-3SG=IPFV REL seven tray gold
    mar wizəm
    1SG.DAT bring.2PL
    'He says to his son: oh, he says to bring him seven golden trays.'

In N04 "Noah" s28, the bird's perception is foregrounded because of its salience for the progression of the story (see section 2.3.5 for the rationale of the gloss EMPH for the particle a).

(3) a ˈdr-a-ə ər-ɪtʰaˈin ˈkʰtʰ jʊpkʰ kʰam kʰam jʊpkʰ
    EMPH there-DEM3-CON perceive do-PST water little little water
    ˈkʰam=ʂ wɔs-d ətʰ **wəsk=ʂ** wɔs-d
    little=IPFV become-3SG and dry=IPFV become-3SG
    'There it perceived that the water becomes less and less, and it becomes dry.'

In N03 "Naser Khesrau" s5, explanatory background concerning the greatness of Naser is given. It is foregrounded because the story develops around his eminence.

(4) **jaʊ=əʂ** ya ar ˈtʃiz-ə ˈdɪʃ-tʰ ətʰ ˈjanə də
    3SG=IPFV very every thing-OBJ know-3SG and that.is in
    ɣɔˈib=əʂ jaʊ qʰəˈsa-ə dɪʃ-tʰ
    foresight=IPFV 3SG story-OBJ know-3SG
    'He knows everything, that is, he knows things in foresight.'

2.3.1.2 Change of tense for backgrounding

The default storyline tense of fictional and semi-fictional narratives (folktales, uncertain history) is the present. For narratives that are considered a true representation of events, such as personal experience and religious narratives which are part of the doctrine (Abraham, Noah), it is the past tense.

---

[3] The illustrated features are indicated with bold print.
[4] Present tense is unmarked. When no tense occurs in the gloss, the verb is in the present tense.

2.3 Foregrounding and backgrounding

If the story line is in the present tense, the background setting, explanation, and evaluation are given in the perfect. This agrees with Bashir's assessment concerning Wakhi: "The basic indicative function of the perfect is resultative-stative" (Bashir 2009:839). Likewise in Persian, the perfect presents background information (Roberts 2009:265). In narratives, the change of tense from present to perfect coincides with one of the common uses of the perfect aspect; however, the change of tense is realized differently in other text types (see sections 2.3.2.2 and 2.3.2.3). In Wakhi, this kind of change in tense frequently occurs at the beginning or end of a story.

In N01 "King's Daughter" the introduction (s1–2) gives the setting in perfect (Pancheva 2003:1). This is shown in example (5).

(5) **twətkʰ** kʰə pʰɔtʲʃɔ i pʰɔdaˈbɔn jəm pʰɔtʲʃɔ-ən **twətkʰ**
 AUX.PRF REL king one shepherd DEM1 king-ABL AUX.PRF
 i ðəʋjd
 one daughter
 'There has been a king and a shepherd. The king has had a daughter.'

The setting of N06 "Emigration to Wakhan" is likewise in perfect tense, S1–4a. This is shown in example (6).

(6) s1 'The saying (is) like this: that there has been a king by the name of Sanskrit. s2 This king had been in Iran. s3 One time an enemy has appeared to him, and this enemy has waged war against him. s4a Then he has oppressed him.'

S5 describes the flight from Iran in present tense; the evaluation follows in perfect. This is shown in example (7).

(7) s7 'Then he has found a solution and he has come, and arrived in the area of the Wakhan; and he has settled here. s8 Now there (is) the saying that this Wakhi generation has remained from that king Sanskrit. s9 And this Wakhi language has remained from that king Sanskrit. s10 And he has been king of Iran.'

S1–2 and s10 respectively give or confirm the general setting, while the perfect of s8–9 has resultative aspect. To s3, s4, and s7 (the verbs are not typical background state verbs) applies Kibort's (2009:1396) reinterpretation of Reichenbach, as she explains the perfect tense as being event time and reference time not being simultaneous. If the mainline of the story represents the reference time, the events of the sentences concerned take place either before or after the reference time.

The setting of N03 "Naser Khesrau" is s1–2 shown in example (8).

(8) 'Another story is this one: It is a talk that I have heard, and it is what has happened in the valley of Chakhan. Naser Khesrau has gone to Chakhan.'

S3 sets off the storyline in present tense (he enters the village and is invited), then background information is resumed, adding explanation in perfect, underlining the fame of Naser in s4 as displayed in example (9).

(9) 'Everyone has heard the name of Naser Khesrau.'

S1 and s4 are experiential perfect[5], while Kibort's thesis applies to s2.

However, if the mainline of a story is in past tense, the setting is in present tense, as in N08 "Bear story". In this story, the present tense has gnomic aspect[6], as the setting alludes to the danger of bears, s1–2. This is shown in example (10).

(10) 'Well, I tell you a story about a bear which is an animal that is found in the Pamir. It is an animal people are very much afraid of.'

Tense does not change for performative and collateral background. In N05 "Abraham", the storyline and collateral background are in past tense. S8 displayed as example (11) shows this.

(11) jəm azˈɾiatʰ ɪbɾɔˈɪmɪ pʰayʊmˈbar kʰʊnd-ə χaˈbar nə
DEM1 Saint Abraham prophet wife-OBJ news NEG
ˈkʰər-tʰ-ɪ ˈsaɾ-ə a saɾg qʰʊɾbɔˈnɪ tʰʊ
do-PST head-CON EMPH tomorrow sacrifice AUX.PST
'Saint Abraham, the prophet, did not tell his wife that there was to be a sacrifice the next day.'

In N08 "Bear Story", the storyline and performative background (s19) are in past tense. This is shown in example (12).

(12) jəm tʰum tʰʊ kʰə qʰəˈsaɪ-ə nɔyɔɾˈdʊm kʰə də pʰɔˈmir
DEM1 like AUX.PST REL story-CON bear REL in Pamir
tsə zəndaˈgɪ tsaɾ-tʰ wʊz-əm tʰa-ɾk ˈçʰa-tʰɪ
of life do-3SG 1SG-1SG 2PL-DAT say-PST
'The story, that I told you – about the bear, living in the Pamir – was like this.'

2.3.1.3 Background information in sentence-final adverbials

A regular adverbial position is sentence final, but only for spatial adverbials. This is shown in example (13).

(13) (a) fəɾɔɾ tsəɾakər twətk **tər pɔkəstɔn nag**
'They went on flight **towards Pakistan**' (E03, s14);

(b) tʃaʈve waχt wəzəmd **tə χun**
'He brought the cows **home** early' (N01, s6).

If other adverbials occur in this position, they are considered postposed, and often relate brief details of setting, explanatory material, or evaluative background, resulting in a presentational sentence.

---

[5] Experiential perfect aspect is a grammaticalization of the current relevance, at the moment of utterance, of an event or state that occurred prior to the moment of utterance. (Comrie 1976:58).

[6] "Gnomic" means that a proposition is generic and holds true in the past, present, and future (Bybee et al. 1994:319).

2.3 Foregrounding and backgrounding

In example (14), taken from N06 "Emigration to Wakhan", s1 supplies background information. The crucial part is a sentence-final adverbial; it adds specific explanatory background to the general setting.

(14)   i   pʰɔtˈʃɔ   twətkʰ   bə   ˈnuŋg-ə   sansˈkɽitʰ
       one   king   time   by   name-CON   Sanskrit
       'There was a king by the name of Sanskrit.'

In N08 "Bear Story", the narrator tells how he shot a bear, which is no longer permitted. Therefore the background information concerning the time of the event, which was fifteen years earlier, is important. This is seen in S18 shown in example (15).

(15)   çatʰ   ɔzɔˈdi   waχtʰtʰu   də   ˈsɔl-ə   kʰə   1378
       own   freedom   timeAUX.PST   in   year-CON   REL   1378
       'It was a time of freedom in the year 1378.'

In N09 "The Accident" s1, the adverb giving background information adds credibility to the story, as the narrator speaks about himself.

(16)   wʊz   i   qʰ   tʰaəˈsa-ɽ   ˈtsaɽ-əm   ˈwalə   tsə   çtʰø   saɽgʊˈzaʃ-ən
       1SG   one   story   2SG-DAT   tell-1SG   so   of   own   experience-ABL
       'I tell you a story of my own experience.'

2.3.1.4 The preposition tsə "of" in background material

The preposition *tsə* "of"/"from" has a derivative meaning; the head noun is in the ablative case[7], for example, *qɽʊt tsə ʒaɽʒən wɔst* "dried yoghurt is made **of** milk" (P06, s1), or *tsə dɪɔɽən wəzdɪ* "he came **from** the village". The preposition also occurs before verbs, predominantly in subordinate clauses, mostly relative. Such sentences tend to give explanatory background, frequently identificational or spatial, occasionally evaluational. When a clause is thus marked, the preceding or subsequent clause increases in salience – as a clause is by definition backgrounded against its environment.

Spatial and identificational explanations illustrate the extension of the original derivative function of *tsə*: of all places, or of all people, the one referred to in the clause marked by *tsə* is the one further explained. As a preposition and as a backgrounding device, *tsə* expresses separation of some kind. Native speakers perceive the particle occurring before a noun as a regular preposition or before a verb as the same word.

N03 "Naser Khesrau" s2 gives spatial explanatory background, indicated by the preposition *tsə* and perfect tense (see section 2.3.1.2). S2 is reproduced in example (17).

(17)   nɔˈsərə   χəsˈrau   də   tʃɔˈχɔn-ə   tsə   ɽəç-kʰ
       Naser   Khesrau   in   Chakhan   of   go-PRF
       'Naser Khesrau went to Chakhan.'

In N04 "Noah" s17, the preposition occurs in two relative clauses, identifying the people who fled from the waters. Due to the backgrounding

---

[7] In linguistic literature, the case is analyzed and glossed as genitive or ablative. Bashir (2009) uses ablative.

of the relative clauses, the main clause is more salient (*ts-əɪ* is a fusion of the preposition *tsə* and the auxiliary *təɪ*). S17 is shown in example (18).

(18) i   tʰəˈdɔ   mərˈdʊm-ə   kʰə   gʊˈnɔ   **tsə** khər-tʰu   wə   χʊˈdɔ
      one   amount   people-CON REL   sin   of   do-PPST   and God
      amrəˈb   qhəˈbʉl nə   kʰər-tʰɪ   **ts-əɪ**   ˈjəm-əʃ   də   kʰo
      command   accept   NEG   do-PST   of-AUX   DEM1-PL   in   mountain
      ˈnag-əv   ˈrø-nɪ
      towards-2PL   flee-PST
      'And the people who had sinned and have not accepted God's command, they fled towards the mountain.'

In N08 "Bear Story" s4, both clauses give spatial explanatory background information. The second clause explains the location of the place named in the first clause. It is backgrounded by the use of *tsə*, and thus creates a hierarchy of the clauses. S4 is displayed in example (19).

(19) də   i   dʒaɪ   ˈnʊŋg-ə   qhəˈbalɣar   ʊtʰ   də   ˈbaɪn-ə
      in   one   place   name-CON   Qabelghar   AUX.PST   in   between-CON
      dəˈrəɪn-ə   tʰʂɔrˈgɔ   dəˈraɪ-ə   χʊʂɔˈbɔd   **tsə**   ʊtʰ
      valley-CON   Shkarga   valley-CON   Khusabad   of   AUX.PST
      'It was a place by the name of Qabelghar, it was between the valley of Shkarga and the valley of Khusabad.'

Example (20) shows N01 "King's Daughter" s11. In it the narrator summarizes the son's attempt to persuade his father, thus giving evaluational background.

(20) ts-um   kʰə   **tsə**   çan-d   qhəˈbʉl   nə   tsar-tʰ
      Whatever   REL   of   say-3SG   accept   NEG   do-3SG
      'Whatever he (the father) says, he (the son) does not accept.'

2.3.1.5 *"Announced" background information*

Occasionally explanatory background information is explicitly announced, marked by the verb "say" in the third person plural. This feature is rare.

In N09 "The accident" s7, the narrator points out the name of the path. Example (21) shows s7.

(21) belɔχeˈra   ˈsakʰ-ən   skʰə   bən   vəˈdʊkʰ   ˈrəʉj-dɪ   skʰə
      finally   1PL-1PL   towards   lower   path   go-PST   towards
      ˈgɔzχun   vəˈdʊkʰ   ˈçan-ən
      gazkhan   path   say-3PL
      'Finally we went via the lower path, it is called the "Gazkhan-path".'

2.3 Foregrounding and backgrounding

2.3.2 Procedural

2.3.2.1 The enclitic =ṣ to foreground background material

In procedurals, the clitic =ṣ serves the same function as in narratives: It foregrounds material that is usually considered background on account of its salience in the text for either the narrator or the audience.

In P01 "Wedding Ceremony", s11 would be background as it is a speech clause. However, the question is foregrounded as it is crucial for the marriage negotiation! This is the only instance the clitic is used in the 4.2 minute-long text. The groom addresses the parents of the bride in example (22).

(22) thu=ṣ   qʰəˈbɨl   ˈtsaɾ-a   ˈnəɪ-a
      2SG-IPFV accept   do-Q   NEG-Q
      'Do you accept? Or not?'

In P04 "Farming" s23–25, explanatory background is given concerning the difficulty people face because of lack of water. S26 in example (23) expresses the urgency of having water at the right time (here the clitic occurs for the first time in the text).

(23) jəm   jʊpkʰ də   saɾaˈtʰɔn=ṣ   ˈwizɪ-d   ja   bə   χub   ətʰ
      DEM1 water in   Saraton=IPFV come-3SG   DEM3 also good and
      nəɪ   kʰə tsə   saɾaˈtʰɔn=ṣ   bə   tʰər   wɔs-tʰ   tʰər ˈdʒaʊzɔ
      NEG   REL of   Saraton=IPFV   also PASS   become-3SG   onto Jauza
      ˈpʊtʂəs-tʰ
      demand-3SG
      'The water comes in (the month of) Saraton, this is also good, but if (the month of) Saraton also passes, then it (the dry period) extends into (the month of) Jauza.'

The clitic occurs only once more, again in explanatory background concerning water, s34. This is shown in example (24).

(24) jiɾkʰ   dʒun   tʰə   jʊpkʰ kʰam   pi-tʰ=ṣ
      barley however REL   water little drink-3SG=IPFV
      'Barley, however, only needs a little water.'

In P08 "Prayer", the clitic is used once, in the conclusion. Evaluational background is foregrounded as it describes the foundation for every prayer, s19. Example (25) shows s19.

(25) χʊˈdɔ   ɾəwɔˈɾi   gɔç-tʰ   tʰə   wɔz=ṣ   tʃiz   wɔs-tʰ
      God   daytime   make-3SG   REL   again=IPFV   thing   become-3SG
      'God makes the days and what happens again.' (Everything is in God's hand.)

2.3.2.2 Change of tense for backgrounding

Procedurals are given in the present tense with habitual aspect since procedures describe how things are habitually done by everyone within the given cultural context. Backgrounded information about setting or clarification of the order of events is expressed in the past tense, usually in a subordinate clause. The main clause follows in the present tense. However, clear examples are rare.

In P04 "Farming" s1 (example (26)), the background setting sets off the procedural, stating the time of the year.

(26) zəmə'sthɔn kʰə   spʰɔ   ðarth   'pʰərvə-tʰɪ   sakʰ
     winter   REL   1PL.GEN animal.dung hit-PST   1PL
     kʰər'jar   'gɔn-ən
     labour.group   make-1PL
     'In winter when the animal dung is ready, we put a group of labourers together.'

Later in P04 "Farming" s4 (example (27)), the same structure expresses the timeframe.

(27) ʃɔ'gʉn-ən   kʰə   ja   rə'wɔr   **kʰər-tʰ** spʰɔ
     new.year-1PL REL DEM3 day   do-PST   1PL.GEN
     jutʰ   'tʰʊχəm   'nəʉəz-d
     handful.of.wheat   seed   come.out-3SG
     'When we have celebrated New Year's day, then we bring out a handful of wheat.'

2.3.2.3 Background information in sentence-final adverbials

In procedurals, this feature is employed as it is in narratives.

In P04 "Farming" s6, explanatory background is given concerning the way oxen have to be acclimated to work in spring.

In P06 "Making Qrut" s1, the adverbial provides explanatory background concerning the kind of milk.

In P07 "Slaughtering a Cow" s6 (example (28)), the speaker gives background information about the way a cow is skinned.

(28) jan   'jau-ə   pʰistʰ 'tsar-ən **tsə** a'wal-ən   tʰɔ ɔ'χer
     then 3SG-OBJ   skin   do-1PL   of   first-ABL to   last
     'Then we skin it, from front to back.'

2.3.2.4 The preposition tsə 'of' in background material

The preposition *tsə* marks background material in procedurals as it does in narratives.

In P01 "Wedding Ceremony", the relative clause (beginning with the second *kə*) gives identificational background, s1. P05 "Baking Bread" s24 employs the preposition in the first clause giving conditional explanatory background, thus drawing the listener's attention to the second clause of the sentence.

In P10 "Death of an Adult" s3, the subordinate clause is backgrounded because the listener is already aware of the theme. More salient, therefore, is the subsequent clause which relates the actions taken after a death. Example (29) shows s3.

2.3 Foregrounding and backgrounding

(29) agaɾ ajɔˈnan i kʰɔr ɔl   jɔ i χalg də zø
     if   suddenly one work present or one person in 1SG.GEN
     χun tsə ˈbəɪn-ən **tsə** ɾəʂ-tʰ wʊz basˈwəzi-əm kʰə
     house of middle-ABL of go-3SG 1SG can-1SG   REL-EMPH
     a-ˈd-ətʰ   ɾəˈwɔɾ a-ˈjətʰ   çø   ˈqʰaʊm-ə   χəˈbaɾ
     EMPH-in-DEM2 day EMPH-DEM2 own relatives-OBJ news
     ˈtsaɾ-əm
     do-1SG
     'If there is suddenly some work or if a person dies in my house,
     then at that day I inform my relatives.'

In P10 "Death of an Adult" s13, the background setting expresses a condition in a subordinate clause. More salient is the consequence given in the main clause. Example (30) shows s13.

(30) ˈamɔ ˈχalg-ə   kʰə lʊp-ˈtʰəɾ **ts-əɪ** amsɔˈja-əʃ atˈmi
     but person-CON REL big-COMP of-AUX neighbour-PL certainly
     ˈiʊ bʊɪ kʰəˈla tʃɥç-tʰ
     one two sheep/goat slaughter-3SG
     'But when the person was important, then the neighbours definitely
     slaughter one or two sheep/goats.'

2.3.2.5 "Announced" background information

The "announcement" of background information is used much more frequently in procedurals than in narratives. Procedurals are naturally geared towards a listener who is not familiar with the procedure; therefore, he needs further background information, usually cultural, to be able to follow the procedure. The lexical indicators used are 'it is tradition', 'for that reason', 'it is commanded', or the third person plural of the verb 'say'. The explicit announcement can either be a cataphoric reference or within the clause.

In P02 "Beginning of Harvest" s4, the cultural explanatory background is introduced by a cataphoric reference.

(31) wɔz dzi **anaˈnotʰ-ə** **spʰɔ**   ˈdʒaɪ-ən kʰə iˈjun
     again alike tradition-OBJ 1PL.GEN place-ABL REL some
     tʃɪˈnɪ   jɔ alaˈbi   ʒaɾʒ ˈkʰatʰ-ən
     china.bowl or metal.bowl milk put-3PL
     'Then we have this tradition at our place, that we put milk in some
     china bowls or metal bowls.'

In P10 "Death of an Adult" s31, the speaker announces with a cataphoric reference that he will explain a tradition.
In P09 "Death of a Child" s4, the speaker points out that the prayer for the dead is a religious command.
In P09 "Death of a Child" s19, background information names the prayer for the given occasion, and is marked by a speech verb.

2.3.3 Behavioural

2.3.3.1 The Enclitic =ṣ to foreground background material

In behaviourals, the clitic =ṣ serves the same function as in narratives, that is, foregrounding material that would normally be considered background.

In B02 "How to Teach" s4 (example (32)), the speaker gives explanatory background information as he points out his experience. He foregrounds it since it qualifies him to advise about teaching.

(32) ˈjanə tsə ʐø   tʰadʒɾuˈba-ən a-ˈdzi **maˈlem-ṣ**
      then of experience-ABL EMPH   alike teacher=IPFV
      ˈwɔs-tʰI
      become-PST
      'Then, according to my experience, a teacher was like that:....'

In B04 "Difficulties in the Village" s46, the speaker hints by adding the clitic in a subordinate clause that he considers it the government's responsibility to give the money to repair a certain road and house.

B08 "Attending Prayer", s2 has the typical structure of a hortatory thesis: the main claim is in imperative mode, and the supporting reasons are in present tense. However, they are foregrounded since they are considered crucial and thus taken up again in s3–4, and also in the summary of the text (s9).

2.3.3.2 Change of tense for backgrounding

The mainline of behaviourals is in imperative mode as the speaker addresses the listener with his exhortations. Background information is either in present indicative giving reasons why these claims should be followed, or in past tense expressing the setting in the form of brief subordinate conditional clauses. Behavioural stories deviate from this rule but follow those of narrative (see section 2.3.1.2), while the hortatory passages – usually speech clauses of one of the participants – follow the rules given for behaviourals.

In B02 "How to Teach" s3, the speaker gives background information about himself in the past tense, which qualifies him to instruct others.

In B03 "A Girl's Lessons" s7, the subordinate conditional clause is in past tense; it is background setting. The sentence supports the hortatory claims concerning how girls need to be brought up.

The same structure is present in B04 "Difficulties in the Village" s52. The argument supports the main claim: Live peacefully together in the village!

Again this structure is employed in B05 "Opium Story" s22. The sentence supports the central advice: Get rid of your opium addiction!

2.3.3.3 Background information in sentence-final adverbials

This feature has the same function in behaviourals as it has in narratives.

B04 "Difficulties in the Village" gives evaluational background summarizing the result of the mediating effort of the narrator indicated by the past tense and by a sentence-final adverbial. However, the sentence in example (33) is foregrounded by the imperfective marker to emphasize the success, s33.

2.3 Foregrounding and backgrounding

(33) jəm jaɾkʰ-ṣ   ˈvi-tʰ ɪ   pʰʊˈɾa
     DEM1 work-IPFV become-PST complete
     'This work was completed.'

Again in B04 "Difficulties in the Village", the speaker illustrates his main advice (to support each other in the village) with an example about a road construction project. In s46, he gives background information.

2.3.3.4 The preposition tsə 'of' in background material

In behaviourals, the preposition serves the same purpose as in narratives.

B01 "Rules of the Aga Khan" has two parts. Each lists five commands given to the Ismaeli people. The first sentence of each part is a cataphoric reference with the preposition *tsə*. As they are backgrounded, the actual content of the commands becomes salient. S1 introduces the first block.

S4 introduces the second block; here, the preposition occurs in a main clause.

In B02 "How to Teach" s9, the first clause is backgrounded to stress the positive consequences of having at least limited literacy skills, as stated in the second clause.

In B05 "Opium Story" s27, the relative clause is backgrounded because the listener already knows that opium addicts are addressed. This serves to stress the subsequent clause.

2.3.3.5 "Announced" background information

In behaviourals, this feature is rare. In B01 "Rules of the Aga Khan" s3, a relative pronoun and a speech verb in the third person plural are combined; the speaker explains the meaning of a lexical item.

2.3.4 Expository text

2.3.4.1 The enclitic =ṣ to foreground background material

In behaviourals, the clitic =ṣ serves the same function as it does in narratives.

In E03 "Living under Oppression" s6, the first clause is subordinate, supplying spatial explanatory background. The foregrounding achieved by the clitic indicates that indeed all places where people went are included.

E05 "Clans of the Wakhan", s5 is a subordinate clause; it is foregrounded since the crucial theme of oppression is introduced in the text.

(34) ˈamɔ ˈts-əm-ən   ə   ˈjkʰaʊ-əʃ məɾˈdʊm-əɾ=ṣ   ɣaftʃ ɣaftʃ
     but of-DEM1-ABL REL 3SG-PL   people-DAT=IPFV   very very
     ˈzələm   kʰəɾ-kʰ
     oppression do-PRF
     'But since they oppressed the people very much...'

E03 "Living under Oppression" s27 gives evaluational background, confirming the credibility of the report. The clitic indicates the validity of what the father has told.

E07 "Hotsprings" s2 gives explanatory background information concerning the reason why hotsprings are considered a miracle. It is foregrounded since they are crucial in the daily life of the Wakhi people.

(35) mʊdʒɪˈza-ɪə ˈjaʊ-ə ə kʰə də i **dʒaɪ-əʂ** jaʊ sʉr
    miracle-CON 3SG-c on REL in one place=IPFV 3SG cold
    ˈjʊpkʰ-ə sʉr jupkʰ-ʂ banˈda bə tʃiz mʊʃkʰɪləth bə
    water-OBJ cold water=IPFV servant by thing difficulty by
    tʃiz ˈdʒabr-əʂ ˈjaʊ-ə θin tsar-tʰ
    thing effort=IPFV 3SG-OBJ hot do-3SG
    'The miracle is that in one place – cold water, cold water, servants (of God) with what sort of difficulty and what sort of effort do they heat it!'

2.3.4.2 Change of tense for backgrounding

The tense of expository texts is the present since the speaker makes claims that he considers to be generally true. However, the tense frequently changes to perfect in background material, especially when the speaker argues from past experience. This parallels the feature of background setting in narrative.

E02 "Life in Old Times" contrasts past with present conditions. The past serves as a dark background for a slightly brighter present. The whole text is an illustration of the statement in s1.

In E03 "Living under Oppression" s13, as the speaker explains the fate of young men during a certain time in history, he supplies background information.

E06 "Knowledge of the Hour" s3 presents background information concerning the origin of a book, giving credibility to the information of the text. Additionally, the preposition *tsə* marks the information as backgrounded (see section 2.3.1.4).

2.3.4.3 Background information in sentence-final adverbials

This feature is used in the same way as it is in narrative texts.

In E03 "Living under Oppression", the speaker relates his father's experience with oppression in the past. S18 serves as a summary of the preceding paragraph; thus, it is evaluational background. Within the sentence, the time frame is given as sentence-final background setting. At the same time, the adverbial is highlighted by its position at the core of an *inclusio*.[8]

In E04 "Life of the Ismaeli" s1, the extended adverbial at the end of the first clause provides explanatory background since it orients the listener to what he is about to hear; the adverbial in the second clause adds setting background referring to the time of events. Additionally, the whole sentence is backgrounded by the preposition *tsə* in both clauses.

---

[8] "*Inclusio* structures involve the bracketing of a unit by making a statement at the beginning, an approximation of which is repeated at the end." (Levinsohn 2023:157n5) Compare also section 2.5.1.2.

2.3 Foregrounding and backgrounding 67

2.3.4.4 The preposition tsə *'of'* in background material

This preposition serves the same purpose as it does in narrative texts.

In E01 "History of Ismaeli Islam" s13, a relative clause adds identificational background information, clarifying which branch the narrator refers to.

In E03 "Living under Oppression", s15 gives identification background concerning two people groups: those who left, and those who remained at home. This adds salience to the severity of the main clause.

E06 "Book of the Hour" discusses the use of the book. In s3, the speaker gives identificational background information concerning the source of the information in a relative clause.

In E09 "Health Courses" s1, the speaker backgrounds the first clause because the existence of health courses is assumed. Therefore, more weight is on the second clause, which gives reasons for the courses.

2.3.4.5 'Announced' background information

'Announced' background is seldom used in expository texts. The lexical item announcing the background information is 'that is'.

In E10 "Banking", s5 gives a brief background explanation introduced with 'by (the following) meaning'. It is a cataphoric reference.

(36) a-ˈjəm   ˈbɔŋkʰ-ə   χəˈdi   ˈjanə kʰə bə məˈnɔ-ə
      EMPH-DEM1   bank-CON   relatives that.is REL by meaning-CON

   a-ˈjəm-ə   ˈçatʰ-ə   ˈχalg-ən   çøn
   EMPH-DEM1-OBJ   own-OBJ   person-ABL towards

   'The bank of the relatives, that is, it means that it belongs to the people themselves.'

In E03 "Living under Oppression" s14, the meaning of a word is explained, indicated by 'that is'.

2.3.5 Summary

Table 2.2. Foregrounding and backgrounding features in the four genres

Feature + Function	Narrative 10 texts	Procedure 10 texts	Behavioural 8 texts	Exposition 10 texts
Enclitic =ṣ̌ to foreground background material[a]	In 9 texts	In 5 texts	In 6 texts	In 8 texts
Change of tense for backgrounding setting, evaluation, explanatory background[b]	a) PRS to PRF b) PST to PRS In 8 texts	PRS to PST in 8 texts	PRS IMP to PRS IND or PST IND, In 8 texts	PRS or PST to PRF, In 10 texts
Sentence-final adverbial for brief background comments (setting, evaluation, explanatory)[c]	In 2 texts	In 4 texts	In 1 text	In 4 texts
Preposition tsə for explanatory, identificational background, backgrounding against more salient context[d]	In 6 texts	In 5 texts	In 7 texts	In 9 texts
Announced background mainly for cultural and religious background information[e]	In 3 texts	In 6 texts	In 3 texts	In 3 texts

[a] This is very common in all genres, except in procedures which have less complex foreground-background structures. More research is needed concerning the choice of constituent the clitic is attached to.
[b] This is very common in all genres.
[c] Overall this appears only occasionally.
[d] This is more common in behaviourals and exposition which are structured around arguments. It occurs mostly within relative clauses.
[e] This is most common in procedures which naturally relate cultural conventions. It could alternatively be labeled performative background. It can have the form of a cataphoric reference.

2.4 Prominence summary

Prominence relates to a process in language which directs attention to a particular constituent of a sentence. Four features are used in Wakhi to indicate prominence. These are summarized for the four genres in table 2.3.

Table 2.3. Features used to indicate prominence in the four genres

Feature + Function	Narrative 10 texts	Procedure 10 texts	Behavioural 8 texts	Exposition 10 texts
Focal and contrastive prominence using preposing or postposing[a]	In 8 texts	In 9 texts	In 8 texts	In 10 texts
Focal and contrastive prominence using emphatic marker a[b]	In 10 texts	In 9 texts	In 5 texts	In 9 texts
Thematic prominence expressed through extensive or minimal occurrence of key words[c]	Main character is named extensively or minimally	Theme introduction in first sentence, key words throughout text	Theme named in opening or closing, key words throughout text, especially paragraph breaks	Theme named in opening *and* closing, key words throughout text, especially paragraph breaks
Emphatic prominence expressed through emphatic lexical items[d]	In 4 texts	In 1 text	In 3 texts	In 5 texts

[a] This is very common in all genres. It applies mostly to the object. Preposing vs. postposing is determined by which position is farther from the original one.
[b] This is very common in all genres. It is mostly anaphoric, sometimes cataphoric.
[c] This naturally occurs in all text of all genres, however, with slight variations.
[d] This is relatively rare, especially in procedures where the speaker naturally tends not to be strongly involved emotionally. Adjectives, pairs of similar nouns, word repetitions, or strong negations are used.

2.5 Highlighting

Highlighting or a peak in a narrative is essentially a zone of turbulence in regard to the flow of the discourse (Longacre 1996:38). In Wakhi, such turbulence can be produced by several syntactic means, usually at crucial points in the text such as the climax or evaluation. In contrast, prominence directs attention to one constituent of a sentence (possibly the same constituent throughout a story). However, there is overlap between highlighting and prominence, especially concerning their function within a text. Following the discussion in sections 2.5.1 through 2.5.4 of features marking highlighting in the four genres, table 2.4 in section 2.5.5 presents a summary, including the number of occurrences of each feature in the various genres.

2.5.1 Narrative

2.5.1.1 Deviation from the main tense

As seen above, tense may deviate from the default to achieve backgrounding (see section 2.3.1.2). A similar device can be employed within the storyline.

In narratives, deviation from the default tense within the mainline, which can be present or past tense (see section 2.3.1.2), indicates highlighting. The mainline of N01 "King's Daughter" is in present tense. It changes to the past tense to underline the king's surprise that the farmer has fulfilled the condition set for the marriage of their children. The subsequent subordinate phrase is in past tense again, since the reader already knows that the farmer's son has managed to obtain gold, S42.

The mainline of N03 "Naser Khesrau" is in the present tense as well. As the nature of the test which the host puts before his guest becomes apparent, the tense changes to the past. In this case, it is the verb on the mainline which is a speech orienter. S10 in example (37) shows this deviation from the main tense.

(37) jəm   ðaɪ   ˈçan-dɪ χɔ   wʊz nev   ˈjəm-ər   i   skʰən
     DEM1   man   say-PST intj 1SG now   DEM1-DAT one puppy
     ˈtʃʉç-əm   ˈbɔjad
     slaughter-1SG   must
     'The man said: Well, I now have to slaughter a puppy for him.'

In stories with the storyline in past the tense, the present tense indicates highlighting. In N08 "Bear story", the only verb in the present tense in the mainline is the howling of the bear – apparently the climax for the narrator, s13.

2.5.1.2 Parallelisms and inclusio

Key stages of a text, such as the peak of the problem or the conclusion, may be marked by a parallelism, in which the second line may be identical, be altered in content or word order, or expand on the first (compare Klutz 1999:261 for similar features in Koiné Greek). Some texts are framed with multiple *inclusio*. This feature is employed in a number of variants, as illustrated in the examples.

2.5 Highlighting

To highlight the problem in N05 "Abraham", three identically structured sentences with different objects are juxtaposed, s3. These are depicted in example (38).

(38) (a) ˈstur-ə qʰʊrbɔˈnɪ gɔç-tʰɪ nə ˈvɪ-tʰɪ[9]
camel-OBJ sacrifice make-PST NEG become-PST

(b) ˈdruks̩-ə qʰʊrbɔˈnɪ gɔç-tʰɪ nə ˈvɪ-tʰɪ
bull-OBJ sacrifice make-PST NEG become-PST

(c) ˈqla-rə qʰʊrbɔˈnɪ gɔç-tʰɪ nə ˈvɪ-tʰɪ
sheep/goat-OBJ sacrifice make-PST NEG become-PST

a. 'He sacrificed a camel; it was not (acceptable).

b. He sacrificed a bull; it was not (acceptable).

c. He sacrificed a sheep/goat; it was not (acceptable).'

The confirmation of the problem employs a similar structure, changing perspective to the first person (God speaking), s5.

Parallel sentences in N08 "Bear Story" highlight the incident's danger. The order of adverbial and object is inverted in the second clause, s7.

(39) nɔyɔrˈdʊm ts-a nag ˈmaẓ-ə nə ˈwɪn-dɪ ˈmagam
bear of-DEM3 towards 1SG-OBJ NEG see-PST but

ˈwʊz-əm ˈjau-ə tʰərˈmis ˈwɪn-dɪ
1SG-1SG 3SG.OBJ before see-PST

'The bear did not see me until then, but I saw him before.'

In the denouement of N03 "Naser Khesrau" s20–21, the name of the village is postposed in the first clause, then preposed in the second clause.

2.5.1.3 Rhetorical questions

Rhetorical questions are only occasionally used as a discourse device within the corpus. However, they are used frequently in daily speech, predominantly in the negative, for example, "Won't you come and drink tea?" The person addressed knows that he is usually expected to decline the offer.[10]

In N01 "King's Daughter" s15, the king uses a rhetorical question towards the shepherd to stress the absurdity of the proposal. The implied answer is "no"!

(40) jəm ˈçan-dɪ zø ðəɥjd-s̩ tʰər tʰau ˈjatʰ-a
DEM1 say-PST 1SG.GEN daughter-IPFV about 2SG.OBJ arrive-Q

'He (the king) said: Does my daughter reach you?'

In N07 "War of the Kyrgyz" s33, the mother addresses the pursuers of her son, intending to confront them with the vileness of their behaviour.

---

[9] In section 2.5.1.2 Parallelisms and *Inclusio*, identical lexical items in multiple lines are bold; corresponding lexical items are italicized.

[10] If the host wants to serve tea, he just prepares the tea and urges the guest to drink without asking first.

2.5.1.4 Subordinate clauses in the storyline

Information in subordinate clauses is usually backgrounded (Gee 2011:93). In narratives they add background information, while the verbs in the main clauses are on the timeline. However, if verbs in subordinate clauses are on the timeline, they do other, additional discourse work (Thompson 1987:445). Progression of the storyline in subordinate clauses indicates highlighting in Wakhi. This feature may be used near the climax to keep the listener in suspense, since subordinate clauses slow down the progression of events.

In N02 "Nesandaljon", s178 describes a crucial incident before the denouement. If the king's daughter hands over the flowers, the death of the main character will result. The fact that the king and the old man pressure her is part of the storyline in a subordinate clause. The listener is kept in suspense whether the king's daughter will give in to the pressure.

In N04 "Noah", the settling of the people on the mountain is in a subordinate clause. The desperateness of their condition is highlighted. The listener is kept in suspense concerning their fate, s20–21.

The timeline of the climax in N05 "Abraham" is God commands him not to harm Ishmael, then the animal appears, then it kneels down. The appearance of the substitute sacrifice is in a subordinate clause. The narrator highlights the fact that it arrived just at the right time, supported by the emphatic marker *a*, s29.

2.5.1.5 Final cataphoric reference

The denouement of a narrative may be introduced by a cataphoric reference highlighting the conclusion.

In N04 "Noah", a cataphoric reference introduces the final sentence, strengthened by an emphatic marker, s31.

In N06 "Emigration to Wakhan" in the conclusion following the cataphoric reference, likewise emphatic markers are added to "Wakhi generation" and to "king Sanskrit", s9.

2.5.2 Procedural

2.5.2.1 Deviation from the main tense

This feature does not occur in the present corpus in procedurals.

2.5.2.2 Parallelisms and inclusio

As in narratives, this feature is used at crucial stages of procedures.

In P01 "Wedding Ceremony", s11 employs an *inclusio* as the betrothal of the daughter is discussed. The parallelism of the frame is achieved by words with similar meanings ("agreement", "acceptance") and the negative particle combined with the emphatic marker *a* as "question tag". The closing sentence of the frame receives urgency from the imperfective marker (see section 2.3.1.1).

Later in P01 "Wedding Ceremony" in s20, a parallelism describes the trouble of a groom. In the main clause, "household goods" are left-dislocated; they are expanded on in the subsequent subordinate clauses.

2.5 Highlighting

In P05 "Baking Bread", a parallelism in s3 describes the importance of the right temperature of water for the dough. The sentence provides highlighted explanatory background information.

P09 "Death of a Child", s6 displays a parallel structure, with the indirect and direct object reversed in the second clause. The verb and the indirect object are repeated, and the direct object ('grave') is replaced by a synonym as shown in example (41).

(41) (a) wə amsɔˈja-əʃ   ja-r   ˈqʰabər dʒir   ˈtsar-ən
           and neighbour-PL 3SG-DAT grave ready do-3PL

     (b) χɔkʰ χɔkʰ ja-r   dʒir   ˈtsar-ən
           grave grave 3SG-DAT ready field
           a. 'And the neighbours prepare him a grave,
           b. They make a grave for him.'

2.5.2.3 Rhetorical questions

This feature does not occur in the present corpus in procedurals.

2.5.2.4 Subordinate clauses in the storyline

As in narratives, progression of a procedure's mainline with a subordinate clause indicates highlighting. However, this is rare.

In P01 "Wedding Ceremony" s11, the suitor phrases his purpose in a subordinate clause, highlighting his pursuit. Grammatically, it could have been expressed equally well in a main clause.

2.5.2.5 Final cataphoric reference

This feature does not occur in the present corpus in procedurals.

2.5.3 Behavioural

2.5.3.1 Deviation from the main tense

The tense and mode of the main assertions in behaviourals is the present imperative. When an incident from the past has strong implications for the future in support of the hortatory thesis, it can be highlighted using the perfect tense. This can be distinguished from backgrounding with perfect tense as background information predominantly uses state verbs, while accomplishment and achievement verbs in perfect tense indicate highlighting (compare Foley and Van Valin 1984:371). A series of verbs in perfect tense can form a strong argument, as in B03 "A Girl's Lessons" s8–10.

In B05 "Opium Story", the reason against smoking opium is highlighted in s23.

In B06 "Cleaning Teeth", s10-12 highlights the reason for toothache – building up to the main behavioural thesis which discourages eating sweets and promotes brushing teeth.

2.5.3.2 Parallelisms and inclusio

Analogous to narratives, in behaviourals this feature is used to support the main hortatory thesis.

In B2 "How to Teach", the benefit of studying is highlighted by a tri-part parallel structure. The if-clause is backgrounded in s7-8 (see section 2.3.1.4) against the three short main clauses by the use of the preposition *tsə*, as seen in example (42).

(42) (a) ˈagar tʰu wudg dʒɔɪ ts-əɪ ˈvrɔkʰər
if 2SG today study of-AUX tomorrow

(b) i dɔkˈtʰar ˈnəʉəz
one doctor come.out

(c) i maˈlem ˈnəʉəz
one teacher come.out

(d) i mɔˈmur ˈnəʉəz
one clerk come.out

'If you study today, tomorrow …

… a doctor will become of you,

… a teacher will become of you,

… a clerk will become of you.'

In B04 "Difficulties in the Village" s18, the negation particle is preposed from preceding the verb to preceding the direct object in both parts of the parallel pair, resulting in emphatic prominence (see section 2.4). The sentence is highlighted as it expresses the urgency to solve a conflict and to live peacefully with each other.

In B05 "Opium Story" s28, the friend tries to reason with the opium addict.

In B03 "A Girl's Lessons" s20-21 uses a positive-negative pair to highlight the responsibility of the mother.

The whole text B08 "Attending Prayer" is an *inclusio*, starting with the main behavioural claim, s1.

The following sentences stress the importance of listening to the admonition of the people and point out that only occasional attendance is insufficient. The final sentence, s9, repeats the main claim, expanding it by the repetition of the main supporting argument. The object ("this people's talk") is preposed to strengthen that this is in fact the purpose of attending prayer. In B02 "How to Teach", several *inclusio* explain how students should be encouraged, starting with s7: "A student must be encouraged!"

2.5 Highlighting

S8–15 point out professional prospects and the honour one receives in the village for being educated. S16 closes the first frame, as well as opening the second frame: "For that reason a student must be encouraged."

S16–17 express that no help can be expected from outsiders and concludes with the same message, s18: "Therefore, a student should be encouraged and should study."

This sentence also opens the third frame. S18–32 point out that today's teaching methods place the student at the center of the lesson instead of the teacher. S33, the closing of the third frame, reiterates: "… so that the student becomes encouraged."

2.5.3.3 Rhetorical questions

Behaviourals are the only genre besides narratives that use rhetorical questions to highlight significant parts of the text.

In B03 "A Girl's Lessons" s26–27, a rhetorical question with its answer, is at the core of a paragraph comparing good and bad behaviour as shown in example (43).

(43) tsə ˈχalg-ən   tʃiz   ˈwəɾəṣ-th   χuˈb-iɟ
     of person-ABL thing remain-3SG good-NOM
     'What remains of a person? Goodness!' (a person's good deeds)

In B07 "Wheat and Potatoes" s5, the son poses a rhetorical question to his father, expressing the main behavioural claim of the text. It introduces the subsequent explanation of the benefit of vegetables.

2.5.3.4 Subordinate clauses in the argument line

In behaviourals, subordinate clauses usually support the main hortatory claims. Main arguments in subordinate clauses indicate highlighting.

In B06 "Cleaning Teeth" s18, the crucial information is phrased in a subordinate clause following a main clause ("can"). The syntax would have been more straightforward if the speaker had omitted the main clause and had expressed the content of the subordinate clause in the main clause instead. Here the structure obviously highlights the importance of the content ("clean teeth").

B07 "Wheat and Potatoes", s7 expresses the main aim of the behavioural (to cultivate vegetables) in a subordinate clause.

2.5.4 Expository text

2.5.4.1 Deviation from the main tense

As in behaviourals, important issues can be highlighted in expository texts by using the perfect tense. However, the distinction between background information and highlighting using the perfect tense must be made from the context, as state verbs are used for main arguments in expository texts more commonly than in other genres.

E01 "History of Ismaeli Islam" is in the present tense, expressing today's practices, and in past tense, relating historic events. The tense changes to perfect in s5, highlighting the common roots of Ismaeli and Sunni Muslims.

In the same text, s15–18 summarize in the perfect tense the important issues of the preceding paragraph (which is in past and present tense), emphasizing the commonality between Ismaelis and Sunni Muslims (in a practical sense, this highlighting might have been done in order to be "politically correct").

In E08 "Ways of Teaching" the speaker compares previous teaching methods with present teaching methods. He describes the present methods in the present tense; only s16 is in perfect tense, highlighting the benefits of the new method.

In E10 "Banking", s3 makes a strong point in favor of the community banking system. The perfect tense highlights that someone who has saved in the past benefits in the future – in contrast to the arbitrary dealings of money lenders.

2.5.4.2 Parallelisms and inclusio

As in the other genres, this feature supports the main theses of expository texts.

In E01 "History of Ismaeli Islam" s12, the speaker explains the historical root of the difference between 12th-Shia and Ismaeli using a parallelism. The direct object is postposed in both clauses.

E02 "Life in Old Times" employs an *inclusio*; the centre is a tri-part parallelism. The frame contrasts the past with the present in the centre, s9–11.

The *inclusio* in E03 "Living under Oppression" stretches over several sentences, highlighting the hardness of the oppression during the time of Zaher Shah. The opening of the frame is s21–22 shown in example (44).

(44) 'Those of our relatives who went to Tajikistan, they went because of oppression at that time. It was the time of Zaher Sha.'

The speaker proceeds to describe that people fled from military recruitment. S24 in example (45), the closing of the frame reiterates.

(45) 'It was the time of Zaher Sha. Our people went to Pakistan. They went to Tajikistan as well because of oppression.'

In fact, the structure of the passage is chiastic.

A They went to Tajikistan because of oppression. (s21)
  B It was the time of Zaher Sha. (s22)
    C Danger of military recruitment (s23)
  B' It was the time of Zaher Sha. (s24)
A' They went to Pakistan and Tajikistan because of oppression. (s24)

E06 "Book of the Hour" stresses the importance of complying with the rules of the "book of the hour" using a parallelism, s5–6.

For example at what time to take out the carpets, we consult the 'book of the hour'.
For example at what time to go outdoors, we consult the 'book of the hour'.

2.5 Highlighting

In E10 "Banking" s27, the speaker illustrates the benefit of the community bank, using the contrast of happy and sad occasions.

2.5.4.3 Subordinate clauses in the argument line

In expository text, as in behaviourals, subordinate clauses usually support the main arguments. Main arguments in subordinate clauses indicate highlighting.

In E07 "Hotsprings" s4, each subordinate clause exceeds the salience of the preceding one in the strength of the argument.

In E08 "Ways of Teaching" the narrator, a teacher, relates how students should be treated. To strengthen his point rhetorically, he employs a tri-part parallelism of subordinate clauses, s11: "The new method tells us, that the student cannot be hit, the student cannot be commanded, the student cannot be accused."

2.5.4.4 Final cataphoric reference

As in narratives, a cataphoric reference can highlight the final conclusion of an expository text.

In E06 "Book of the Hour", the final sentence provides a summary, highlighted by a cataphoric reference, s17.

2.5.5 Summary

Table 2.4. Features used to indicate highlighting in the four genres

Feature + function	Narrative 10 texts	Procedure 10 texts	Behavioural 8 texts	Exposition 10 texts
Deviation from mainline tense to highlight problem or peak[a]	a) PST to PRS b) PRS to PST In 6 texts	None	PRS IMP to PRF IND In 4 texts	PRS or PST to PRF In 4 texts
Parallelism and inclusio to highlight problem, peak or strong argument[b]	Only here also used for evaluation, In 8 texts	In 8 texts	In 7 texts	In 7 texts
Rhetorical questions for rebuke or encouragement[c]	In 7 texts	None	In 7 texts	None

Table 2.4. (*continued*)

Feature + function	Narrative 10 texts	Procedure 10 texts	Behavioural 8 texts	Exposition 10 texts
Subordinate clause in storyline or argument line to keep up suspense or strengthen central claim[d]	In 6 texts	In 4 texts	In 3 texts	In 4 texts
Final cataphoric reference to highlight conclusion or consequence[e]	In 4 texts	None	None	In 2 texts

[a] This is fairly common in narratives, and less common in behaviourals and expositions; due to their argument structure, they have a greater percentage of supporting material and therefore less tense variation within the mainline.
[b] This is common in all genres. It appears in multiple varieties, including chiasm and positive-negative pairs. It is often combined with EMPH or IMPV markers.
[c] This might also appear in procedurals and expositions if the corpus were more extensive.
[d] This occurs occasionally in all genres.
[e] This might also appear in procedurals and behaviourals if the corpus were more extensive.

2.6 Conclusion

Wakhi has multiple means at its disposal to express foregrounding and backgrounding, highlighting, and prominence. They are used in similar ways in all four genres.

- Foregrounding of background material is achieved by the clitic =ṣ.
- Perfect tense indicates setting or explanatory or evaluational background.

For brief pieces of background information, an adverbial can be postposed. The preposition *tsə* indicates that material is backgrounded against its more salient environment. Furthermore, background information can be explicitly announced.

To ascribe focal or contrastive prominence to a constituent, it may be preposed or postposed (applied to objects), or the emphatic marker *a* may be attached (applied to all constituents). To achieve thematic prominence throughout a text, the relevant entity is mentioned extensively, or in narratives, alternatively coded minimally. In addition, it can be marked repeatedly with focal prominence. Emphatic prominence indicates heightened emotion; it is coded lexically by adjectives or by noun repetitions.

2.6 Conclusion

Highlighting can be applied to crucial parts of the progression of a text. This is achieved by deviation from the main tense either when the problem is posed or at the peak. Parallelisms and similar structures, such as *inclusio* and chiasm, occur at the peak, or to propose a strong argument.

Rather rarely used means are rhetorical questions to express encouragement or rebuke, subordinate clauses as part of the mainline to keep up suspense, and cataphoric references pointing to the conclusion of a text.

The described features can be combined in a multitude of ways. For backgrounding the preposition *tsə* can occur with change of tense, or with a sentence final adverbial.

Likewise, means of foregrounding, prominence, and highlighting can accumulate to achieve an even stronger impact, especially when the particles combine with other devices. The emphatic marker *a* occurs with contrastive postposing 0 (68)[11], with the naming of the theme of prominence (127), with deviation from the mainline tense 0, with the imperfective marker, (122), with parallelism (142), or with a final cataphoric reference (149). The imperfective marker =*š* occurs with preposing (79), with a rhetorical question (143), with parallelism (150), or with a subordinate clause on the argument line (182). Furthermore, parallelism give emphatic prominence (131).

Backgrounding devices are combined with devices for prominence and highlighting when background information is considered crucial for the subsequent development of the text. Change of tense for backgrounding occurs with the emphatic marker *a* (11). A sentence-final adverbial is used with emphatic prominence (27), or with the imperfective marker (45) The preposition *tsə* occurs with the imperfective marker (31), or with the emphatic marker (61), and announced background information with the emphatic marker (35). Further combinations might be found in a larger text corpus, and their effects might be distinguishable according to genre.

The described features and their combinations show that Wakhi speakers have a rich variety of means at their disposal acting jointly to make texts understandable and to convey the purpose of their speech. These features cause narratives to be vivid, procedurals traceable, behaviourals persuasive, and expository texts convincing.

More research is needed concerning whether preposing versus postposing is merely determined by the original position of the constituent, or whether it serves additional distinguishable ends. Furthermore, the position of the clitic =*š* in the sentence should be researched. It would also be interesting to see whether rhetorical questions occur in procedural and expository texts, and whether a final cataphoric reference occurs in procedurals and behaviourals in a bigger corpus. Eventually, more research is needed to detect how the different combinations of features are used and what effect they achieve in the different genres.

---

[11] The following numbers refer to examples in the original master's thesis. The following examples are included in this short chapter: 143 (= example 40 in this chapter), 45 (= 33), 34 (= 31).

References

Backstrom, Peter. 2009. Gojal Wakhi grammar sketch. Ms.

Bashir, Elena. 2009. Wakhi. In Gernot Windfuhr (ed.), *The Iranian languages*, 825–861. London: Routledge.

Buddruss, Georg. 1974. Neuiranische Wortstudien. Zur Wakhi-Sprache in Hunza [New-Iranian word studies. About the Wakhi language in Hunza]. *Münchener Studien zur Sprachwissenschaft*, 32:9–40.

Bybee, Joan, Revere Perkins, and William Pagliuca. 1994. *Tense, aspect, and modality in the languages of the world*. Chicago: University of Chicago Press.

Cambridge Dictionaries Online. 2011. Cambridge dictionaries online. http://dictionary.cambridge.org/.

Comrie, Bernard. 1976. *Aspect: An introduction to verbal aspect and related problems*. Cambridge: Cambridge University Press.

Duncan, Alexander, and Eleanor Duncan. 2002. Report of survey of Wakhan District, Badakhshan Province, Afghanistan. Report prepared for Orphans, Refugees and Aid International. Ms.

Erschler, David. 2010. On optionality in grammar: The case of East Iranian almost Wackernagel clitics. Paper presented at the Syntax of the World's Languages IV, Lyon, September 23, 2010.

Foley, William A., and Robert D. Van Valin, Jr. 1984. *Functional syntax and universal grammar*. Cambridge Studies in Linguistics 38. Cambridge: Cambridge University Press.

Gee, James Paul. 2011. *How to do discourse analysis: A toolkit*. New York: Routledge.

Givón, T. 1987. Beyond foreground and background. In Russell S. Tomlin (ed.), *Coherence and grounding in discourse: Outcome of a symposium, Eugene, Oregon, June 1984*, 175–188. Amsterdam: John Benjamins.

Grjunberg, Alexander L., and I. M. Stéblin-Kamensky. 1988. *La langue wakhi*. Paris: Éditions de la Maison des sciences de l'homme.

Haspelmath, Martin, ed. 2001. *Language typology and language universals: An international handbook*. Vol. 1. Berlin: De Gruyter.

Hopkirk, Peter. 1992. *The great game: The struggle for empire in Central Asia*. New York: Kodansha.

Kibort, Anna. 2009. Modelling the 'perfect', a category between tense and aspect. In *Current issues in unity and diversity of languages. Collection of the papers selected from the CIL 18th*, held at Korea University in Seoul on July 21-26, 2008, 1390–1404. Seoul: The Linguistic Society of Korea.

Kieffer, Charles M. 1978. Einführung in die Wakhi-Sprache und Glossar. In R. Senarclens de Grancy and R. Kostka (eds.), *Grosser Pamir. Österreichisches Forscchungsunternehmen 1975 in Wakhan-Pamir Afghanistan*, 345–374. Graz: Akademische Druck- und Verlagsanstalt.

Klutz, Todd. 1999. "Naked and wounded": Foregrounding, relevance and situation in Acts 19.13–20. In Stanley E. Porter and Jeffrey T. Reed (eds.), *Discourse analysis and the New Testament: Approaches and results*, 258–279. Sheffield: Sheffield Academic.

References

Kreutzmann, Hermann. 1996. *Ethnizität im Entwicklungsprozess. Die Wakhi in Hochasien* [Ethnicity in the process of development: The Wakhi in High Altitude Asia]. Berlin: Reimer.

Kreutzmann, Hermann. 2003. Ethnic minorities and marginality in the Pamirian Knot: Survival of Wakhi and Kirghiz in a harsh environment and global contexts. *The Geographical Journal*, 169(3):215–235. Erlangen-Nuremberg: Institute of Geography.

Levinsohn, Stephen H. 2023a. *Self-instruction materials on narrative discourse analysis*. Dallas: SIL International.

Levinsohn, Stephen H. 2023b. *Self-instruction materials on non-narrative discourse analysis*. Dallas: SIL International.

Lewis, M. Paul, Gary F. Simons, and Charlie D. Fennig. 2013. *Ethnologue: Languages of the world*. Dallas: SIL International. http://www.ethnologue.com.

Longacre, Robert E. 1996. *The grammar of discourse*. New York: Plenum Press.

Longacre, Robert E., and Frances Woods, eds. 1976. *Discourse grammar: Studies in indigenous languages of Colombia, Panama, and Ecuador*. Part 3. Dallas: Summer Institute of Linguistics and University of Texas at Arlington.

Lorimer, David L. R. 1958. *The Wakhi language*. Vol. 1. London: School of Oriental and African Studies.

Morgenstierne, Georg. 1938. *Iranian Pamir languages: Yidgha-Munji, Sanglechi-Ishkashmi and Wakhi*. Indo-Iranian Frontier Languages 2. Oslo: Instituttet for sammenlignende kulturforskning.

Moseley, Christopher. 2010. *Atlas of the world's languages in danger*. Paris: UNESCO Publishing. http://www.unesco.org/culture/en/endangeredlanguages/atlas.

Pakhalina, T. N. 1975. *Vakhanskii iazyk* [The Wakhi language]. Moskva: Nauka.

Pancheva, Roumyana. 2003. The aspectual makeup of perfect participles and the interpretations of the perfect. In Artemis Alexiadou, Monika Rathert, and Arnim von Stechow (eds.), *Perfect explorations*, 277–306. Berlin: De Gruyter Mouton.

Payne, John R. 1989. Pamir languages. In Rüdiger R. Schmitt (ed.), *Compendium Linguarum Iranicarum*, 417–444. Wiesbaden: Ludwig Reichert.

Reinhold, Beate. 2006. Neue Entwicklungen in der Wakhi-Sprache Von Gojal (Nordpakistan). *Journal of the Royal Asiatic Society*, 19:254–256.

Roberts, John R. 2009. *A study of Persian discourse structure*. Uppsala: Uppsala Universitet.

Rowe, William C. 2010. The Wakhan Corridor: Endgame of the great game. In Alexander C. Diener and Joshua Hagen (eds.), *Borderlines and borderlands: Political oddities at the edge of the nation-state*, 53–68. Plymouth: Rowman and Littlefield.

Shaw, Robert Barkley. 1876. On the Ghalchah languages (Wakhi and Sarikoli). *Journal of the Asiatic Society of Bengal*, 45(1–2):139–278.

Skjaervø, Prods Oktor. 1989. Modern East Iranian languages. In Rüdiger Schmitt (ed.), *Compendium linguarum Iranicarum*, 370–383. Wiesbaden: Dr. Ludwig Reichert Verlag.

Thompson, Sandra A. 1987. Subordination and narrative event structure. In Russell S. Tomlin (ed.), *Typological studies in language*, 11:435–454. Amsterdam: John Benjamins.

Walberg, Eric. 2011. *Postmodern imperialism: Geopolitics and the great game*. Atlanta: Clarity Press.

3

Linguistic Areality in Northeastern Afghanistan

Henrik Liljegren
Stockholm University

3.1 Introduction

Diversity, be it ethnic, linguistic or cultural, is characterizing Afghanistan as a country. Zeroing in on the northeastern part of the country, diversity is taken to yet another level. This region, which comprises a mere tenth of the total area of the country and has a population of less than four million (as compared to Afghanistan's totally thirty-six million), is home to two-thirds of all languages spoken on Afghan soil, representing four phylogenetic groupings: Iranian, Nuristani, Indo-Aryan and Turkic.

Much linguistic work carried out in this region has been descriptive, mainly analyzing and describing individual languages and language communities in terms of their structural and lexical properties, and to some extent addressing issues related to their respective classification within the phylogenies referred to above. Much less attention has been given to language contact or the possible presence of areal features that would characterize all or some subsets of the languages of the region. Is it, for instance, possible to discern any significant patterns of convergence or divergence, either within or across established groupings?

In the present study, an attempt is made at producing an areal-typological profile of the languages of that particular region, based on recently collected data from a tight sample of twenty-nine varieties. Traditional language classification is revisited and problematized in the light of linguistic areality and what appear to be effects of historical contact patterns, both in the region and beyond its confines. In section 3.2, the geographical region and its languages are given a brief introduction. Section 3.3 presents the data set and the methods applied in the study. Section 3.4 revisits and discusses previous classification of the languages under study. In section 3.5, that classification is tested against lexical data collected in the present study, and section 3.6, which forms the main analytical part of this study, presents a systematic comparison of the sample languages, covering five structural domains (word order, nominal categories, simple clauses, phonology, and lexical structure). Section 3.7 summarizes and discusses the findings, particularly those of section 3.6, and offers some preliminary conclusions.

3.2 The region and its linguistic landscape

Northeastern Afghanistan (henceforth abbreviated as NEA), as defined in the present study, covers the provinces of Badakhshan, Nuristan, Kunar, Nangarhar, Laghman and Kapisa. All of the language varieties presently investigated are spoken in one or more of those six provinces (figure 3.1). Geographically, the region is characterized by the high mountains of the Hindu Kush range, reaching its highest elevation at approximately 7,500 metres (Noshaq Peak) near the border between Badakhshan and Pakistan's Upper Chitral district.

These partly impenetrable mountains are cut through by numerous rivers and streams, and it is primarily in the many valleys, in some areas extremely narrow, where the region's population is concentrated. In the north, the region shares a long border with Tajikistan, and in the east with Pakistan. At the eastern end of the Wakhan Corridor, the narrow sliver of Afghan territory that separates northern Pakistan from Tajikistan, the region also shares a tiny stretch of border with China's Xinjiang province.

Figure 3.1. Map of northeastern Afghanistan with geographical locations of sample varieties.

The topography itself can be considered one of the main reasons for the region's linguistic diversity, as the myriad of inaccessible and secluded valleys for centuries have provided their inhabitants with relative isolation from other groups and influences and successively offered refuge to groups fleeing the onslaught of the more dominant societies and linguistic groups associated with the political centres. Until as late as the 1890s, the ancestors of today's Nuristanis retained their traditional pre-Muslim religion, of which a related form still survives among the Kalasha in Pakistan's Chitral valley.

While the three southern-most provinces, Nangarhar, Kunar and Laghman, as of today, are heavily influenced by Pashto and the Pashtuns as an ethnic group, this is home to a range of Indo-Aryan varieties commonly referred to as Pashai, although their respective speech forms are not mutually intelligible across the whole continuum. The westernmost extension of Pashai is Kapisa, a province to the west of Laghman, where the Pashtun presence is much less pronounced than in the former three provinces and instead Tajiks constitute the major ethnic component and Dari is the most important medium of communication. Apart from Pashai, a few other minor linguistic communities are represented. In Kapisa, the Iranian language Parachi is spoken by a community of a few thousand individuals, and in Kunar province we find a few other, mostly numerically minor, Indo-Aryan languages, some of them also spoken on the Pakistan side of the border.

To the immediate north of Laghman and Kunar, and to the south of Badakhshan, lies Nuristan, the only province in the NEA region in which neither Pashtuns nor Tajiks is a major ethnic component. The overwhelming majority of the inhabitants of this mountainous and partly forested area, are Nuristanis and speak one of the five or six distinct Nuristani languages.

Badakhshan is the northernmost and easternmost province of Afghanistan. Although Tajiks make up the ethnic majority, it is a diverse area, in many respects, linguistically, geographically and culturally. Dari, in numerous local forms, is a major language, but there are important pockets of a number of other Iranian languages: Shughni and Roshani in the Shughnan, mostly along the Tajikistan border; Ishkashimi and Sanglechi at the western end of the Wakhan Corridor; Wakhi throughout the Wakhan Corridor; and Munji in the southernmost part of the province. There are also sizeable Uzbek communities in the central parts of the province, and a numerically minor group of Kyrgyz herders residing at the higher altitudes of the Wakhan Corridor.

Linguistic survey, documentation and description of the many languages in this part of Afghanistan has a long history (Rzehak 2016), but when it comes to areal typology and contact linguistics, much detailed and systematic study still remains to be carried out. The linguistic profile of the larger mountain region that NEA is part of and its significance as a contact zone or convergence area has been touched upon by several scholars in the past (Baart 2014; Bashir 1996a, 1996b, 2003:823, 2016; Èdel'man 1980, 1983:16; Koptjevskaja-Tamm and Liljegren 2017:215–223; Tikkanen 1999, 2008; Toporov 1970), although the tendency has been to focus on individual features and phenomena, sometimes based on relatively sparse data, and seldom have there been attempts at applying a higher degree of feature aggregation with tight sampling.

3.3 Data and methods

In the spring of 2017, the author had the privilege of working with speakers of twenty-nine distinct language varieties of northeastern Afghanistan (table 3.1).[1] Under the auspices of Samar, three collaborative research workshops, two

---

[1] Many language names, particularly those referring to small ethnolinguistic communities, occur in various forms or with various spellings. I have normally chosen the form most frequently used in trusted sources, but those should in no way be interpreted as prescriptive, and I apologize in advance for any unintended negative connotations that any of those forms may have locally. A few language names deserve some further comments: Sawi (or Savi) is the form used in most sources while Sauji is the name that the modern-day speakers appear to prefer, including the consultant in this study. A few of the language names (particularly referring to Iranian languages) currently appear as an ethnonymic base and a

in Kabul and one in Faizabad, were arranged, to which community members were recruited and invited.[2] Each workshop was held for five consecutive days, involving one to three speakers of each sample language. An elicitation package had already, prior to the workshops, been translated from English into Dari and Pashto (the two most common second languages among the participants) to facilitate the data collection process. The material collected (by means of written, in most cases Arabic-based representation, provided by the speakers themselves, and by audio- and/or video recording conducted by the researcher) included wordlists, questionnaires, the translation of a parallel text and some stimulus-based elicitation. The workshop also included a number of interactive components in which the participants contributed, compared across the varieties represented or discussed words and constructions.

Table 3.1. Language varieties in the data sample

Indo-Aryan (12)		
Gawar-Bati, Naray [gwt]	Pashai, Alishang [glh (ag)]	Pashai, Korangal [aee (kg)]
Gojri, Naray [gju]	Pashai, Amla [psi (am)]	Pashai, Sanjan, Kohistan [glh (sn)]
Pashai, Alasai [psh]	Pashai, Aret [aee (at)]	Pashai, Shemal [aee (sh)]
Pashai, Alingar [psi (ar)]	Pashai, Chalas [aee (ch)]	Sawi, Naray [sdg]
Iranian (9)		
Dari, Darwazi [prs]	Parachi, Nijrab [prc]	Sanglechi, Sanglech [sgy]
Ishkashimi, Ishkashim [isk]	Pashto (northern), Tagab [pbu]	Shughni, Shughnan [sgh (a)]

---

suffixed derivation -*ani*, rather than in their more established i-ending forms, such as Wakhani rather than Wakhi, and Munjani rather than Munji; I have consistently chosen the latter. Kati, in the present study represented by a western and an eastern variety, is also referred to as Kataviri or Katë. Waigali, at least the variety that was included in the sample, is also (and preferably) referred to as Kalasha, but in order to avoid unnecessary confusion with the Indo-Aryan language referred to as Kalasha, spoken in neighbouring Pakistan, the name Waigali was kept for this Nuristani language. An alternate way of referring to the language would be to specify it as Nuristani Kalasha. Prasun was consistently referred to as Paruni by the consultant involved in the study.

[2] It was in connection with my visit to Kabul in 2017 that I met and spoke with our dear colleague Simone for the last time. Three wordlists were collected: a) a 40-item basic vocabulary list; b) a word list including 95 kinship terms; and c) a list of cardinal numerals. Two questionnaires were used: a) a sentence questionnaire representing 87 verb meanings; and b) a demonstrative questionnaire or elicitation kit through which expressions were captured (by audio and video) as the speaker was presented with objects situated at various distances. The parallel text used was the traditional fable The North Wind and the Sun. For capturing natural or semi-natural speech, the speakers were asked to retell the contents of the six-minute *Pear Film*.

3.3 Data and methods

Table 3.1. (*continued*)

Munji, Munjan [mnj]	Roshani, Roshan [sgh (r)]	Wakhi, Wakhan [wbl]
Nuristani (6)		
Ashkun, Nurgram [ask]	Kati, Bargi Matal [bsh (e)]	Prasun, Parun [prn]
Kamviri, Kamdesh [xvi]	Kati, Duab [bsh (w)]	Waigali, Waygal [wbk]
Turkic (2)		
Kyrgyz, Wakhan [kir]	Uzbek (southern), Argo [uzs]	

Note: The data are sorted by genera, with language name and further specification of speaker location, and its 3-letter ISO 639-3 code. Additional letters in parentheses are the author's own subcategory coding.

Not all of the twenty-nine varieties are considered languages in their own right. However, it was deemed beneficial in some cases to make even finer differentiations than warranted by available language lists. This was, for instance, a consideration when choosing a higher resolution for a number of lesser researched geographical continua with a long history in the region, than for larger languages or macrolanguages (such as Pashto) with well-documented and, in comparison, relatively moderate levels of internal variation across regions well beyond the scope of this study. Nuristani Kati was, for instance, represented by a western variety (Duab) as well as an eastern (Bargi Matal), and Iranian Shughni was represented by the speech of Shughni proper as well as the speech of Roshan, a variety that locally is perceived as a language in its own right, Roshani. The spectrum of Indo-Aryan varieties sometimes referred to collectively as Pashai, which on basis of earlier scholarly work has been categorized into four "languages", northeastern, northwestern, southeastern and southwestern Pashai (Morgenstierne 1967), was in this study represented by as many as nine local varieties, rather evenly spread out from west to east. The alignment of each one of these with one of Morgenstierne's four Pashais, and thereby with a particular three-letter code, is a mere approximation.

Some relevant but numerically small language communities were not represented at all, either due to difficulties in recruiting speakers or simply because they do not seem to be spoken any longer. In the first category, we count Tregami, a Nuristani language, Grangali, an Indo-Aryan language, and possibly Shumashti [sts], another Indo-Aryan language. In the second, Tirahi and Wotapuri-Katarqalai, both Indo-Aryan languages documented in the past, most likely are not spoken at all any longer.

Some of the varieties included represent local varieties of languages spoken in a much wider region, mainly beyond the borders of northeastern Afghanistan as defined here. That is true of Gojri (sometimes written as Gujari), the Indo-Aryan speech of a largely nomadic group, Gujars, found in scattered pockets as well as in a few more concentrated populations from northeastern Afghanistan, across northern Pakistan, to Jammu and Kashmir and adjacent parts of northwestern and central India (Hallberg and O'Leary 1992:91, 96–98). While Dari in itself is a major variety of Persian, the variety of Dari represented in this study is the speech of Darwaz, a local community of northernmost Badakhshan, locally referred to as Darwazi. The variety of Pashto included here is the language used by ethnic Pashtuns in Tagab district of Kapisa province.

While Wakhi is a comparatively small language, its speakers are spread across several international borders. Apart from the population residing in the Wakhan Corridor in Afghanistan, it is spoken in adjacent areas of northernmost Pakistan, in the Pamir Mountains of Tajikistan as well as by a group in China's Xinjiang Autonomous Region. The two Turkic varieties, likewise, are local varieties of two major languages spoken in large areas of Central Asia.

3.4 Language classification

Three of the linguistic genera included in this study are beyond doubt Indo-European: Indo-Aryan (or Indic as it is also referred to), Iranian and Nuristani. There is also no modern-day controversy related to their inclusion in the Indo-Iranian subfamily (Degener 2002:103). The geographical distribution of this subfamily as a whole is the result of expansion into West and South Asia from an original homeland on the Eurasian steppe north of the Black and Caspian Seas, already at that time (about 2000 B.C.) displaying a dialectal differentiation corresponding to the later division into Indo-Aryan and Iranian (Parpola 2003:79–80). There is much less consensus on the exact placement of Nuristani in relation to the other two branches. While few scholars after Morgenstierne (1961:139) question the classificatory validity of Nuristani as a distinct group, thus overruling, for example, Grierson's (1919) earlier identifications of a separate Dardic sub-branch of Indo-Aryan including both the Nuristani (or Kafiri) languages and many of the clearly Indo-Aryan languages spoken in the mountainous Northwest of the Indian subcontinent, there are basically three remaining hypotheses regarding Nuristani (figure 3.2), following Degener (2002:140): a) a "third branch" hypothesis, which holds that it is indeed a third family or branch, alongside Indo-Aryan and Iranian, b) an "Indian" hypothesis, which holds that it is part of the Indo-Aryan family but branched off already during the pre-Vedic period from mainstream Indo-Aryan, and c) an "Iranian" hypothesis, which holds that it is part of the Iranian family but branched off at an early stage from the rest of the Iranian languages.

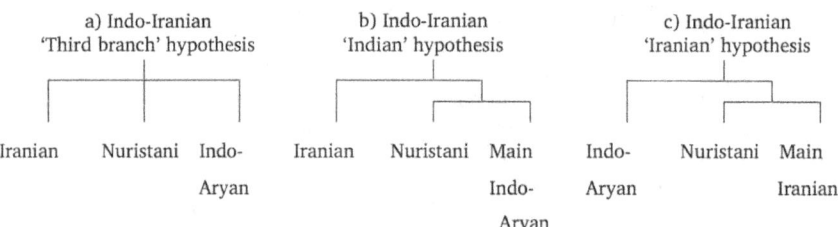

Figure 3.2. Three hypotheses regarding Nuristani Indo-Iranian classification.

Each of these three hypotheses has its proponents, and whichever is preferred, the general situation remains that Nuristani shares features with

3.4 Language classification

Indo-Aryan as well as with Iranian, although modern Nuristani is somewhat more "Indic" than "Iranian". Degener, whose inclinations are generally in favour of the "Indian" hypothesis, holds that mere linguistic data would make all of them equally plausible but that the addition of non-linguistic data, such as archeological and ethnographic evidence, suggest that the carriers of a proto-language common to Indo-Aryan and Nuristani split off from Iranian in the plains of Central Asia, moved on in the direction of the Indian subcontinent, that some of them, the ancestors of today's Nuristani speakers, remained behind, presumably somewhere in today's Afghanistan, not too far from their present localities in the high Hindu Kush, but came in renewed contact with advancing Iranians, resulting in, for example, the de-aspiration common to Nuristani and Iranian. This is also the line I will pursue in my classification below. However, in the long period following that interaction, the Nuristanis settled in (or perhaps escaped into) their present mountainous habitat and remained in relative isolation save for some low-intensity contact with neighbouring Indo-Aryan groups (Degener 2002:112–116). However, what that latter interaction actually entailed, is something that we will have reason to come back to later. The Nuristani languages have also been given an internal classification, with a main division between a Southern and a Northern group, with five distinct "languages" identified on the next level, in most cases corresponding to the 3-letter ISO 639-3 codes associated with Nuristani. Kamviri, however, is considered a sub-variety of Kati (corresponding to Strand's Kâmk'ata-viri). In our sample, Ashkun and Waigali are South Nuristani, and the two Kati (or more correctly Kataviri) varieties, Kamviri and Prasun are North Nuristani.

As for the clearly Indo-Aryan component, that is, the languages of northeastern Afghanistan that in modern-day descriptions are labelled as Indo-Aryan, we need to say something about their internal classification. The term "Dardic", already mentioned above, has often been applied to all of the Indo-Aryan varieties in our sample (apart from Gojri), as well as to the remnant (or possibly extinct) languages Shumashti, Grangali, Wotapuri-Katarqalai and Tirahi, along with some twenty other language varieties spoken across the entire mountainous region of northern Pakistan and Kashmir. In his *Linguistic Survey of India*, Grierson (1919) applied the term Dardic, initially coined and used as a linguistic label by Leitner (1877), in a classificatory sense, treating it as a "sub-family" of Indo-Aryan, but the term has also been, and is sometimes still, applied without taking some of the complexities into account, to signify an entity other than Indo-Aryan (Munshi 2006). After decades of meticulous fieldwork and detailed analysis of a large number of those languages, Morgenstierne (1961:139) concluded that "[t]here is not a single common feature distinguishing Dardic, as a whole, from the rest of the IA [Indo-Aryan] languages, and the Dardic area itself is intersected by a network of isoglosses, often of historical interest as indicating ancient lines of communication as well as barriers. Dardic is simply a convenient term to denote a bundle of aberrant IA hill-languages", a statement echoed subsequently by a number of scholars, some of them recycling "Dardic" as a mere geographic or areal expression (Bashir 2003:821–822; Strand 1973:298), others preferring to drop the term altogether to avoid further confusion (Strand 2001:251; Liljegren 2014:135; Petersen 2015:23). In any case, there is probably little reason to include a single intermediate level between Indo-Aryan and some six to eight (mostly uncontroversial) lower-level groupings of Indo-Aryan which were also suggested by Morgenstierne (1961:138–139), and have been confirmed and presented, in slightly different versions, by others.

Leaving aside the Indo-Aryan languages in adjacent areas across international borders, the varieties in this sample belong in four clearly separate groups. Gojri is, as earlier described, not primarily associated with this mountainous region; instead, most of its closest relatives are found in Indian Rajasthan (Sharma 2002:44–45). All of the varieties labelled "Pashai" are part of an established group, spoken exclusively by communities in the mountain regions immediately to the north of Kabul and Jalalabad, but "split up into a large number of in many cases mutually incomprehensible dialects" (Morgenstierne 1967a:6). While the four-way division of this group, already referred to above, is based on Morgenstierne's extensive work, and still considered authoritative, he himself readily admits that "[a] satisfactory classification of Pash. dialects would require a much fuller knowledge of them than we possess at present", and that the four-way division is a "practical" division based on a combination of phonological and morphological rather than lexical features (Morgenstierne 1967b:12–13). Lexically, there appears to be a main division between East (NE and SE) and West (NW and SW), or more specifically between varieties spoken to the west of Alingar river vis-à-vis varieties spoken to the east and south of that river (Morgenstierne 1967c:8–11; Strand 2001:251). Gawar-Bati, in our sample represented by a variety spoken in Naray in the Kunar valley, spills over into an adjacent area in Pakistan, while the only other closely related varieties are (or perhaps used to be) spoken in Pashai-dominated areas. Its relatedness to Dameli, a language spoken in close proximity to the Gawar-Bati community on the Pakistani side of the border, is uncertain (Morgenstierne 1961:138), although Bashir (2003:824) places them together in the same Kunar group, while Strand considers Gawar-Bati and its two sister languages (Grangali and Shumashti) as a group in its own right (Pech group), whereas he classifies Dameli as Western Kohistani (Strand 2001:258). Finally, among the Indo-Aryan languages, Sawi (locally often referred to as Sauji) constitutes the western extreme of a large continuum, Shina, found in various forms in smaller pockets as well as in concentrations with several hundred thousands of speakers along the Indus river in northern Pakistan, all the way to Ladakh at the eastern end (Schmidt 2004:33). In addition to Sawi, two particularly closely related varieties are spoken in northern Pakistan: Palula in Chitral and Kalkoti in Dir Kohistan (Liljegren 2013; 2016:18–20). The three varieties represent the end point of one or two small-scale migrations, taking place only a few centuries ago, originating in the vicinity of Chilas in the Indus valley (Liljegren 2009:54–59).

While there are slightly less Iranian varieties in this sample as compared to Indo-Aryan, these represent a rather wide range of languages, classification-wise. As for the major east-west divide of Iranian, only one of the varieties can be considered western, or more specifically southwestern, namely Darwazi, or the Dari of Darwaz, this in spite of its geographical location in the very northern part of this region. It is essentially a variety of Dari, Afghan Farsi, and is also considered as such by the speaker community (Beck and Beyer 2013:22–23). The rest of the languages are Eastern (Skjaervø 1989a:370). Among the latter, Pashto is the numerically dominant and also the geographically most widespread, spoken in large parts of northwestern Pakistan and in southern and eastern Afghanistan. The variety represented here, spoken locally in Tagab,

3.4 Language classification

Kapisa, is a northern, or more specifically northwestern, dialect (Skjaervø 1989b:386; MacKenzie 1959). Six of the varieties included in this study – Shughni, Roshani, Wakhi, Munji, Ishkashimi and Sanglechi – belong to a group of East Iranian usually referred to as Pamir languages (Payne 1989:417; Èdel'man and Dodykhudoeva 2009:773). Figure 3.3 diagrams the relatedness of all of the languages under consideration.

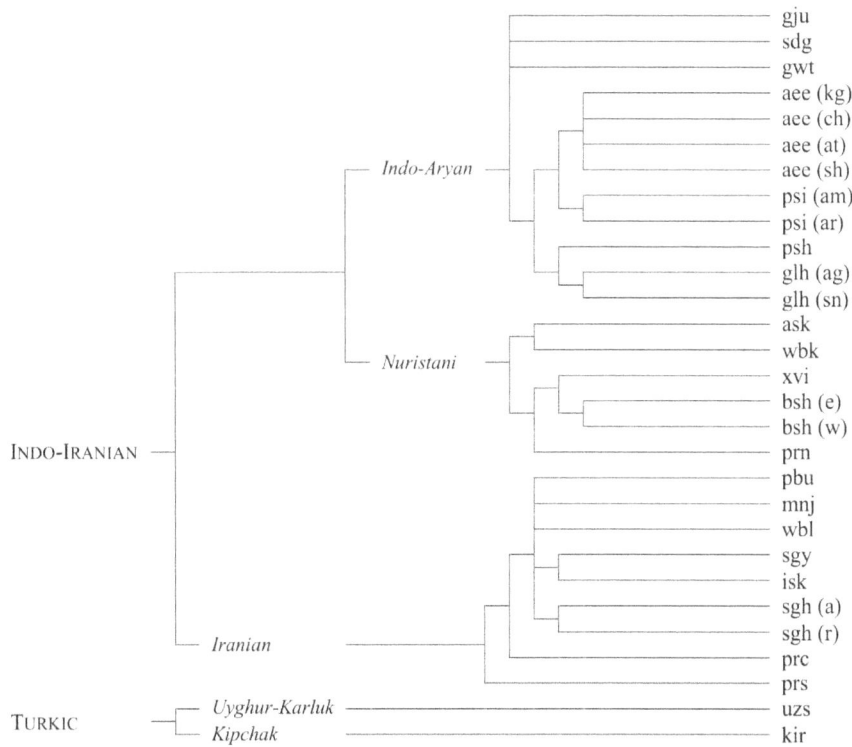

Figure 3.3. Language relatedness according to traditional classification.

However, a situation similar to that of "Dardic" (see above) is at hand, in which present-day similarities between languages spoken in a relatively confined region might be attributable to areality rather than to inheritance from an intermediate "Pamir" proto-language separate from the rest of East Iranian (Bashir 2009:857). Instead, "the Pamir languages constitute distinct genetic sub-groups that derive from several distinct proto-dialects of East Iranian origin" (Èdel'man and Dodykhudoeva 2009:776). What is clear is that some of these varieties are indeed closely related to one another: Shughni with Roshani, as are Ishkashimi with Sanglechi (Payne 1989:417–420). Munji is closely related to Yidgha, a speaker community across the border in Pakistan's Chitral district (Morgenstierne 1938:3).

It appears that Wakhi is somewhat more distantly related to the rest of the East Iranian varieties of Pamir (Èdel'man and Dodykhudoeva 2009:777), and that Munji-Yidgha, if considering Iranian outside the Pamir region, stands closest to Pashto (Morgenstierne 1938:25). The remaining Iranian variety to be discussed is Parachi. While in general terms belonging to the East Iranian languages (Skjaervø 1989:370), and more specifically to a southeastern subgroup (Kieffer 2009:693), the classification of Parachi poses problems of a particular kind, as there are features that reveal deep historical affinities with northwestern languages, such as Mazandarani and Kurdish (Morgenstierne 1926:27-28). It is only closely related to one other Iranian language, namely Ormuri, another small speaker community, found in Logar province and across the border in Pakistan's Waziristan (Skjaervø 1989:370), a linguistic island surrounded by Pashto.

As mentioned above, two Turkic varieties were included in the study: a dialect of southern (or Afghan) Uzbek, spoken in Badakhshan's Argo district, and a variety of Kyrgyz spoken by herdsmen in the far-flung highland regions of the Wakhan Corridor. Uzbek and Kyrgyz belong to two separate branches of Turkic. Uzbek is part of a southeastern branch, also referred to as Uyghur-Karluk, and is most closely related to Uyghur (Johanson 2006:287-288) with which it shares many linguistic features (Boeschoten 1998:357) while also displaying a great deal of Iranian interference (Reichl 1983:481). Kyrgyz, on the other hand, is northwestern Turkic, or Kipchak, and is closely related to Kazakh, but it also shares some features with South Siberian Turkic (Kirchner 1998:344).

In figure 3.3 an attempt is made at displaying the relatedness between our twenty-nine sample varieties, following the above-discussed classification. No lower-level branch labels have been inserted, and only differentiation with direct relevance to the sample has been included.

3.5 Lexical analysis

In an attempt to test the validity of the classification in figure 3.3, a word list was compiled, aimed at including such basic lexical terms which tend to be inherited rather than (easily) borrowed. A subset of this list is identical to the forty items used by the Automated Similarity Judgment Program (Wichmann, Brown and Holman 2018) in their attempts to classify languages computationally. To that, lower numerals (those not already in the 40-list) and the numerals "ten" and "twenty" were added, as well as thirty-five kinship terms and eleven basic verbs from the elicited material. The resulting list consisted of ninety-five items. Each term, in each variety, was subsequently assigned a numerical cognacy class, mainly based on reasonable phonological similarity across the varieties. With the help of SplitsTree 4.14.6 (Huson and Bryant 2006), a NeighborNet representation was generated (figure 3.4), in which the length of the branches corresponds to the degree of similarity or difference (that is, the relative proportion of shared cognacy classes) between the individual varieties that were included. The representation differs from the treelike classification in figure 3.3 by visualizing multiple paths between two points, taking conflicting signals into account, thus in a more meaningful way showing significant clusters.

The "tree" confirms, to a large extent, the previous phylogenetic classification. The two Turkic varieties are tightly aligned to each other but clearly branch off from the rest of the languages, although not dramatically so. Most of the Iranian varieties cluster together, although only four of them, all "Pamir" languages (Roshani, Shughni, Ishkashimi, Sanglechi), show

3.6 Structural analysis

a relatively close affinity with one another. The exception among the Iranian varieties is Pashto, which neither clusters with Iranian in general, nor with the other northeastern languages. Five of the Nuristani languages form another perceivable cluster, while Prasun, contrary to expectation, is not part of it. As for Indo-Aryan, two separate groups can be identified. Gojri, Sawi and Gawar-Bati occur together, but not tightly so (which is indeed expected, considering that they have been assigned to different sub-groups), and all of the nine Pashai varieties form a tight and very convincing cluster of their own, even internally clustering according to the suggested east-west divide. It is also possible to interpret the representation as confirming a closer affinity between Nuristani and (at least some) Indo-Aryan as compared to the one between Nuristani and Iranian.

Figure 3.4. Lexical similarities in NEA languages.[3]

3.6 Structural analysis

Turning to language structure, a few features intended to represent different linguistic sub-systems have been investigated across the varieties. For each such feature, each individual variety has been classified as displaying a distinctive value. Apart from presenting a quantitative distribution of values across the sample as a whole, notes have been made about their geographical distribution as well as typical associations between a certain feature value and a particular phylogenetic grouping. The subsystems represented are word order, nominal categories, simple clauses, phonology and lexical structure.

---

[3] NeighborNet representation based on cognacy coding of 95 basic vocabulary items, visualized by means of SplitsTree 4.14.6.

3.6.1 Word order

A fundamental typological feature is the order of object and verb in transitive clauses. Globally, languages tend to have a dominant order that is either the object preceding the verb (OV) or the object following the verb (VO), with each value being almost equally frequent in the world's languages (Dryer 2013). Languages in which there is no dominant order are considerably less common. In the NEA region, however, languages are exclusively OV. Considering that this is also the case in the larger Asian macro-area surrounding this region, it is hardly a surprising result (Masica 2001:240–243). Instead it confirms that the region in this respect lines up fully with the larger area that it is part of.

The following examples, (1) to (4), from Kyrgyz (Turkic), Ishkashimi (Iranian), Western Kati (Nuristani) and Alishang Pashai (Indo-Aryan) illustrate this hegemony as far as the basic word order SOV in the region is concerned. The verb-final order is also typical of Turkic, Iranian, Nuristani and Indo-Aryan in general (Kashmiri being a notable exception among the Indo-Aryan languages).

(1) Kyrgyz (Turkic) (KIR-ValQuestYB:001)
    bala mewa-ni dʑe-de
    boy fruit-ACC eat-PST

(2) Ishkashimi (Iranian) (ISK-ValQuestSO:001)
    zɑːwman av= meːwa χuːl
    boy   ACC fruit   eat.PST

(3) Western Kati (Nuristani) (BSHw-ValQuestAU:001)
    pəzə mijoː jaɽ-a
    boy fruit eat.PST-M.SG

(4) Alishang Pashai (Indo-Aryan) (GLHag-ValQuestSF:001)
    baːɽoː meːwa ẓiniː-(j)a
    boy   fruit eat.PST-M.SG
    'The boy ate the fruit.'

Another word order feature, the order of adposition and noun phrase, is known to correlate to a large extent with the order of object and verb (Dryer 1992:81), meaning that OV languages tend to make use of postpositions, while VO languages instead use prepositions. Contrary to expectation, however, there is no exclusive use of postpositions in NEA (table 3.2). While the use of only postpositions dominates, see example (5), two varieties use prepositions, see example (6), and in as many as six of them both postpositions and prepositions occur, see example (7).[4]

---

[4] The material did not allow for a definite conclusion regarding the use of adpositions in Nuristani Waigali.

3.6 Structural analysis

Table 3.2. Order of adposition and noun phrase in NEA

Feature value	# of varieties displaying it	%
Postpositions	20	69
Prepositions	2	7
Postpositions and prepositions	6	21

All of the varieties with prepositions (whether exclusively so, as in Munji and Wakhi, or along with postpositions, as in Darwazi, Pashto, Sanglechi, Ishkashimi, Shughni and Roshani) are Iranian. That both prepositions and postpositions are used, does not necessarily entail that both are used simultaneously in one and the same adpositional phrase, although that is indeed the case in some Pashto adpositional phrases (example (7)).

(5) Gawar-Bati (Indo-Aryan)
 maːnuç-eː taːnu ḍijaː =*pinaː* rupaj gut-as
 man-ERG REFL friend.OBL from money take.PST-3SG
 'The man took the money from his friend.' (GWTa-ValQuestAG:031)

(6) Munji (Iranian)
 meːr-en *ʒe=* duːstənəʃ ve= pajse ʁərəvd
 man-ERG from friend ACC money take.PST
 'The man took the money from his friend.' (MNJ-ValQuestAJ:031)

(7) Pashto (Iranian)
 saɽiː la= χpəliː məlgiriː =*tsaχa* pisiː waːχst-əl-iː
 man.ERG of REFL friend from money take.PST-IPFV-F.PL
 'The man took the money from his friend.' (PBUa-ValQuestKO:031)

The co-occurrence of OV word order and prepositions is found in Iranian in a larger area also outside NEA, pointed out by Stilo (2005) as characteristic of a transition zone between two macro-areas, in this case the largely Iranian-dominated area of West Asia which is "sandwiched" between typically VO languages (Arabic and other languages in the Mediterranean region) and typically OV languages (in much of the rest of Asia to the North and to the East, whether Turkic or Indo-Aryan).

3.6.2 Nominal categories

Cross-linguistic variation with respect to the number of morphological cases uniquely expressed is displayed in table 3.3. This is not taking a full inflectional paradigm into account, but is instead limited to case differentiation for the grammatical relations of A (transitive subjects), S (intransitive subjects), P (direct objects) and R (recipients) for full nouns.[5] No attempt has been made

---

[5] A = agent-like argument of canonical transitive verb; S = single argument of canonical intransitive verb; P = patient-like argument of canonical transitive verb; R = recipient.

to differentiate between case inflection in a strict sense and adpositional (or clitical) case marking.

Table 3.3. Number of cases (based on: A, S, P, R) used by varieties in NEA

Feature value	# of varieties displaying it	%
2 case forms	6	21
3 case forms	**19**	**66**
4 case forms	4	14

Nominal case differentiation as a feature is present in all of the NEA varieties, although realized in a variety of ways. A few examples of language-specific case distributions are shown in table 3.4. In the majority of varieties, that is, in nineteen of the varieties studied, three distinct forms are used. In all but five of the varieties, S is non-uniquely coded, while as many as twenty-five of the varieties express the R relation with a form separate from the other three relations.

Table 3.4. Case distribution exemplified with the noun "boy" in Roshani, Chalas Pashai, Ashkun, Sanglechi and Munji

Language	# of forms	A	S	P	R
Roshani	2	ʁaða	ʁaða	ʁaða	ʁaða-re
Chalas Pashai	2	kaːkuː-(w)ə	kaːkuː	kaːkuː	kaːkuː-(w)ə
Ashkun	3	məraːk-ə	məraːk	məraːk	məraːk =ɕej
Sanglechi	3	zəmənuːk	zəmənuːk	wə= zəmənuːk	zəmənuːk =bə
Munji	4	zunjiʁaː-(c)en	zunjiʁaː	ve= zunjiʁaː	ne= zunjiʁaː-(c)en

For the languages with three case forms, two main patterns are in place, one accusative (coding A and S in the same way but P differently, as in Sanglechi) and one ergative (coding S and P in the same way but A differently, as in Ashkun), a matter we will return to in further detail below. As for the geographical distribution of the respective feature values there is nothing really significant, and the category with three forms includes varieties from all four genera.

Taking agreement as the defining characteristic of grammatical gender, a majority of our sample varieties display evidence of two or more genders lexically associated with nouns, while only eight of them lack this property altogether (table 3.5).

3.6 Structural analysis

Table 3.5. Number of genders in NEA

Feature value	# of varieties displaying it	%
No gender	8	28
2 genders	15	6
4 genders	6	21

The typical NEA language differentiates between two sex-based genders, masculine and feminine.

These languages are exclusively Indo-Iranian, while both of the Turkic languages in the sample, like Turkic in general, lack gender differentiation. In Sawi, an Indo-Aryan language, verbs agree in gender (and number), as can be seen in example (8). The noun 'thief' in (8a) triggers masculine verb agreement in the form of a suffix *-u*, and 'girl' in (8b) feminine agreement, with a suffix *-i*. This masculine—feminine differentiation also extends into the inanimate realm: 'rain', in (8c), is assigned masculine, and 'sun', in (8d), feminine gender. A similar system is found in many Indo-Aryan languages, also outside of NEA, with agreement morphemes reminiscent of those in Sawi (Masica 1991:220–223).

(8) Sawi (Indo-Aryan)

   (a) jak ***muṣaːṭu*** waːl-***u*** ṭaːŋguwaːnã: dʒul-i ṭi
       IDEF thief(M) come.PFV-M.SG of.pear tree-OBL up
       ukɑːt-***u***
       get.up.PFV-M.SG
       'A thief came and climbed up a pear tree.' (SDG-PearStoryFR:002)

   (b) ***puje*** riŋg-il-***i***
       girl(F) cry-PFV-F.SG
       'The girl cried.' (SDG-ValQuestFR:083)

   (c) ***baṣ*** uṭiṭ-***u***
       rain(M) fall.PFV-M.SG
       'It rained.' (SDG-ValQuestFR:069)

   (d) ***suri*** ukeːt-***iː***
       sun(F) get.up.PFV-F.SG
       'The sun rose.' (SDG-NorthwindFR:004a)

However, although grammatical gender is an inherited feature in those Indo-Iranian languages that have it, far from all modern Indo-Iranian languages have retained this feature. As many as five of the Iranian varieties in our sample (Darwazi, Ishkashimi, Parachi, Sanglechi, and Wakhi) and one of the Nuristani languages (Prasun) appear to lack gender differentiation of any kind. The loss of gender reflects a development common to a large number of Iranian languages also outside of this region (Windfuhr 2009:22). On the other hand, six of the Indo-Aryan languages, all of them eastern varieties of Pashai (Amla, Alingar, Aret, Chalas, Shemal, Korangal), display additional gender-like features. Apart from the masculine vs feminine agreement, mostly with several targets within the noun phrase as well as verbal agreement, there is also an animate vs inanimate differentiation, although exclusively tied to a copula verb or a copula-derived auxiliary. It would probably make most sense to consider these as two overlapping gender systems (two sex-based genders, each with two animacy-based subgenders, animate and inanimate,) as suggested by Lehr for the southeastern variety that she describes (2014:176–177)) rather than as four distinct categories. As shown in example (9) from the Alingar variety of Pashai, there are three singular forms of the copula verb in the present tense, a masculine animate as in (9a), agreeing with 'man', a feminine animate as in (9b), agreeing with 'sister', and an inanimate form as in (9c), agreeing with 'ground'. As for other targets, such as adjectives and possessive pronouns, agreement is in masculine (with 'man' and 'ground') or in feminine only (with 'sister').

(9) Pashai Alingar (Indo-Aryan)

(a) ala ***bənda:*** bɑ:zɑ:ri: ***a:s***
 this man(M.AN) hunter be.PRS.M.AN.SG
 'This man is a hunter.' (PSIar-ValQuestHA:070)

(b) me:n-*i:* ***saja:m*** tɕənd-*i:* ***e:s***
 my-F.SG sister(F.AN) small-F.SG be.PRS.F.AN.SG
 'My sister is small.' (PSIar-ElicGenHA:002)

(c) ***zəmi:n*** su:su:w-*a:* ***si:***
 ground dry-M.SG be.PRS.INAN.SG
 'The ground is dry.' (PSIar-ValQuestHA:068)

To what extent sex-based gender differentiation is upheld also with inanimates in all of these varieties is an issue needing more detailed research, especially in the case of Chalas and Shemal Pashai. A possibility is that these varieties in fact make a three-way, but target-wise very limited, differentiation between masculine animates, feminine animates and inanimates, much along the lines of Dameli (Perder 2013:50–55), an Indo-Aryan language spoken not too far away, across the border in Pakistan's Chitral district, in which sex-based gender is still present but appears to be declining in favour of a more semantic-based system, perhaps eventually resulting in the complete loss of sex-based gender, as in Khowar and Kalasha, two other Indo-Aryan languages spoken in the same district (Liljegren 2017:131).

3.6.3 Simple clauses

Returning to the issue of noun case but now from an alignment perspective, the figures in table 3.6 indicate a great deal of diversity with no feature-value being typical of the region as a whole. What is interesting to note, however, is the high frequency of ergativity, as compared to what is found globally; while less than a fifth of the languages in Comrie's (2013) sample are classified as

3.6 Structural analysis

ergative (or more correctly split-ergative), close to half of our NEA sample belong in that category.

Table 3.6. Case alignment (nouns)

Feature value	# of varieties displaying it	%
Ergative {A}{S P}	13	45
Accusative {A S}{P}	10	34
Tripartite {A}{S}{P}	3	10
Neutral {A S P}	3	10

The application of a non-nominative case-marking of transitive subjects in the perfective (or past tenses) and a direct object coded as nominative (or direct), as exemplified by Eastern Kati in (10), is a feature inherited from earlier stages of Indo-Aryan, Iranian and Nuristani.[6] It can therefore be assumed that the Indo-Iranian varieties in this sample with nominative-accusative or neutral alignment patterns have lost the ergativity once characterizing their respective ancestral languages, while the accusativity of the two Turkic varieties is an inherited feature value.

(10) Eastern Kati (Nuristani)

(a) pərmaɽ-i: dʐuk kəni:
 small-F girl laugh.PST.3F.SG
 'The little girl laughed.' (BSHe-ValQuestZA:057)

(b) dʐuk-ə i:kə pi:ç a:wi:
 girl-OBL 1SG.DAT flower bring.PST.3F.SG
 'The girl brought flowers to me.' (BSHe-ValQuestZA:075)

(c) məɽə dʐuk a:wə-ta pəjiçi:
 boy girl water-goal push.PST.3F.SG
 'The boy pushed the girl into the water.' (BSHw-ValQuestZA:074)

The development of non-nominative case-marking of direct objects, as in example (11) from Parachi, found in as many as eleven of the Indo-Iranian varieties studied, is a separate development, and it differs from the marking of transitive subjects in the variability of its application.

---

[6] The origin of ergative constructions in these languages and in the wider region have been dealt with in many previous works. For a comprehensive summary, see Bashir (2016:451–454).

(11) Parachi (Iranian)

    (a) kaʃte mariːz hoːst
           girl patient be.PST
           'The girl was ill.' (PRC-ValQuestSH:082)

    (b) kaʃte kitɑːb-ike safha pɑːra koṛ
           girl book-OBL page tearing do.PST
           'The girl tore the page from the book.' (PRC-ValQuestSH:032)

    (c) bɑːluː **ma**= kaʃte min aw-kun dehelak koṛ
           boy ACC girl in water-to push do.PST
           'The boy pushed the girl into the water.' (PRC-ValQuestSH:074)

While the "A flagging" is governed, at least largely, by tense or aspect, "P flagging" appears to be governed by a cluster of features having to do primarily with referentiality (Subbarao 2016:459). The latter is often referred to as differential object marking, something that is characterizing a macro-area of a similar scope as we noted for OV word order (Masica 2001:243–246). The geographical distribution of the values is significant. All of the ergative varieties are situated in the southeastern part of NEA (in Nuristan, Kunar, Nangarhar and Laghman), while the accusative varieties are in the north and southwest. Tripartite case alignment in three of the varieties (Gojri, Gawar-Bati and Munji) can be seen as the combined result of retained ergativity and the development of differential object marking.

Canonically, ergativity is associated with "A flagging" as well as with verbal agreement with direct objects (here referred to as P agreement), while accusativity is associated with "P flagging" and verbal agreement with the subject, whether transitive (that is, A agreement) or intransitive. A cursory look at table 3.7 might seem to confirm that equation. However, by comparing the two features for each individual variety, a few interesting discrepancies appear. In fact, four of the varieties with an ergative case marking system display accusative verbal agreement (Waigali, Korangal Pashai, Shemal Pashai, Aret Pashai). Also, two of the languages with tripartite case alignment are accusatively aligned when it comes to verbal agreement (Gawar-Bati and Munji). All of those languages are pretty much clustered along the border with Pakistan.

3.6 Structural analysis

Table 3.7. Agreement patterns (verbs in pfv/pst)

Feature value	# of varieties displaying it	%
A agreement	12	41
P agreement	8	28
A & P agreement	5	17
No agreement	4	14

As many as five of the varieties, all of them belonging to the Pashai cluster, agree partly with A, and partly with P. As can be seen in example (12) from Amla Pashai, the verb agrees in gender, number and person with the direct object, 'help' in (a) and 'talking' in (b), and in person and number with the transitive subject, 'I' in (a) and 'girl' in (b). The P agreement is mainly by means of stem modification, and the A agreement is by means of a following suffix.

(12) Pashai, Amla (Indo-Aryan)

(a) mam ba:l-ku:la məntan ku:mak kijak-əm
1SG.OBL boy-PL with help(M) did.3M.SG.P-1SG.A
'I helped the boys.' (PSIam-ValQuestNG:015)

(b) kiṭa:lik-a kila: məntan ta:nik ɕuʈaŋ ba:ra:j aʁad
girl-OBL boy with REFL dog about talking(F)
ke:tɕ-in
did.3F.SG.P-3SG.A
'The girl talked to the boy about her dog.' (PSIam-ValQuestNG:018)

3.6.4 Phonology

A feature of particular areal interest is the presence of retroflex sounds. As shown in table 3.8,[7] all but four of the varieties in NEA have either retroflex plosives, or retroflex fricatives/affricates,[8] or both included in their inventories. While languages with retroflex plosives as well as retroflex fricatives/affricates are cross-linguistically rare (only about 2 percent of the languages in UPSID[9]), about a third of our sample varieties have them.

---

[7] The material did not allow for a definite conclusion regarding the use of retroflex consonants in Nuristani Waigali.
[8] Because retroflex fricatives and affricates in some of the languages are part of the same subset (in some cases variants or allophonically related realizations of the same phonemes), there has been no attempt made to differentiate between them in this study.
[9] UPSID, the UCLA Phonological Segment Inventory Database, includes segmental data from 451 languages around the world and is provided online: http://web.phonetik.uni-frankfurt.de/upsid.html.

Table 3.8. Retroflex consonants in NEA

Feature value	# of varieties displaying it	%
No retroflex plosives or fricatives/affricates	4	14
Retroflex plosives only	10	34
Retroflex plosives and fricatives/affricates	10	34
Retroflex fricatives/affricates only	4	14

The only varieties that lack retroflex consonants are the two Turkic varieties and two of the Iranian languages (Darwazi and Ishkashimi) spoken in the northern part of the region.

A related issue is the prevalence of affricates in the languages. As can be seen in table 3.9, all of the languages have affricates in their segmental inventory. The ones occurring are associated with three places of articulation: palatal (or alveolo-palatal), dental and retroflex. Those that only have one place of articulation are palatal (7 of the languages), those with two are palatal and dental (14 of the languages), and those with three are palatal, dental and retroflex (7 of the languages). Again, from the perspective of global distribution, this is unusual, as only 18 percent of the UPSID languages have palatal and dental affricates, and as few as 2 percent have affricates in all three places of articulation.

Table 3.9. Affricates in NEA

Feature value	# of varieties displaying it	%
No affricates	0	0
Palatal (or alveolo-palatal) affricates only	7	24
Palatal and dental plosives only	14	48
Palatal, dental and retroflex affricates	7	24

Segment inventories that include many retroflex sounds as well as a tripartite affricate differentiation characterize the wider mountain region to the east of NEA and is typical of many of the Indo-Aryan languages of the "Dardic" type (while not characterizing Indo-Aryan in general) but also include some Iranian "Pamir" languages and the language isolate Burushaski spoken in northern-most Pakistan, and to a lesser extent adjacent varieties of Tibetan (Toporov 1970; Hock 2015; Liljegren 2017:116–119). In NEA itself, the centre of gravity for this type of inventory seems to be in eastern Nuristan and adjacent areas, mainly including Nuristani and Indo-Aryan. A partial inventory of Indo-Aryan Gawar-Bati is taken as an example in table 3.10.[10] Among the plosives, a dental pronunciation contrasts with a retroflex one (or more correctly an apical post-alveolar pronunciation) with an added contrast in voicing, and with

---

[10] The analysis in this case is mainly based on data collected separately from consultants in Arandu, in the Gawar-Bati-speaking area in Pakistan.

3.6 Structural analysis

affricates a tripartite differentiation is upheld, while voicing is only marginally contrastive. The set of affricates is, at least partly, distinct from a set of fricatives that also makes a three-way differentiation. There are indications that the voiced fricatives and affricates stand in an allophonic relationship to one another. An added, inherited, contrast in aspiration may still be upheld with the voiceless plosives and affricates but appears to have been neutralized in many positions.

Table 3.10. The inventory of dental, retroflex and palatal plosives, affricates and fricatives in Gawar-Bati (Indo-Aryan)

Manner	Dental	Retroflex (apical)	Palatal (laminal)
Plosive	t d	ʈ ɖ	
Affricate	ts	ʈʂ (ɖʐ)	tɕ dʑ
Fricative	s z	ʂ ʐ	ɕ

3.6.5 Lexical structure

The slight dominance of numeral systems in NEA with a vigesimal base (table 3.11) is of particular interest, as it contrasts with the global preference for systems with a decimal base (Comrie 2013). In sixteen of the NEA sample varieties, twenty occurs as a base, along with a decimal base. Those are almost exclusively Nuristani and Indo-Aryan. Wakhi is the only Iranian language exemplifying it in NEA.

Table 3.11. Numeral bases in NEA

Feature value	# of varieties displaying it	%
Decimal base (only)	12	41
Vigesimal base	16	55
Digital	1	3

Just as we noted in connection with the phonological features discussed above, this kind of numeral system, exemplified by Nuristani Ashkun in table 3.12, is typical of a larger region, beyond NEA and dominates much of the mountainous region encompassing northeastern Afghanistan, northern Pakistan and Kashmir regardless of phylogenetic classification (Bashir 2003:823; Tikkanen 2008:257; Liljegren 2017:143–145).

Table 3.12. Numerals in Ashkun (Nuristani)

Number	Vernacular	Structure
10	dos	
20	wiçi	
30	wiça: dos	= 20 and 10
40	du:çi	= two 20
50	du:ça: dos	= two 20 and 10
60	treçi	= three 20
70	treça: dos	= three 20 and 10
80	tsəta:çi	= four 20
90	tsəta:ça: dos	= four 20 and 10
100	puntçi	= five 20

Another structural aspect of numeral systems is the internal composition of higher numerals, whether these are formed with the order base + n or n+base, or happen to apply a different order for the numerals 11 to 19 as compared to the numerals 21 to 29. In fact, The NEA varieties are very diverse in this respect (table 3.13), and we notice an interesting sub-areal distribution of the types observed. All of the varieties with a consistent order base+n are found in the northernmost part of the region, while the varieties with a consistent order n+base are found in the south, regardless of them using a decimal system or a vigesimal. In the rest of the varieties (which is indeed the large majority) a hybrid system is in place, and these are all geographically in between the two consistent poles.

Table 3.13. The numerals 6, 16, 26 and 36 in seven languages

Language	Structure	6	16	26	36
Shughni	10+n, 20+n, D	χo:ɣ	ji ði:sat χo:ɣ	ðə ði:sat χo:ɣ	haraj ði:sat χo:ɣ
Wakhi	10+n, 20+n, V	ça:d	ðas ça:d	i: bistet ça:d	i: bistet ðas ça:d
Sanjan Pashai	n+10, 20+n, D	ṣɛ	ṣuj	wəstə ṣɛ	triju ṣɛ
Chalas Pashai	n+10, 20+n, V	tçʰə	ṣu:ʈ	wistə bi tçʰə	wistə bi ṣu:ʈ
Gojri	n+10, n+20, D	tçʰi:	su:ʈa	tʃʰe:tabi:	tʃʰe:ta tri:
Prasun	n+10, n+20, V	wo:ṣ:ə	wəṣlu:z	wuṣ:e:ẓ	wuṣluze:ẓ
Munji	n+n, Digital	a:χʃɛ	juwo a:χʃɛ	ləwo a:χʃɛ	çirɛj o a:χʃɛ

3.6 Structural analysis

A special case as far as numeral bases and composition are concerned is Iranian Munji. In principle, a decimal organization is applied, but without actually having a dedicated morpheme signifying 'ten' or '-teen'. Instead, the lower numerals ('one' to 'nine'), along with a 'zero', are used as digits for referring to any numbers above nine, and these occur in exactly the same order as in writing: *çirɛj o aːχʃɛ* 'thirty six' (lit. 'three and six'), *juː o lə sifɛriː* '100' (lit. 'one and two zeros'), *juː o çirɛj sifɛriː* '1000' (lit. 'one and three zeros'). While restricted numeral systems, or the total lack of numerals, have been noted for individual languages, a "digital strategy" such as the one applied in Munji, has not, to my knowledge, been documented for spoken languages, whereas it does occur in individual sign languages (Zeshan et al. 2013:364). It appears that Munji earlier (or perhaps still by some speakers) made use of the Persian numerals above 'nine', according to a decimal system (Morgenstierne 1938:125–126), while the inherited numerals 'ten' and 'twenty' are still in use in closely related Yidgha (the author's own data), spoken in Pakistan, but in that case applied according to a vigesimal system, and in its compositional structure identical to the numeral system of Khowar, the neighbouring, and locally influential, Indo-Aryan language.

Kinship terminology is a vast area of investigation, and for the NEA region it is one which appears particularly promising. In this study, only a sub-domain has been studied, namely the terms used in the community when referring to one's parents and their respective siblings, and the polysemy patterns that can be observed. In this respect, the varieties, again, display great diversity among themselves. As many as nine different configurations of kinship terms occur (table 3.14), a few of which are only exemplified by a single variety.[11]

Table 3.14. Kinship terms for one's parents and their siblings in NEA

Feature value	# of varieties displaying it	%
F ≠ FB ≠ MB & M ≠ MZ ≠ FZ (i)	12	41
F ≠ FB = MB & M ≠ MZ = FZ (ii)	1	3
F = FB ≠ MB & M = MZ ≠ FZ (iii)	2	7
F ≠ FB- ≠ MB & M ≠ MZ = FZ (iv)	6	21
F = FB ≠ MB & M ≠ MZ ≠ FZ (v)	1	3
F = FB ≠ MB & M ≠ MZ = FZ (vi)	1	3
F = FB ≠ MB & M = MZ = FZ (vii)	3	10
F ≠ FB ≠ MB & M = MZ ≠ FZ (viii)	1	3
F ≠ FB ≠ MB & M = MZ = FZ (ix)	1	3

However, it would make more sense to consider three of the configurations as main types, occurring in a prototypical way in some of the languages, but as mixed systems in others. The first main type, the configuration labelled as (i) in

---
[11] The material did not allow for a definite conclusion regarding the kinship configuration in Indo-Aryan Shemal Pashai.

table 3.14, makes a full lexical differentiation between the six relations. Three completely different terms are used for one's father (F), one's father's brother (FB) and one's mother's brother (MB); and likewise, three different terms are used for one's mother (M), one's mother's sister (MZ) and one's father's sister (FZ). The terms used in Uzbek (figure 3.5) is an example. This is the system used in as many as twelve of the NEA varieties, but it is also applied to the male relatives but not to the female relatives in the configurations labelled (iv), (viii) and (ix); it is applied to the female relatives but not to the male relatives in configuration (v).

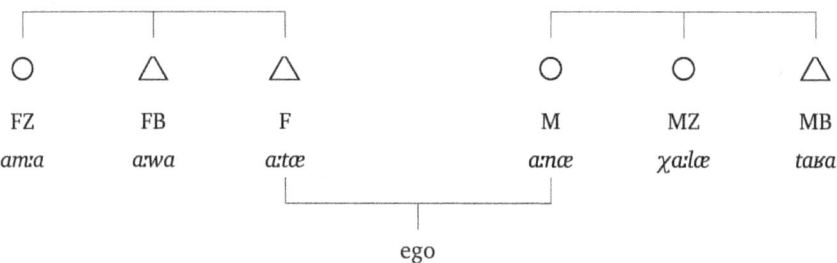

Figure 3.5. Parents and their siblings: full differentiation, Uzbek (Turkic).

The second main type is, in its prototypical form, the one labelled (ii) and exemplified by Munji in figure 3.6. The term for one's father's brother is the same as the one applied for one's mother's brother, while that is lexically distinct from 'father'. In the same way, one's mother's sister and one's father's sister are referred to with the same term. I will refer to this as an "uncles-aunts-terminology". It is restricted to "aunts" in the configurations labelled (iv) and (vi).

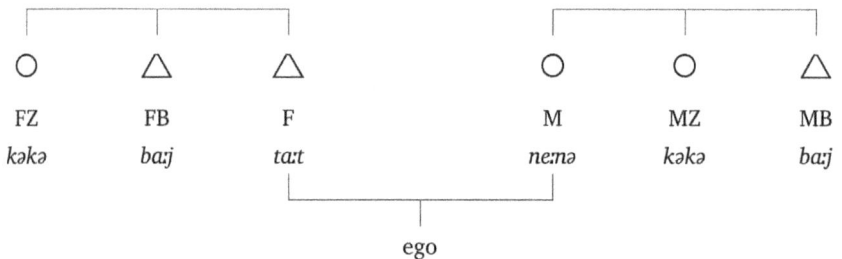

Figure 3.6. Parents and their siblings: "uncles-aunts-terminology", Munji (Iranian).

A third main type is prototypically the one labelled (iii). In this case, one's father's brother is also a "father", and one's mother's sister a "mother".

As exemplified by Waigali in figure 3.7, the usual way of applying this is by using a clarifying modifier "big" or "little" to signify siblings older or younger than one's own father or mother. A paternal uncle who is older than one's father is therefore a "big father", and one younger than one's father is a "little father". I will refer to this as a "fathers-mothers-terminology".

3.6 Structural analysis

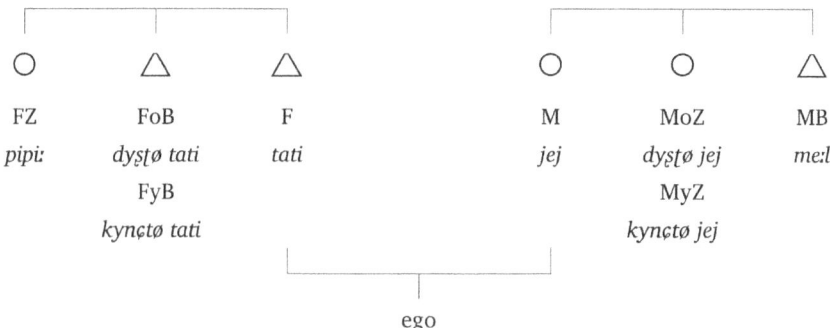

Figure 3.7. Parents and their siblings: "mothers-fathers-terminology", Waigali (Nuristani).

There may be other, alternative terms used exclusively for paternal uncles in those languages, lexically distinct from "father". Even in this case, there are configurations only partly reflecting this system; those labelled (v) and (vi) only apply it to male relatives. A special case, which alternatively may be regarded an important system in its own right, that is present in four of the NEA varieties, is represented by those that apply a "mother"term to one's mother's sister and one's father's sister alike, as in configurations (vii) and (ix), exemplified by Korangali Pashai in figure 3.8.

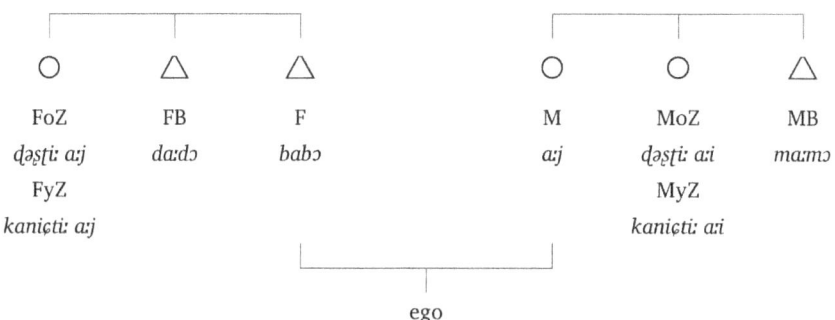

Figure 3.8. Parents and their siblings: "mothers-terminology", Korangali Pashai (Indo-Aryan).

Vestiges of such terminology is perhaps reflected even in the kinship terms themselves in languages that, at least from a purely synchronic perspective, have been classified as belonging to other types. Sanjan Pashai, for instance, makes a full lexical differentiation between the six relations, but the form similarity between the FB and MZ terms suggests an earlier special treatment, perhaps as "parents", vis-à-vis FZ and MB: *ba:ba:* 'father', *a:i:* 'mother', *mambu:* 'father's brother', *a:mə* 'father's sister', *mawlu:* 'mother's brother', *ma:mbi:* 'mother's sister'. Alasai Pashai, although here classified as a language with an "aunt-terminology," shows form similarities between the terms for FB, FZ and MZ, again suggesting an earlier special treatment along the lines of the "fathers-mothers-terminology:" *ba:w* 'father', *a:jə* 'mother', *mambu:* 'father's brother', *ma:mbi:* 'father's sister', *ma:ma:* 'mother's brother', *ma:mbi:* 'mother's sister'.

There is no single clear evidence of a kinship system in which the polysemy of the "father" term extends to one's mother's brother. However, the forms of the kinship terms in Prasun can be seen as vestiges of such a system: *jej* 'father', *nan* 'mother', *gəndərjej* 'father's older brother', *banjej* 'father's younger brother', *banan* 'father's sister', *me:ljej* 'mother's brother', *nan* 'mother's older sister', *banan* 'mother's younger sister'.

The geographical distribution of the three main systems is somewhat difficult to interpret without also taking surrounding regions into account. As for the first system, it is mainly found in the north, in many of the Iranian languages as well as in the other geographical peripheries. It is also dominant in much of northern India. While the "uncles-aunts-terminology" is present in its prototypical form only in Munji in NEA, it is indeed the system of a few varieties (Indo-Aryan and Iranian alike) spoken in adjacent areas of northern Pakistan, bordering on the Wakhan Corridor. The "fathers-mothers-terminology" is in NEA only represented in its "pure" form in parts of Nuristan, but there are several other languages in a central axis stretching through the Hindukush-Karakoram from east to west that have it, including a number of Indo-Aryan languages as well as adjacent Tibetan varieties and the language isolate Burushaski, suggesting that it may have an old historical connection particularly tied to the larger mountain region but probably exclusive of the Pamirs (Liljegren 2017:146–147; Parkin 1987:165).

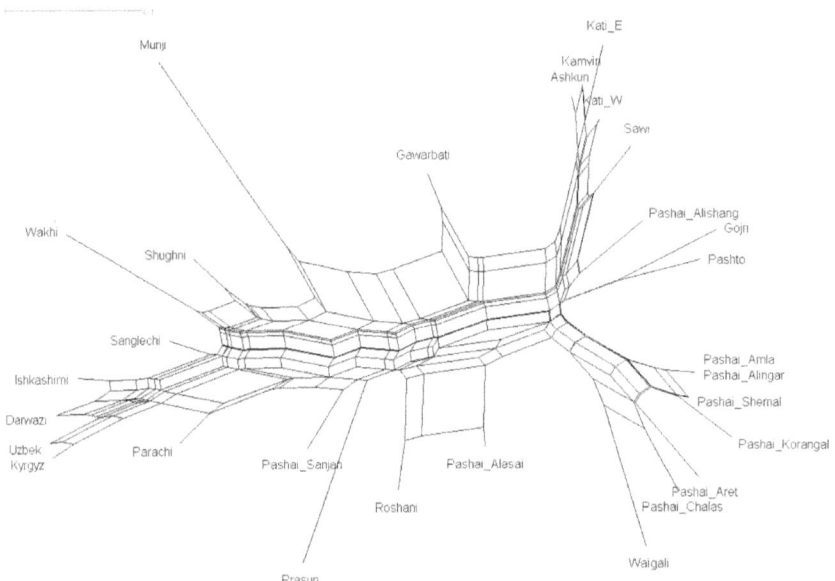

Figure 3.9. Structural similarities in NEA languages.[12]

---

[12] NeighborNet representation based on 28 binary features, visualized by means of SplitsTree 4.14.6.

In an attempt to measure structural similarity or diversity in NEA, the properties discussed above were broken down into binary features, resulting in a set of twenty-eight features (4 relating to word order, 7 relating to nominal categories, 4 relating to simple clauses, 5 relating to phonology and 8 relating to lexical structure). For instance, in regard to the kinship terms used for one's parents and their siblings, four separate binary features were established: a) whether or not polysemy exists between F and FB, resulting in a numeric value 0 or 1; b) whether or not polysemy exists between FB and MB, resulting in a numeric value 0 or 1; c) whether or not polysemy exists between M and MZ, resulting in a numeric value 0 or 1; and d) whether or not polysemy exists between MZ and FZ, resulting in a numeric value 0 or 1. Like in the lexical analysis, a NeighborNet representation was generated (figure 3.9).

Two important questions to ask when interpreting this representation are: a) how does this representation compare with the one generated from basic lexical data? (figure 3.4) and b) what significant clusters can be observed, if any? In comparison with the lexical analysis, a more sprawling image is noticeable, and the clusters that are there are generally smaller, that is, comprise fewer varieties each. Another general observation is that, although some of the languages that are considered closely related group together structurally too, there are several deviations from that pattern. For example, while all nine Pashai varieties, without exception, clustered very distinctly and very tightly in the lexical analysis, only six of them come out as structurally similar to one another, all of them at home in the eastern half of the Pashai continuum. Sanjan Pashai, Alasai Pashai and Alishang Pashai are structurally more similar to non-Pashai varieties than to their closest genetic "relatives". While four of the Nuristani varieties form a dense cluster, two of them are definitely not part of it or even close to it. Waigali is more closely aligned to the eastern Pashai cluster, and Prasun does not cluster tightly with any other variety, which was the case in the lexical representation too. Conversely, varieties that were relatively clearly distinguished from the rest in the lexical analysis, show a closer affinity to other, non-related or not particularly closely related, varieties as far as structure is concerned. The two Turkic varieties, Uzbek and Kyrgyz, group together with each other, just as in the lexical representation, but the two interestingly also cluster with a few Iranian varieties, particularly with Darwazi and Ishkashimi. Pashto, which does not line up particularly closely with any other variety lexically, groups structurally with a few Indo-Aryan languages. Perhaps the most interesting correlation appears to be geographical, in which the left half (in figure 3.9) almost exclusively comprises languages in the north and west (or Badakhshan and Kapisa), and the right half languages in the southeast (or Nangarhar, Laghman, Kunar and most of Nuristan).

3.7 Concluding discussion

The survey of structural features presented above and the subsequent analysis of their respective distributions quantitatively as well as geographically suggest areal diffusion on a number of levels, and possibly at various time depths, involving language contact both within and across phylogenetic groupings represented in NEA.

Some of the properties are reflexes of macroareal configurations well beyond the confines of NEA. That is the case with both of the word-order features that were analyzed in 3.6.1. The exclusive display of the head-final order Object-Verb is a feature characterizing languages of various genera in Asia from the southern tip of India to Turkey in the west, to northeastern-most Siberia in Asia's extreme northeast, in what Masica has named the "Indo-Turanian" area (2001:240–243). In most parts of that macro area, this feature lines up with the (similarly head-final) use of postpositions rather than prepositions, except for an Iranian-dominated area of Western Asia in which OV-order instead is combined with postpositions, characterizing a "buffer" between the OV-area and the adjacent VO-dominated Mediterranean world (Stilo 2005). The fault line between postpositions and prepositions happens to cut through NEA, as most of the Iranian languages in this area either use prepositions or a combination of prepositions and postpositions, while the rest of the languages are purely postpositional. Other features reflecting overlaps of wider areal influences are the alignment properties discussed in 3.6.3. On the one hand, NEA is part of an "ergativity belt" linking parts of South Asia with Western Asia (Masica 2001:248–250), characterized by a special "agent" case and verbal agreement with the "patient". This is a conservative feature, realized in a variety of ways, as full, split or decayed ergativity, across a number of genera, although never including Turkic. In NEA itself, it is maintained partly or fully in the Indo-Iranian languages in the southeastern part of the area, whereas in many of the Indo-Iranian languages in the north and west, particularly in Iranian, ergativity has decayed, or is still decaying, in favour of accusativity (Payne 1980). On the other hand, NEA is part of another macro-area characterized by definite or differential object marking, comprising many (but far from all) South and Central Asian languages (Masica 2001:243–246). Diffusion is, in this case, much more recent and less pervasive, possibly originating in Central Asia, but propelled and accelerated by a few influential languages of wider communication, such as Persian. The ongoing competition between two strong areal influences is apparent from overlapping phenomena, particularly in the southern part of NEA, in which several varieties display tripartite case differentiation and double agreement, the latter confined to Pashai, although the same phenomenon is present in Indo-Aryan Kashmiri, spoken at another local fault line between ergativity and accusativity, and in yet another set of languages, in NEA as well as in adjacent areas of northern Pakistan and northern India, ergative case alignment co-occurs with accusative verb agreement (Deo and Sharma 2006:374–376; Verbeke 2013:248–267; Liljegren 2014:156–159). Although tightly linked to alignment features, yet in some ways constituting a separate phenomenon, is the presence of nominal case marking and a large case inventory (discussed in 3.6.2). This is a property typical of northern and central Eurasia (Iggesen 2013). All of the languages in NEA make use of case differentiation, and the majority of them extensively so, clearly showing that the area is indeed part of this wider macro-area.

A feature that, perhaps more than any other one discussed above, is tied to a particular phylogenetic grouping is grammatical gender (3.6.2). It is almost exclusively an inherited feature, although it may have been subject to various language-specific developments, including its erosion and eventual abandonment. Its complete absence in the two Turkic varieties is therefore only to be expected, as Turkic along with a number of other genera typical of central and northern Eurasia are non-gender as a whole. Its presence in twenty-one of the twenty-seven Indo-Iranian languages is not a surprise either,

3.7 Concluding discussion

as this inherited property is fairly stable throughout Indo-European as a whole (Nichols 2003:285). As already mentioned, the loss of gender, which in the case of NEA is an almost exclusively Iranian development, is part of a wider tendency in the Iranian world. Whether the loss of gender in Nuristani Prasun is a result of Iranian language contact or is due to internal developments, perhaps of substratal origin, is yet to be determined. The added presence of animacy-differentiation, on top of the inherited sex-based differentiation, in as many as six of the varieties is of particular interest and may be related to similar (possibly substratal) phenomena noted in other parts of the mountainous region beyond NEA (Payne 1989:423; Bashir 1988:408–419), thus evidencing a significant subarea including the language isolate Burushaski with its four-gender system which reflects sex-based as well as animacy-based differentiation (Berger 1998:33–34).

Apart from the grammaticalization of animacy, the strongest evidence of areality tied to the region itself, or rather to the wider Hindu Kush-Pamir-Karakoram mountain region as a whole, relates to phonology (3.6.4) and lexical structure (3.6.5). While the presence of retroflex consonants in general is an essential characteristic of the South Asian linguistic area (Masica 2001:254–257), of which NEA constitutes its northwestern periphery, the presence of retroflex plosives and fricatives/affricates alike, is a feature of the mountain region itself. Along with that goes another important feature, shared by many mountain languages, namely a tripartite affricate (and/or) fricative contrast (Hock 2015a:127–130). While it probably makes most sense to regard this as the result of multiple causation (2015b:130), partly as the result of an area-specific parallel innovation without any one language being responsible (Grossman and Nikolaev 2018), the language isolate Burushaski, or a proto-language related to it, or even some other unknown substratum, most likely played a role in the development of such consonant sets in many Indo-Iranian languages (Tikkanen 1999:146–147). In the case of NEA, neither one of those two values (retroflex plosives + retroflex fricatives/affricates; tripartite affricate contrast) is a majority feature; rather they are features characterizing a "hard core". As for retroflexion, the varieties with retroflex plosives only are all found at the southern end of NEA, the varieties with retroflex fricatives/affricates only are all found at the northern end of NEA, whereas the languages with both are located at the centre of the region. This can be compared with Tikkanen's (2008) characterization of the wider mountain area as a phonological transit zone between Central Asia and South Asia, in which the overlapping features in themselves appear to be area-defining.

The lexical features studied are probably representing one or more ancient layers of areality. In the case of numeral systems, the varieties with a vigesimal base are in the majority, contrasting with the systems used in the surrounding lower altitude regions, including those of the influential languages of wider communication. Vigesimal systems are also dominant in the adjacent mountain areas to the east of NEA. The compositional nature of those systems, however, have a clearly subareal distribution, with base + n characterizing the north, n + base characterizing the south, and a number of varieties in between evidencing a hybrid type. Again, this is a distributional pattern found in the rest of the Hindukush-Karakoram mountain region. The kinship subsystems investigated, reveal at first glance an astonishing degree of diversity across NEA, but are essentially pointing to two specific subareas, each reflecting a prototypical configuration with plenty of smaller variations, while a third system, mainly found at the peripheries aligns itself with more dominant surrounding cultures and languages.

By taking all of the investigated structural features into account in one go (figure 3.9), we were able to discern an interesting geographical pattern, namely one that sets the southeastern part of NEA apart as a similarity cluster versus a northern/western one. By plotting the individual varieties as belonging to one or the other, the pattern stands out even more clearly, as shown in figure 3.10.

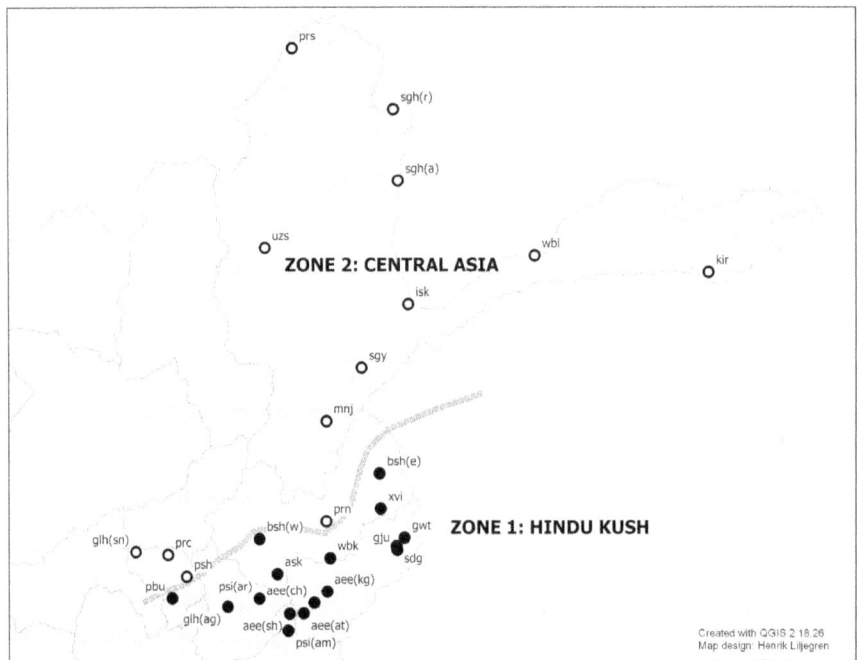

Figure 3.10. Map of northeastern Afghanistan with sample varieties plotted as belonging to one of two diffusion zones.

This may be taken as an indication of two distinct diffusion zones, in a few cases cutting right through established phylogenetic groupings: a) setting Pashto apart structurally from the rest of the Iranian languages in the region, b) setting Prasun apart from the rest of Nuristani, and c) setting at least two of the Pashai varieties, that of Sanjan and of Alasai, apart from the other Indo-Aryan languages as well as from their closest Pashai relatives. Zone 1: Hindu Kush, comprising the southeast, is a zone which is characterized by properties shared with languages in much of the rest of the wider Hindu Kush region to the east of NEA (particularly in a belt stretching through northern Pakistan's mountain region). Some of those are typical of the region itself, whereas other features are found in South Asia in general. The other, Zone 2: Central Asia, linking the western part of NEA diagonally with the north, is characterized by properties partly shared with languages in much of the rest of Central or West Asia, but there are also a number of features that appears to be characteristic of the Pamir region. It is probably not a mere coincidence that the two zones, as far as NEA is concerned, in general line up each with a different language of wider communication, Pashto in Zone 1 and Dari in Zone 2.

Further studies, adding more linguistic features to the analysis, will show us whether this preliminary picture remains stable, or would need to be adjusted or given a more fine-grained areal or sub-areal characterization.

3.8 Acknowledgements

A special thanks to all forty speakers of various languages who contributed valuable first-hand data and to Samar (Kabul and Faizabad) for excellent collaboration in facilitating the workshops. While we would like to acknowledge all of them personally, we have for safety reasons decided to let them remain anonymous. I would also like to thank Noa Lange, Stockholm, for assistance in transcribing and annotating recordings, and to Nina Knobloch, Stockholm, who as part of a half-term project course organized and processed the collected data, and contributed substantially to cognacy by coding the lexical data.

This work is part of the project *Language contact and relatedness in the Hindukush region*, supported by the Swedish Research Council (421-2014-631).

References

Baart, Joan L. G. 2014. Tone and stress in North-West Indo-Aryan: A survey. In Johanneke Caspers, Yiya Chen, Willemijn Heeren, Jos Pacilly, Niels O. Schiller, and Ellen Zanten (eds.), *Above and beyond the segments*, 1–13. Amsterdam: John Benjamins.

Bashir, Elena. 1988. Topics in Kalasha syntax: An areal and typological perspective. PhD dissertation. University of Michigan, Ann Arbor.

Bashir, Elena. 1996a. Mosaic of tongues: Quotatives and complementizers in Northwest Indo-Aryan, Burushaski, and Balti. In William L. Hanaway and Wilma Heston (eds.), *Studies in Pakistani popular culture*, 187–286. Lahore: Lok Virsa Publishing House and Sang-e-Meel Publications.

Bashir, Elena. 1996b. The areal position of Khowar: South Asian and other affinities. In Elena Bashir and Israr-ud-Din (eds.), *Proceedings of the Second International Hindukush Cultural Conference*, 167–179. Karachi: Oxford University Press.

Bashir, Elena. 2003. Dardic. In George Cardona and Danesh Jain (eds.), *The Indo-Aryan languages*, 818–894. London: Routledge.

Bashir, Elena. 2009. Wakhi. In Gernot Windfuhr (ed.), *The Iranian languages*, 825–861. London: Routledge.

Bashir, Elena. 2016a. Agent marking. In Hans Henrich Hock and Elena Bashir (eds.), *The languages and linguistics of South Asia: A comprehensive guide*, 450–459. Boston: De Gruyter Mouton.

Bashir, Elena. 2016b. Pre-1947 convergences. In Hans Henrich Hock and Elena Bashir (eds.), *The languages and linguistics of South Asia: A comprehensive guide*, 264–284. Boston: De Gruyter Mouton.

Beck, Simone, and Daniela Beyer. 2013. A sociolinguistic assessment of the Darwazi speech variety in Afghanistan. *Linguistic Discovery*, 11(1):22–82.

Berger, Hermann. 1998. *Die Burushaski-Sprache von Hunza und Nager*. Neuindische Studien 13. Wiesbaden: Harrassowitz Verlag.

Boeschoten, Hendrik. 1998. Uzbek. In Lars Johanson and Éva Á Csató (eds.), *The Turkic languages*, 357–378. London: Routledge.

Comrie, Bernard. 2013a. Alignment of case marking of full noun phrases. In Matthew S. Dryer and Martin Haspelmath (eds.), *The world atlas of language structures online*. Leipzig: Max Planck Institute for Evolutionary Anthropology. http://wals.info/chapter/98.

Comrie, Bernard. 2013b. Numeral bases. In Matthew S. Dryer and Martin Haspelmath (eds.), *The world atlas of language structures online*. Leipzig: Max Planck Institute for Evolutionary Anthropology. https://wals.info/chapter/131.

Degener, Almuth. 2002. The Nuristani languages. In Nicholas Sims-Williams (ed.), *Indo-Iranian languages and peoples*, 103–117. Proceedings of the British Academy 116. Oxford: Oxford University Press.

Deo, Ashwini, and Devyani Sharma. 2006. Typological variation in the ergative morphology of Indo-Aryan languages. *Linguistic Typology*, 10(3):369–418.

Dryer, Matthew S. 1992. The Greenbergian word order correlations. *Language*, 68(1):81–138.

Dryer, Matthew S. 2013. Order of object and verb. In Matthew S. Dryer and Martin Haspelmath (eds.), *The world atlas of language structures online*. Leipzig: Max Planck Institute for Evolutionary Anthropology. http://wals.info/chapter/83.

Èdel'man, Džoi Iosifovna. 1980. K substratnomu nasledijù central'no-aziatskogo jazykovogo sojuza [Towards the substrate heritage of the Central Asian linguistic union]. *Voprosy jazykoznanija*, 5:21–32.

Èdel'man, Džoi Iosifovna. 1983. *The Dardic and Nuristani languages*. Languages of Asia and Africa. Moscow: Nauka.

Èdel'man, Džoi Iosifovna, and Leila R. Dodykhudoeva. 2009. The Pamir languages. In Gernot Windfuhr (ed.), *The Iranian languages*, 773–786. London: Routledge.

Grierson, George A. 1919. *Indo-Aryan family: North-Western Group: Specimens of the Dardic or Pisacha languages (including Kashmiri)*. Linguistic Survey of India. Vol. VIII(II). Calcutta: Office of the Superintendent of Government Printing.

Grossman, Eitan, and Dmitry Nikolaev. 2018. Areal sound change and the distributional typology of affricate richness in Eurasia. *Studies in Language*, 42(3):562–599.

Hallberg, Calinda E., and Clare F. O'Leary. 1992. Dialect variation and multilingualism among Gujars of Pakistan. In Calvin R. Rensch, Calinda E. Hallberg, and Clare F. O'Leary (eds.), *Hindko and Gujari sociolinguistic survey of Northern Pakistan* 3, 91–194, 259–302. Islamabad: National Institute of Pakistan Studies Quaid-i-Azam University and Summer Institute of Linguistics.

References

Hock, Hans Henrich. 2015. The Northwest of South Asia and beyond: The issue of Indo-Aryan retroflexion yet again. *Journal of South Asian Languages and Linguistics*, 2(1):111–135.

Huson, Daniel H., and David Bryant. 2006. Application of phylogenetic networks in evolutionary studies. *Molecular Biology and Evolution*, 23(2):254–267.

Iggesen, Oliver A. 2013. Number of cases. In Matthew S. Dryer and Martin Haspelmath (eds.), *The world atlas of language structures online*. Leipzig: Max Planck Institute for Evolutionary Anthropology. https://wals.info/chapter/49.

Johanson, Lars. 2006. Uzbek. In Keith Brown (ed.), *Encyclopedia of language and linguistics*, 287–290. Amsterdam: Elsevier.

Kieffer, Charles M. 2009. Parachi. In Gernot Windfuhr (ed.), *The Iranian languages*, 693–720. London: Routledge.

Kirchner, Mark. 1998. Kyrgyz. In Lars Johanson and Éva Á. Csató (eds.), *The Turkic languages*, 344–356. London: Routledge.

Koptjevskaja-Tamm, Maria, and Henrik Liljegren. 2017. Semantic patterns from an areal perspective. In Raymond Hickey (ed.), *The Cambridge handbook of areal linguistics*, 204–236. Cambridge: Cambridge University Press.

Lehr, Rachel. 2014. A descriptive grammar of Pashai: The language and speech community of Darrai Nur. PhD dissertation. University of Chicago.

Leitner, Gottlieb Wilhelm. 1877. *The languages and races of Dardistan*. Lahore: Government Central Book Depot.

Liljegren, Henrik. 2009. The Dangari tongue of Choke and Machoke: Tracing the proto-language of Shina enclaves in the Hindu Kush. *Acta Orientalia*, 70:7–62.

Liljegren, Henrik. 2013. Notes on Kalkoti: A Shina language with strong Kohistani influences. *Linguistic Discovery*, 11(1):129–160.

Liljegren, Henrik. 2014. A survey of alignment features in the Greater Hindukush with special references to Indo-Aryan. In Pirkko Suihkonen and Lindsay J. Whaley (eds.), *On diversity and complexity of languages spoken in Europe and North and Central Asia*, 133–174. Studies in Language Companion Series 164. Amsterdam: John Benjamins.

Liljegren, Henrik. 2016. *A grammar of Palula*. Studies in Diversity Linguistics 8. Berlin: Language Science Press.

Liljegren, Henrik. 2017. Profiling Indo-Aryan in the Hindukush-Karakoram: A preliminary study of micro-typological patterns. *Journal of South Asian Languages and Linguistics*, 4(1):107–156.

MacKenzie, David Neil. 1959. A standard Pashto. *Bulletin of the School of Oriental and African Studies, University of London*, 22(1/3):231–235.

Masica, Colin P. 1991. *The Indo-Aryan languages*. Cambridge: Cambridge University Press.

Masica, Colin P. 2001. The definition and significance of linguistic areas: Methods, pitfalls, and possibilities (with special reference to the validity of South Asia as a linguistic area). In Peri Bhaskararao (ed.), *The yearbook of South Asian languages and linguistics 2001*, 205–267. London: SAGE.

Morgenstierne, Georg. 1926. *Report on a linguistic mission to Afghanistan*. Serie C 1-2. Oslo: Instituttet for sammenlignende kulturforskning.

Morgenstierne, Georg. 1938. *Iranian Pamir languages: Yidgha-Munji, Sanglechi-Ishkashmi and Wakhi*. Indo-Iranian Frontier Languages 2. Oslo: Instituttet for sammenlignende kulturforskning.

Morgenstierne, Georg. 1961. Dardic and Kafir languages. In *Encyclopedia of Islam*, 2:138–139. Leiden: Brill.

Morgenstierne, Georg. 1967. *The Pashai language: Part 2: Texts and translations*. Indo-Iranian Frontier Languages 3. Oslo: Universitetsforlaget. Originally published 1944.

Munshi, Sadaf. 2006. Dardic. In Keith Brown (ed.), *Encyclopedia of language and linguistics*, 354–356. Amsterdam: Elsevier.

Nichols, Johanna. 2003. Diversity and stability in language. In Brian D. Joseph and Richard D. Janda (eds.), *The handbook of historical linguistics*, 283–310. Malden: Blackwell.

Parkin, Robert. 1987. Kin classification in the Karakorum. *Man (New Series)*, 22(1):157–170.

Parpola, Asko. 2003. From the dialects of Old Indo-Aryan to Proto-Indo-Aryan and Proto-Iranian. In Nicholas Sims-Williams (ed.), *Indo-Iranian languages and peoples*, 43–102. Proceedings of the British Academy 116. Oxford: Oxford University Press.

Payne, John R. 1980. The decay of ergativity in Pamir languages. *Lingua*, 51(2–3):147–186.

Payne, John R. 1989. Pamir languages. In Rüdiger R. Schmitt (ed.), *Compendium Linguarum Iranicarum*, 417–444. Wiesbaden: Ludwig Reichert.

Perder, Emil. 2013. A grammatical description of Dameli. PhD dissertation. Stockholm University.

Petersen, Jan Heegård. 2015. Kalasha texts – With introductory grammar. *Acta Linguistica Hafniensia*, 47(sup 1):1–275.

Reichl, K. 1983. Syntactic interference in Afghan Uzbek. *Anthropos*, 78(3–4):481–500.

Rzehak, Lutz. 2016. Recent developments in Afghanistan. In Hans Henrich Hock and Elena Bashir (eds.), *The languages and linguistics of South Asia: A comprehensive guide*, 292–299. Boston: De Gruyter Mouton. https://www.degruyter.com/document/doi/10.1515/9783110423303/html.

Schmidt, Ruth Laila. 2004. A grammatical comparison of Shina dialects. In Anju Saxena (ed.), *Studies and Monographs*, 149:33–55. Berlin: De Gruyter Mouton.

Sharma, J. C. 2002. Gojri and its relationship with Rajasthani. *International Journal of Dravidian Linguistics*, 31:27–46.

References

Skjaervø, Prods Oktor. 1989a. Modern East Iranian languages. In Rüdiger Schmitt (ed.), *Compendium linguarum Iranicarum*, 370–383. Wiesbaden: Dr. Ludwig Reichert Verlag.

Skjaervø, Prods Oktor. 1989b. Pashto. In Rüdiger Schmitt (ed.), *Compendium linguarum Iranicarum*, 384–410. Wiesbaden: Dr. Ludwig Reichert Verlag.

Stilo, Donald L. 2005. Iranian as buffer zone between the universal typologies of Turkic and Semitic. In Éva Ágnes Csató Johanson (ed.), *Linguistic convergence and areal diffusion: Case studies from Iranian, Semitic, and Turkic*, 35–63. London: Routledge Curzon.

Strand, Richard F. 1973. Notes on the Nuristani and Dardic languages. *Journal of the American Oriental Society*, 93(3):297–305.

Strand, Richard F. 2001. The tongues of Peristân. Appendix 1. In Alberto Cacopardo and Augusto Cacopardo (eds.), *Gates of Peristan: History, religion and society in the Hindu Kush*, 251–257. Reports and Memoirs 5. Rome: Istituto italiano per l'Africa e l'Oriente.

Subbarao, K. V. 2016. Object marking. In Hans Henrich Hock and Elena Bashir (eds.), *The languages and linguistics of South Asia: A comprehensive guide*, 459–465. Boston: De Gruyter Mouton. https://www.degruyter.com/document/doi/10.1515/9783110423303/html.

Tikkanen, Bertil. 1999. Archaeological-linguistic correlations in the formation of retroflex typologies and correlating areal features in South Asia. In Roger Blench and Matthew Spriggs (eds.), *Archaeology and language IV: Language change and cultural transformation*, 138–148. London: Routledge.

Tikkanen, Bertil. 2008. Some areal phonological isoglosses in the transit zone between South and Central Asia. In Israr-ud-Din (ed.), *Proceedings of the Third International Hindu Kush Cultural Conference, August 26-30, 1995, Chitral (Pakistan)*, 250–262. Karachi: Oxford University Press.

Toporov, Vladimir Nikolayevich. 1970. About the phonological typology of Burushaski. In Roman Jakobson and Shigeo Kawamoto (eds.), *Studies in general and oriental linguistics presented to Shiro Hattori on the occasion of his sixtieth birthday*, 632–647. Tokyo: TEC Corporation for Language and Educational Research.

Verbeke, Saartje. 2013. *Alignment and ergativity in new Indo-Aryan languages*. Berlin: De Gruyter Mouton.

Wichmann, Søren, Cecil H. Brown, and Eric W. Holman. 2018. The ASJP database. Jena: Max Planck Institute for the Science of Human History. https://asjp.clld.org/.

Windfuhr, Gernot. 2009. *The Iranian languages*. London: Routledge.

Zeshan, Ulrike, Cesar Ernesto Escobedo Delgado, Hasan Dikyuva, Sibaji Panda, and Connie de Vose. 2013. Cardinal numerals in rural sign languages: Approaching cross-modal typology. *Linguistic Typology*, 17(3):357–396.

4

Towards a New Analysis of Wakhi Clitics

Erin SanGregory
SIL Global, University of Oregon

Abstract

This paper focuses on clitics in Wakhi, a Pamir language of the Indo-Iranian family.[1] While Wakhi clitics appear to be 2P (second position) in the default case, they can also be found much farther to the right in their clause. Hughes (2011), Erschler (2010), and Fuchs (2015) have taken different approaches to analyzing the wandering Wakhi clitic, which include restricting its hosts and locations, proposing it to be a member of a new category of clitic, and ascribing information structure functions to it. This paper proposes a new phrase structure rule that accounts for the distributional variations of the Wakhi clitic by locating it in SPEC, AUX, where AUX is sister to a recursive VP (verb phrase).

4.1 Introduction

Pamir languages of the Southeastern Iranian family in Central Asia are known to have subject agreement clitics as well as clitics that mark various TAM (tense, aspect, and mood) functions (Erschler 2010:4–6). Clitics in some Pamir languages seem to be true Wackernagel (2P) clitics; however, this is not the case for Wakhi, a Pamir language spoken in Afghanistan, Tajikistan, Pakistan, and China.[2] Like other Pamir languages, Wakhi has both agreement clitics and a TAM clitic, but the distribution of these clitics is freer than is expected of typical Wackernagel clitics. Bashir (2009:835–836) notes that, although the TAM clitic prefers to attach to the first constituent in the clause (2P clitic), both it and the pronominal clitics may in fact attach to any constituent. Furthermore, both types of clitics may appear multiple times in a clause.

Since Bashir, several linguists have tackled the challenge of analyzing Wakhi clitics, with each one proposing a slightly different analysis. Erschler (2010) uses those analyses, as well as examples from other Pamir and Eastern Iranian languages, as the basis for his proposal of a new class of clitic that he calls "Almost Wackernagel Clitics" (AWC). Hughes (2011) rejects Erschler's analysis and uses a combined syntactic and phonological approach to posit the location where Wakhi agreement clitics are base-generated. Most recently, Fuchs (2015) proposes two types of Wakhi pronominal clitics that have different properties, distributional restrictions, and semantic effects.

---

[1] I am deeply indebted to Paul Kroeger for his zealous assistance throughout the process of writing this paper. He has contributed greatly both to the paper and to my understanding of the topic at hand, but I claim all mistakes as solely my own.

[2] ISO 639-3:wbl, Indo-European, Indo-Iranian, Iranian, Eastern, Southeastern, Pamir (Lewis, Simons, and Fennig 2013).

In this paper, I take a different approach to analyzing Wakhi clitics than those used by previous authors. I begin by reviewing the definition of "clitic" and describing how the two types of Wakhi clitics (agreement and TAM) fit into this definition. I then give an overview of the analyses proposed by Erschler, Hughes, and Fuchs. Using data from my own fieldwork,[3] I demonstrate why aspects of these earlier analyses are untenable. Finally, I propose a phrase structure rule that accounts for the distributional variations of the Wakhi clitic by locating it in SPEC, AUX, where AUX is sister to a recursive VP.

4.2 Overview of Wakhi clitics

Before delving into the discussion of Wakhi clitics, it is important to review what clitics are and how their position in the clause has historically been described. I undertake this task in section 4.2.1 before moving on to the specifics of Wakhi clitics. Wakhi has two types of clitics: a set of agreement clitics[4] and a single TAM clitic. The agreement clitics are the subject of section 4.2.2. These clitics indicate agreement with the grammatical subject of the clause in which they occur. Although in both form and function they resemble the inflectional morphology that indicates subject agreement on verbs, they are in fact a distinct class of words, as their wide range of licensed hosts indicates. In section 4.2.3, I introduce the Wakhi TAM clitic and briefly discuss its semantic and discourse effects.

4.2.1 Clitics defined

Linguists have long noted the difference between morphemes that are FREE (can stand independently as prosodic words) and BOUND (must attach to another word / morpheme). Yet there is another set of morphemes that does not seem to fit precisely into either of these categories. These morphemes have been traditionally called CLITICS because, as Zwicky (1977:3) notes, they must "lean on" another prosodic word, known as the HOST, in order to be licit. However, unlike AFFIXES, which are bound morphemes that attach to a host of a specific grammatical category, clitics are "promiscuous"—that is, they can (and do) attach to hosts from a variety of grammatical categories.

Zwicky (1977) describes clitics as belonging to two classes and correlates a clitic's potential location with its class. The first of these classes is called SIMPLE CLITICS. Simple clitics are phonologically reduced forms of full prosodic words, and they obey the syntactic rules governing the free morphemes from which they are derived. For example, the pronoun *he* in the English sentence *Where's he going?*, often reduces in rapid speech to *Where's 'e going?*, but must remain in the same location as the original full pronoun.

---

[3] Previous work on Wakhi has focused on the Tajik and Pakistani dialects but has neglected the dialects from the Wakhan Corridor of Afghanistan, which is the traditional homeland of the Wakhi people and language. With this paper, I hope to enrich the conversation by discussing the results of recent fieldwork done in Afghan Wakhi.

[4] The literature differs as to whether these clitics are pronominal clitics or agreement clitics. Although Hughes (2011) makes several claims that I refute in section 4.3.2.2, I do for the most part concur with his analysis of these clitics as agreement morphemes and accordingly refer to them as such.

4.2 Overview of Wakhi clitics

PHRASAL AFFIXES are a subset of simple clitics (Nevis 1988, cited in Kroeger 2005:322). The morphemes that fall into this category usually carry inflectional (as opposed to lexical) meaning and convey this meaning to an entire constituent (Zwicky 1977:6–7; Kroeger 2005:321–322). That is, although they appear to attach to hosts from a wide variety of grammatical categories, phrasal affixes actually attach to the end of a constituent of a certain category and inflect the constituent as a whole instead of just the word to which they are attached. The English possessive -*s* falls into this category; consider examples such as *the store I like's sale* where the possessive -*s* inflects the entire preceding noun phrase *the store I like*.

SPECIAL CLITICS are unstressed and often bound morphemes that carry the same / similar meaning as a (usually) phonologically related free form, but they are special in that they do not adhere to the normal rules of syntax. This does not mean that they are completely unpredictable in where they locate—they tend to have preferred landing sites, such as near the margin of a constituent, adjacent to the head of a constituent, or at one end or the other of a sentence (Zwicky 1977:18). However, special clitics in different languages exhibit different preferences; therefore, we must write language-specific rules to account for their location.

Since special clitics vary so widely in their behavior, the linguistic community has spent a significant amount of time and effort attempting to describe them and where they can occur. In his seminal work (1892) on clitics, the German linguist Jacob Wackernagel described clitics in ancient Indo-European languages as being SECOND POSITION (2P); that is, that they appeared second in their clause. Clitics of this type have come to be known as "Wackernagel clitics" or as being governed by "Wackernagel's Law." Modern linguists distinguish between two types of Wackernagel clitics. Wackernagel's initial term, SECOND POSITION, is now reserved for a clitic that appears after the first **constituent** in its clause, while a clitic that appears after the first **word** of the clause (like those originally described by Wackernagel himself) is called SECOND WORD (2W).

Special clitics in many languages abide by Wackernagel's Law, but in other languages they exhibit much more freedom in their location, as Zwicky's (1977) definition of them hints. Linguists have attempted to account for clitic placement, Wackernagel or not, in a variety of ways, including morphological (Anderson 1993), syntactic (Klavans 1995), and phonological (Halpern 1995) analyses.

4.2.2 Wakhi verbal agreement suffixes vs. agreement clitics

4.2.2.1 Verbal agreement suffixes

In the nonpast tense (used for both present and future), all Wakhi verbs except for the invariant copula *tǝi* 'be' are inflected for subject agreement via suffixes. An unmarked verb stem indicates 2SG agreement. The suffix -*ǝn* is used for both 1PL and 3PL. Table 4.1, displays the full set of subject agreement markers.[5]

---

[5] The 3SG agreement suffix is realized as -*d* following voiced consonants and as -*t* elsewhere.

Table 4.1. Subject agreement suffixes

Person	Singular	Plural
1	-əm	-ən
2	Ø	-əv
3	-t, -d	-ən

Verbs in tenses other than the nonpast (that is, past and perfect tenses) are inflected for tense but not for subject agreement.[6] Including a subject agreement marker renders a sentence with an inflected verb ungrammatical. This contrast is shown in examples (1) to (3).[7]

(1) jao   nɘu-d
    3SG.NOM cry-3SG
    'He is crying.'

(2) jao   nao-di
    3SG.NOM cry-PST
    'He cried.'

(3) *jao   nao-di-d
    3SG.NOM cry-PST-3SG
    Intended: 'He cried.'

4.2.2.2 Agreement clitics

Wakhi agreement clitics are distinct from the regular subject agreement morphology on verbs. Agreement clitics bear a striking resemblance to the verbal agreement suffixes, but with a few crucial differences. First, the 3SG clitic is extremely rare.[8] Second, whereas the 3PL suffix is identical to the 1PL suffix, the 3PL clitic takes the same form as the 2PL clitic (=əv).[9] The full set of agreement clitics can be seen in table 4.2.

---

[6] A full description of the Wakhi verbal system is beyond the scope of this paper. However, it is helpful to note that verbs generally have two stems, nonpast and past, that are inflected to form the different tenses. In this paper, unmarked verbs are nonpast.

[7] Unless otherwise noted, examples are from my own fieldwork. Examples from other authors have been slightly modified to match my transcription.

[8] I have encountered only one example of the 3SG clitic in my fieldwork thus far. Fuchs notes that use of the 3SG clitic varies by dialect, with a likely trend towards the loss of the clitic. This would certainly seem to be the case for Afghan Wakhi.

[9] Fuchs (2015) cites =iʃ as the 2PL / 3PL clitic in two dialects (Gojali and Murghab) of Wakhi.

4.2 Overview of Wakhi clitics

Table 4.2. Agreement clitics

Person	Singular	Plural
1	=əm	=ən
2	=ət	=əv
3	=i	=əv

Wakhi clitics are in complementary distribution with the agreement suffixes. That is, they cannot appear in a sentence that contains a verb already inflected for subject agreement (nonpast), but they can appear when the verb does not carry an agreement suffix (copula, past, and perfect tenses). Compare the sentences in (1) to (3) to those in (4) to (8). Sentences (4) and (5) both contain a nonpast verb inflected for subject agreement, but the addition of the 1SG clitic =əm makes (5) ungrammatical. In contrast, sentence (6) is grammatical because the past tense verb is uninflected for subject agreement. The sentences in (7) and (8) are also grammatical because they contain the copula, which is uninflected for subject agreement regardless of its tense.

(4) wuz nəʉ-əm
    1SG.NOM cry-1SG
    'I am crying.'

(5) *wuz=**əm** nəʉ-əm
    1SG.NOM=1SG cry-1SG
    Intended: 'I am crying.'

(6) wuz=**əm** nao-di
    1SG.NOM=1SG cry-PST
    'I cried.'

(7) tu xiʃ təi=**ət**
    2SG.NOM happy be=1SG
    'You (sg) are happy.'

(8) tu xiʃ=**ət** tu
    2SG.NOM happy=2SG be.PST
    'You (sg) were happy.'

Wakhi allows for zero-copula constructions in the present tense. Given that zero-copula constructions are verbless clauses and are thus incapable of bearing verbal inflectional morphology, we should expect to find agreement clitics in such sentences. This prediction is borne out by (9) and (10).

(9) wuz airɔn=**əm**
    1SG.NOM surprised=1SG
    'I am surprised.'

(10) tu   xiʃ=ət
     2SG.NOM   happy=2SG
     'You are happy.'

The distribution of Wakhi clitics might cause us to question whether they are in some way related to the agreement suffixes described in section 4.2.2.1. However, they can be distinguished from standard verbal inflectional morphology when we examine their hosts. Remember that an affix must attach only to words of a certain grammatical category, while clitics allow for much more variety in their hosts. When we review the preceding examples, we find that Wakhi clitics can be hosted by a full pronoun subject, as in (6); a verb, as in (7);[10] or an adjective, as in (9) and (10). Additional examples show that clitics can be hosted by nouns (11),[11] conjunctions (12), and various adjunct constituents, such as an adverbial PP (13). Thus, we can safely conclude that this set of Wakhi agreement markers is indeed composed of clitics.

(11) ʃɔt=ən   kɨ[12]   jit-i   çi   qɨtʃa-v-i   wɨzdi-ən
     supper=1PL   COMP   eat-PST   self.GEN   dish-PL-ACC   wash-1PL
     'After we eat supper, we wash our dishes.'

(12) an=ən   ts-a-n   γaftʃ   wɨṣ-ti
     then=1PL   from-DEM3-ABL   INTENS   fear-PST
     'Then we were very afraid of that (bear).'

(13) an   da awal=en   ji   nɔγardum=ən   win-di
     then   at beginning=1PL   one   bear=1PL   see-PST
     'Then, at the beginning, we saw a bear.'

4.2.3 Wakhi TAM clitic

In addition to the agreement clitics, Wakhi also has a single TAM clitic: the morpheme =ṣ. It is somewhat difficult to nail down the exact function of this clitic, in part because it is optional and because its frequency of use therefore varies from speaker to speaker. When reviewing verb paradigms, one language consultant consistently used this clitic to distinguish a present, ongoing activity (as opposed to one anticipated in the future). That is, when prompted for an utterance regarding present activity, she would produce a verb such

---

[10] Although the host in example (7) is a copular verb, the generalization holds for other verbs as well.

[11] Hughes (2011:43) observes that an agreement clitic cannot co-occur with an explicit NP$_{SUBJ}$ in its clause. This is true when that subject is a full noun but not when it is a pronoun, as will be discussed in more detail in section 4.3.2.2.

[12] The word kɨ has several uses. It serves as the complementizer for adverbial time clauses with the meaning 'when' or 'after', as seen here in (11). It can introduce an S-COMP or purposive construction, and it also functions as a relativizer. When used as a relativizer or complementizer for adverbial time clauses, it typically occupies 2P. The topics of relativization and complementization are beyond the scope of this paper, but further study in this area, including the behavior of kɨ as compared to that of the Wakhi agreement and TAM clitics, could shed additional light on the discussion of Wakhi clitic placement.

4.2 Overview of Wakhi clitics

as *ʂkurgəm=əʂ*, which is probably similar in meaning to the English "I am searching". On the other hand, when asked to describe an activity planned for the future, she would drop the clitic and use the verb with only inflectional morphology; that is, *ʂkurgəm* 'I will search'. I choose to follow Beck (2013:14) in glossing =ʂ as 'IPFV' (imperfective), as her example in (14) shows.[13]

(14) jan də sɔbɪq=**əʂ** lup=**əʂ** çat-i kɪ nɔɣardum ətʃ
 then in old.time=IPFV big=IPFV say-PST COMP bear no
 waxt də mɔltɪq-ən ja-r qrib ma rəts-əv
 time with shotgun-ABL 3SG-DAT near NEG.IMP go-2PL
 'Then in old times the old people said: Bears, never go near them (not even) with a shotgun.'[14]

Like the agreement clitics, the Wakhi TAM clitic attaches to a variety of hosts. In (14), we see two instances of the TAM clitic. The first instance of the clitic is hosted by the noun *sɔbɪq* 'old times'; the second instance is hosted by *lup*, an adjective meaning 'big' but used in an abstract sense here to mean 'old people'. The TAM clitic may also attach to a verb, as seen in (15), or to an adjective, as seen in (16) (Beck 2013:13).[15] Furthermore, =ʂ may attach to a pronoun as in (17) (first instance) or to a conjunction as in (18) (Beck, p.c.). Example (18) also shows that the TAM clitic may attach after an agreement clitic, as demonstrated by both instances of the clitic.

(15) çø putr-ər çan-d e çan-d=**əʂ** kɪ ʉb ɣuri
 self.GEN son-DAT say-3SG INTJ say-3SG=IPFV COMP seven tray
 telɔ mar wizəm
 gold 1SG.DAT bring.2SG
 'He says to his son, oh, he says to bring him seven golden trays.'

(16) a=dr-a-ə ta'in kərt-i jupk kam kam jupk
 EMPH=there-DEM3-EZ perceive do-PST water little little water
 kam=**ʂ** wɔs-t
 little=IPFV become-3SG
 'There it perceived that the water becomes less and less, and it dries up.'

---

[13] If we consider this clitic to mark imperfective aspect, we could conceive of its use in the past tense to indicate some kind of continuous (or perhaps habitual) action, which would not be inconsistent with the semantic effects it produces in the present tense. In this case, we could revise the free translation to be 'the old people **used** to say' to reflect the aspectual effect of the clitic more clearly in English.

[14] Beck points out that the Wakhi TAM clitic serves a discourse function as well as an inflectional one. She posits that the use of this clitic foregrounds information that would otherwise have been considered part of the background of a text (2013:12–14). A full discussion of this topic is beyond the scope of the current paper, but her analysis is worth reading for those interested in pursuing the topic further.

[15] The adjective *kam* 'little' is probably part of a light verb construction in this clause, in which case it is interesting to note that the clitic interrupts a constituent, which it is not supposed to do.

(17) jau=əʂ   ɣa   aɾ   tʃiz-ə   diʃ-t   ət   janə
     3SG.NOM=IPFV INTENS every thing-ACC know-3SG and that.is
     də yɔib=əʂ   jau   qəsa-ə   diʃ-t
     in foresight=IPFV 3SG.NOM story-ACC know-3SG
     'He knows everything; that is, he knows things in foresight.'

(18) ˈjan=əv=əʂ   ˈkəɾ-ti   fəˈrɔr   ˈrəɥj-d=əv=əʂ   tr-a
     then=3PL=IPFV   do-PST   escape   go-PST=3PL=IPFV   to-DEM3
     nag
     direction
     'Then they fled, they went over there.'

4.2.4 Classifying Wakhi clitics

Up to this point, I have not attempted to classify Wakhi clitics according to Zwicky's (1977) typology, but have only described how they function in their clause—they either mark agreement with the NP$_{SUBJ}$ or indicate imperfective aspect. From this simple description alone, we can see that Wakhi clitics bear a functional load and do not contribute new lexical content to the sentence. Since one of the characteristics of phrasal affixes is that they contribute inflectional meaning to their clause, Wakhi clitics would seem to fit into this category. However, there are other qualifications of phrasal affixes that Wakhi clitics do not meet. For example, while a phrasal affix exhibits significant freedom in the grammatical category of the individual word it selects as host, that word must be a member of a larger constituent whose category is fixed, such as a noun phrase (as seen in the English example in section 4.2.1). Wakhi clitics of both types regularly violate this stipulation, as noted in section 4.2.2.2 and in section 4.2.3.

Since Wakhi clitics do not match the prototypical description of phrasal affixes, in section 4.3, I consider whether they are special clitics. They fit quite well within this category in that they are exempt from the rules governing regular syntax and instead follow their own peculiar set of rules. In trying to determine what these rules are, linguists have proposed a number of explanations for the distributional variations exhibited by Wakhi clitics. These analyses are the topic of the following section.

4.3 Overview of previous analyses

The Wakhi language as a whole has been the subject of linguistic analysis off and on throughout the past century. Aside from Bashir's (1986) article on ergativity in Wakhi, the majority of these works have been largely typological in nature. Wakhi clitics entered the discussion only recently when Erschler (2010) included them in his study of Eastern Iranian languages that exhibit clitics having Wackernagel-like characteristics. Hughes (2011) and Fuchs (2015) have joined Erschler in the discussion of Wakhi clitics, agreeing that the preferred (but not universal) location for Wakhi clitics is 2P. Indeed, in a survey of the data presented in this paper so far, we find that every clitic (both

4.3 Overview of previous analyses

agreement and TAM) is indeed 2P—except for the doubled clitics in examples (13) and (14) in section 4.2.3.[16] This variation in clitic location is not specific to cases of multiple occurrences, as examples (19) to (21) from Hughes (2011:38) show. Sentence (19) shows the clitic in default 2P, while in sentences (20) and (21), the clitic has attached to a host that occurs later in the sentence.

(19) jəz=əm ʃəpik ɣaftʃ baf çətu
 yesterday=1SG bread INTENS good make.PST.PRF

(20) jəzi ʃəpik=əm ɣaftʃ baf çətu
 yesterday bread=1SG INTENS good make.PST.PRF

(21) jəzi ʃəpik ɣaftʃ baf=əm çətu
 yesterday bread INTENS good=1SG make.PST.PRF
 'Yesterday I made delicious bread.'

It is precisely this variation from a strict Wackernagel position that Erschler, Hughes, and Fuchs attempt to explain; yet each takes a slightly different approach. In the following sections, I overview and critique each analysis in turn.

4.3.1 Erschler's AWC analysis

As mentioned above, clitics described as being Wackernagel clitics occasionally stray from their canonical position. This propensity for wandering is not restricted to Wakhi clitics. Upon comparing data from a number of languages, including Eastern Iranian languages such as Wakhi and several other (closely related) Pamir languages, Erschler (2010) observes that clitics that are supposed to adhere to Wackernagel's Law can be found farther to the right in their clause. He remarks that this "optionality" should not be surprising given that even the prototypical Wackernagel position comes with two standard options: 2W vs. 2P.

To account for this kind of regular clitic wandering, Erschler proposes a new class of clitic: the ALMOST WACKERNAGEL CLITIC (AWC). An AWC is a clitic that by default occupies either the 2W or 2P location in its clause but can optionally appear elsewhere. To explain this behavior, Erschler (2010) builds on Anderson's (2005) intuition that clitics are clause-level morphology and, therefore, "every constituent in the clause receives a bundle of features that can be spelled out as a clitic (or clitic cluster)" (Erschler 2010:9). He suggests that, when taken literally, this approach not only allows clitics to appear farther to the right in their clause, but also predicts multiple manifestations of clitics in a single clause to be possible in some languages. He includes Wakhi as an example of a language where we see this prediction fulfilled, based on examples such as (22) (Grünberg and Stéblin-Kamensky 1976:49 in Erschler 2010:9). This should come as no surprise considering we have already seen multiple spell-out of an agreement clitic in (13) and the TAM clitic in (14).

---

[16] Note that the second pair of clitics in example (18) is 2P, although at first glance it appears otherwise. The host *rəʉj-d* 'go-PST' is the first constituent of the second clause in the sentence.

(22) wuz=əm   pai=əm   ar   çɨ   sar   ɣirɔv-di
     1SG.NOM=1SG   yogurt=1SG   on   self.GEN head   turn.over-PST
     'I spilled the yogurt on my head.'

4.3.2 Hughes's application of the DFCF and PI

4.3.2.1 Overview of Hughes

Although Erschler's proposed ALMOST WACKERNAGEL CLITIC (AWC) category seems to account for both clitic movement and multiple spell-out, his analysis is not accepted by all. Hughes rejects the AWC proposal outright; in fact, he completely forsakes the notion that Wakhi agreement clitics are 2P at all (2011:39).[17] Instead, he proposes that these clitics are the head of an agreement phrase (AGRP) that is base-generated above topic phrase (TP). Several different movement operations can then shift other constituents to a position above that of the clitic in the syntactic tree, thereby locating the clitic in various places in the surface structure of the sentence (2011:53–55). Hughes's analysis crucially depends on his application of two different devices: the DOUBLY FILLED COMP FILTER (DFCF) and PROSODIC INVERSION (PI).

Originally proposed by Koopman (1996), the doubly-filled COMP filter (DFCF) "allows a language to have an overt head and silent specifier in a given projection, or vice versa" (Hughes 2011:55). Critically, only one or the other (that is, head or specifier) can be overtly expressed, not both. The DFCF is important to Hughes's analysis because he claims that these clitics cannot be hosted by a subject determiner phrase (DP); when he invokes the DFCF, he can explain why that should be.

Halpern (1995) uses the theory of prosodic inversion (PI) to explain why 2W clitics locate where they do. Halpern notes that an enclitic that appears at the beginning of a clause is not licensed because it is phonologically and prosodically deficient. However, it has no options for becoming licit because no potential hosts precede it. It is in this situation that he invokes PI. PI moves a clitic only as far as is necessary to provide a licit host; thus, the clitic has only to move after the immediately following word to become licensed.

Hughes appeals to PI to explain why Wakhi agreement clitics occasionally appear after a verb, which according to his analysis should not be allowed. Indeed, he claims that clitics can never attach to the verb unless the verb is the only other phonologically realized word. It is at this point that he calls upon PI as a "mop-up" operation to move the verb before the clitic, an operation that is not ideal, but is preferable to the only other option (namely, leaving the clitic in the initial position without a host) (2011:60).

4.3.2.2 Criticisms of Hughes

Hughes himself recognizes that the quantity of data available to him was marginal (2011:62). Unfortunately, this lack of data has negatively affected his analysis on several points. To begin, his claims limiting the distribution of agreement clitics (upon which his analysis is crucially based) are too strong.

---

[17] Hughes (2011) looks only at Wakhi agreement clitics and does not discuss the TAM clitic at all.

4.3 Overview of previous analyses

As noted above, he claims that a clitic cannot be hosted by any subject DP (whether full pronoun or noun) or by a verb (except when PI intervenes in situations where there is no other constituent before the verb), nor can they appear more than once in their clause. Additionally, he states that a clitic cannot interrupt a constituent and that it may only appear in the past tense. A larger data pool shows that each of these claims is at best too general and at worst inaccurate.

Consider example (23) where the 1PL clitic =ən is hosted by the NP$_{SUBJ}$ *sak* '1PL.NOM', which is a full subject pronoun.

(23) sak=ən   qrib roj-di   kı nɔɣardum mərt-k
     1PL.NOM=1PL near go-PST COMP bear   die-PRF
     'We approached after the bear was dead.'

This example disproves Hughes's claim that a clitic cannot be hosted by a subject DP. However, some qualification is necessary. First, it does appear that a clitic that attaches to a subject DP does so only when that subject is a pronoun—a noun filling this position is not a licit clitic host. Thus, Hughes's claim is half true. Second, I believe the ability of a clitic to attach to a pronoun subject DP to be a result of dialectical variation. Notice that the clitic host in (23) is a nominative case pronoun used in the past tense, which is indicative of a nominative-accusative case system. My fieldwork shows that Afghan Wakhi has the option to follow either a nominative-accusative system or an ergative-absolutive system in the past or perfect tenses (only nominative-accusative is permitted in the nonpast tense). Furthermore, only nominative case subject pronouns can serve as clitic hosts; an ergative pronoun is not a licit host.[18] In all of Hughes's data, NP$_{SUBJ}$ pronouns are in the ergative case. It appears that this is not an accident—tense-conditioned split ergativity is obligatory, not optional, for the Hunza dialect (Backstrom 2015, p.c.).[19] This, then, would explain why my data conflict with Hughes's on this point.

The second issue with Hughes's analysis is his claim that agreement clitics cannot attach to a verb unless the verb is the only full word in the clause. Example (7) from section 4.2.2.2, repeated below as (24), as well as example (25) from Erschler (2010:5), both provide evidence to the contrary. Incidentally, example (24) also refutes Hughes's claim that clitics appear only in the past tense.

(24) tu   xiʃ   təi=ət
     2SG.NOM happy be=1SG
     'You (sg) are happy.'

(25) sak   tə çɨ   ɕui   bar rojd=ən
     1PL.NOM to self.GEN sister door go.PST=1PL
     'We went to my sister's house.'

---

[18] The most likely opportunity for a clitic to attach to a nominal subject would be in the third person. Since the 3SG clitic is quite rare, as mentioned earlier, it could be that the restriction on using a noun subject DP as host is related to the scarcity of the 3SG clitic.
[19] Pakistani.

When Hughes dismissed Erschler's (2010) AWC proposal, he rejected the evidence that Erschler provided for multiple spell-out, presented as example (22) in section 4.3.1. However, I find his dismissal problematic since the evidence, both Erschler's and my own, consistently shows examples of multiple clitics within a single clause. We saw one such example in (13), repeated here as (26).

(26) an da awal=**ən** ji nɔɣardum=ən win-di
then at beginning=1PL one bear==1PL see-PST
'Then, at the beginning, we saw a bear.'

Hughes states that a clitic cannot interrupt a constituent, yet he includes an example that seems to do just that, as shown in (27) (2011:18). He calls this construction a "phrasal verb" and analyzes the nominal component as a separate constituent. I question this analysis because Wakhi is known to have a large inventory of light verb constructions (LVCs), of which this is one.[20] A second example of a clitic interrupting an LVC from Beck (2013, p.c.) can be seen in (28).

(27) jəzi jark=ən çətu
yesterday work=3PL do.PST.PRF
'Yesterday they worked.'

(28) ɣa zamat=ən χəṣ-ətk
INTENS trouble=3PL pull-PRF
'They had a lot of trouble.'

4.3.3 Fuchs's split analysis

4.3.3.1 Overview of Fuchs

Fuchs (2015) is the most recent person to add her voice to the discussion of Wakhi clitics. She deviates from both Erschler (2010) and Hughes (2011) in choosing to adopt what she calls a "split analysis" of Wakhi clitics. Focusing as Hughes did on the agreement clitics, Fuchs divides them into two types of clitics: doubled pronominal clitics and possessive clitics. She states that the pronominal clitics are inherently 2P and that, as such, they are base-generated in SPEC, TP. She also posits both a topic position and a new-information focus position in the left periphery of the sentence. When constituents that would normally appear farther right in a neutral construction are fronted to these positions, they cause the clitic to appear in 3P in the clause. This movement does not pose a problem for the clitic because it imposes no selectional restrictions on its host (Fuchs 2015:10–13).

Fuchs observes that some clitics appear to be involved in an EXTERNAL POSSESSOR construction. An external possessor construction is found where a

---

[20] A full battery of constituency tests for LVCs is beyond the scope of this paper. However, two short examples may be helpful here. First, the LVC moves to the beginning of the clause as a unit when it functions as the subject, as we see in the sentence *jark tsərak qela* 'working is difficult'. Second, the nominalizer *-kɨzg* attaches to the end (heavy verb) of an LVC to derive the meaning 'one who__', as we see in examples such as *jark tsərak-kɨzg* 'worker; one who works'.

4.3 Overview of previous analyses

word possesses something semantically even though it is itself syntactically an argument of the verb. Fuchs notes that external possessor constructions are known to occur in French and that certain Wakhi constructions involving clitics bear a strong resemblance to these French constructions (Fuchs 2015a:15–17). She observes that such clitics occur farther to the right in the sentence than usually expected (beyond 2P) and, critically, that they must refer to an antecedent that both agrees with and is coreferential with the subject (but is not actually the subject) of their clause (2015:9). In other words, although the antecedent is the syntactic possessor, the subject (with which the syntactic antecedent is coreferential) is the semantic, external possessor. Example (29) shows an example of an external possessor construction (Fuchs 2015c:16).[21]

(29) wuz$_i$ çi$_i$ şəw-v-i=**m**$_i$ şkendəvd-i
      1SG.NOM self.GEN horn-PL-ACC=1SG break.TR-PST
      'I broke my horns.'

(30) *wuz$_i$ ti$_j$ şəw-v-i=**m**$_i$ şkendəvd-i
      1SG.NOM 2SG.GEN horn-PL-ACC=1SG break.TR-PST
      'I broke your horns.'

Additional characteristics of constructions involving possessor clitics include 1) that the object being possessed must be highly affected by the activity expressed in the clause (often as a result of inalienable possession), and 2) that the external possessor must be the subject of the clause. Fuchs uses this analysis to explain why example (29) is grammatical while (30) is ungrammatical (Fuchs 2015:16). As the indices show, the clitic in (29) is coreferential with the reflexive pronoun *çi*, which in turn is coreferential with the subject pronoun *wuz*. This works because all three items (clitic, reflexive pronoun, and subject pronoun) agree in person and number. Although the clitic and subject pronoun in (30) agree with each other, they do not agree in person with the genitive pronoun *ti* '2SG.GEN'. This lack of agreement makes it impossible for all three items to be coreferential and thus renders the sentence ungrammatical.

4.3.3.2 Criticisms of Fuchs' analysis

Fuchs's analysis is both elegant and original, yet it is not without flaws. My first criticism regards her account of where the pronominal clitics are base-generated. Although the specific location she posits is different, it is, like that proposed by Hughes (2011), a fixed location above the verb in the syntactic tree. Therefore, Fuchs again relies on PI to account for instances where the verb and the clitic are swapped. As I have already critiqued this approach in section 4.3.2.2, I will not go into all the details again here, but instead refer the reader back to the counterexamples presented in (24) and (25), which demonstrate that the verb can serve as a host even when other potential hosts precede it in the clause.

My second criticism concerns Fuchs's split analysis of possessor clitics. Her external possessor analysis accounts quite neatly for data such as those presented in (29), but consider example (13), repeated here as (31).

---

[21] Bolding and subscript indices added for clarity.

(31) an   da awal=**en**   ji   nɔɣardum=**ən** win-di
     then at beginning=1PL one bear=1PL   see-PST
     'Then, at the beginning, we saw a bear.'

In this example, we see two instances of the clitic =ən '1PL'. According to Fuchs's analysis, we should only see two clitics in the same clause when one is a pronominal 2P clitic and the second is a possessor clitic (2015:18). The first clitic in (31) fits this pattern, but I find it difficult to call the second a possessor since the bear in this clause is clearly not possessed by the (null) subject of the sentence. Furthermore, as example (32) (repeated from (14)) demonstrates, the TAM clitic can also be doubled. It seems illogical to posit that a clitic that indicates imperfective aspect can also indicate possession. Since the TAM clitic and the agreement clitics behave similarly in all other ways, I question the validity of the claim that doubled agreement clitics indicate possession when this interpretation is impossible for the TAM clitic.

(32) jan də sɔbıq=**əş**   lup=**əş**   çat-i   kı   nɔɣardum ətʃ
     then in old.time=IPFV big=IPFV say-PST COMP bear   no
     waxt də mɔltıq-ən   ja-ɾ   qɾib   mə   ɾəts-əv
     time with shotgun-ABL 3SG-DAT near NEG.IMP go-2PL
     'Then in old times the old people said: Bears, never go near them (not even) with a shotgun.'

In summary, in section 4.3 I have taken a cursory look at recent analyses of Wakhi clitics proposed by three linguists. I have examined some of the core arguments of these analyses and presented conflicting data that suggest a new analysis is needed. This analysis is the subject of the next section.

4.4 A preliminary Lexical Functional Grammar analysis of Wakhi clitics

From the overview of other analyses in section 4.3, one thing should be clear, namely, that Wakhi clitics by default prefer 2P regardless of the analysis used to locate them there. Erschler (2010) and Fuchs (2015) both accept this generalization and incorporate it into their analyses. Although Hughes (2011) frees himself from the 2P assumption and attempts to pin down the location of Wakhi clitics by other means, in the end, his analysis still locates them in 2P in the default case whether he admits it or not.

The evidence clearly points towards 2P as the preferred home for Wakhi clitics; however, it also clearly demonstrates that other locations are possible even if they are less favorable. Consider the following examples, all repeated from earlier in this paper and including both types of clitics (agreement and TAM).

(33) jəzi   jark=**əv**   çətu
     yesterday work=3PL do.PST.PRF
     'Yesterday they worked.'

4.4 A preliminary Lexical Functional Grammar analysis of Wakhi clitics

(34) a=dɾ-a-ə   ta'in   kəɾt-i   jupk kam kam jupk
      EMPH=there-DEM3-EZ perceive do-PST water little little water
      kam=ʂ   wɔs-t
      little=IPFV become-3SG
      'There it perceived that the water becomes less and less, and it dries up.'

(35) an   da awal=en   ji   nɔɣardum=ən win-di
      then at beginning=1PL one   bear=1PL   see-PST
      'Then, at the beginning, we saw a bear.'

(36) jan   də sɔbɪq=əʂ   lup=əʂ   çat-i   kɪ   nɔɣardum ətʃ
      then   in old.time=IPFV   big=IPFV   say-PST   COMP bear   no
      waxt   də mɔltɪq-ən   ja-ɾ   qɾib mə   ɾətʂ-əv
      time   with shotgun-ABL   3SG-DAT   near NEG.IMP   go-2PL
      'Then in old times the old people said: Bears, never go near them (not even) with a shotgun.'

Examples (33) and (34) contain one instance of an agreement clitic and a TAM clitic, respectively. Neither of these clitics is 2P, but they both occur immediately before the verb. Moving on to (35) and (36), which both contain two instances of a clitic, we find that in both sentences the first clitic is 2P, while the second is again found immediately before the verb. I do not believe this to be a coincidence. We should recall from Zwicky (1977) that, although special clitics are exempt from normal syntactic rules, they usually gravitate towards a certain position in the sentences—indeed, we have already appealed to this principle by stating that the default location for Wakhi clitics is 2P. Given that a clitic can have a preferred default position, I find it necessary to ask the question, what is to stop it from choosing a preferred secondary location as well? I propose that this is part of the answer to the question of the wandering Wakhi clitic—that it prefers to be 2P, but when it is not, its second-best option is to get as close to the verb as possible (preferably immediately preceding).

I realize that there are still several unexplained examples that contain clitics that are neither 2P nor preverbal. Particularly problematic are examples (20), (22), (25), and (31), repeated below as (37) to (40). In (37), we see a clitic that has attached to the second constituent. Example (38) contains two clitics, the first of which is 2P, but the second of which is not. The clitic has attached to the verb in (39) even though there are several viable hosts higher in the phrase structure. Neither of the clitics in (40) is 2P, although the second clitic is preverbal.

(37) jəzi   ʃəpik=əm   ɣaftʃ   baf   çətu
      yesterday bread=1SG   INTENS   good   make.PST.PRF
      'Yesterday I made delicious bread.'

(38) wuz=əm   pai=əm   ar   çi   sar   ɣiɾɔv-di
      1SG.NOM=1SG   yogurt=1SG   on   self.GEN head   turn.over-PST
      'I spilled the yogurt on my head.'

(39) sak   tə çɨ   çɨi   bar roj̇d=ən
     1PL.NOM to self.GEN sister door go.PST=1PL
     'We went to my sister's house.'

(40) an   da awal=en   ji   nɔɣardum=ən win-di
     then at beginning=1PL   one bear=1PL   see-PST
     'Then, at the beginning, we saw a bear.'

At this point, I see one analysis that holds the potential to account for all of the data, including the problematic examples above. I propose that we write a phrase structure rule (PSR) such as the following.

(41)   VP → VP, Aux

The phrase structure rule above generates a recursive VP with a sister AUX, where the clitic occupies the AUX position. The comma in (41) indicates that the order of VP and AUX is not fixed, but that they can occur in either order. When AUX is the first daughter of the first VP, as we see in the syntax tree in figure 4.1, the clitic attaches to the initial XP constituent (here an NP_{SUBJ}) and appears in 2P.

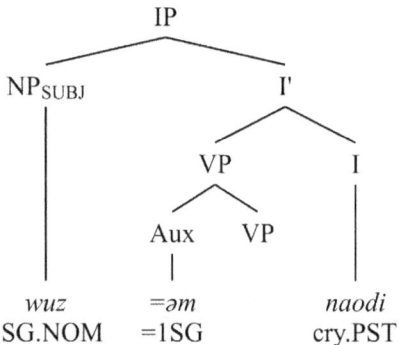

Figure 4.1. C-STR for example (6).

When AUX is the second daughter of the first VP, we get a different result. In this case, the clitic attaches to whichever constituent is immediately lower than AUX in the tree. Thanks to the SOV word order, in this situation that constituent will usually be the verb. We can see an example of this structure in the tree in figure 4.2.

4.4 A preliminary Lexical Functional Grammar analysis of Wakhi clitics

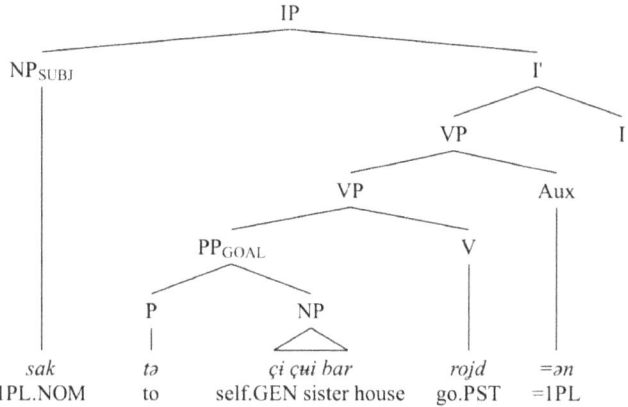

Figure 4.2. C-STR for example (38).

The recursive nature of the phrase structure rule in (41) allows us to generate multiple nested VPs. Not every VP is required to have an AUX sister (other potential sisters are defined by phrase structure rules not included here), but that does not mean that only one VP can have an AUX sister. In fact, AUX can appear multiple times (or in a clause without a clitic, not at all) and at different levels of the tree, thus accounting both for multiple occurrences of a clitic in a single clause and for a clitic that is either non-2P or preverbal. Example trees for a clause including two clitics (including one non-2P clitic) and a preverbal clitic can be seen in figure 4.3 and figure 4.4, respectively.

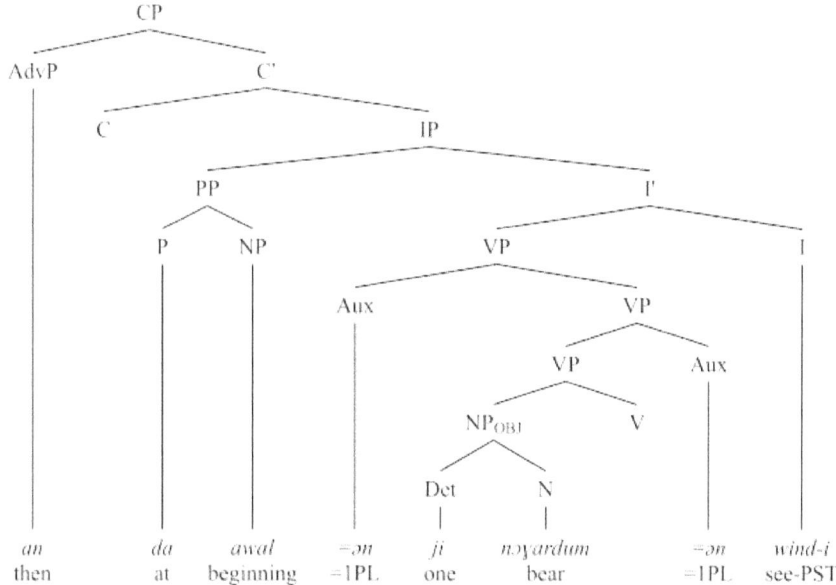

Figure 4.3. C-STR for example (40).

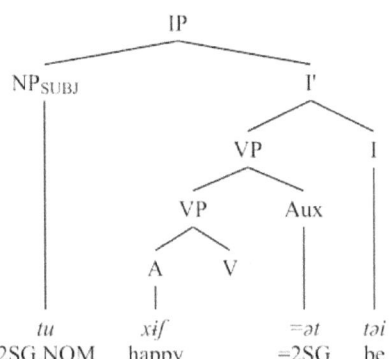

Figure 4.4. C-STR for example (10).[22]

As we can see, locating the clitic in AUX where AUX is the sister of a recursive VP is very powerful. Just this one simple phrase structure rule allows us to account for all of the clitic locations seen in this paper. We need to be careful when writing and applying rules such as this so that we do not give ourselves license to generate unattested or unnatural phrase structures. However, in the case of Wakhi clitics, I believe that the benefits of using such a powerful rule—namely, that it accounts for all of the data uniformly without positing separate classes of clitics or appealing to devices such as the doubly-filled COMP filter (DFCF) or prosodic inversion (PI)—outweigh the drawbacks. Furthermore, it opens the door to further discussion and analysis of Wakhi clitics from within the Lexical Functional Grammar (LFG) framework.

4.5 Conclusion

In conclusion, we have seen that Wakhi has both agreement clitics and TAM clitics. Although these clitics at times appear to move freely within their clause, a closer examination shows that they actually have two main preferred locations, Wackernagel position (2P) and preverbal position. Furthermore, multiple clitics can appear in the same minimal clause. I propose a phrase structure rule that places the Wakhi clitic in an AUX position that is sister to a recursive VP. Such a phrase structure rule includes the options necessary to locate a clitic in 2P, after a non-initial constituent, or in a preverbal or postverbal position and also allows for multiple manifestations of the same clitic within a clause.

---

[22] The copula has been added in this clause although it was null in the example as it was originally presented.

References

Anderson, Stephen R. 1993. Wackernagel's revenge: Clitics, morphology, and the syntax of second position. *Language*, 69(1):68–98.

Anderson, Stephen R. 2005. *Aspects of the theory of clitics*. Oxford: Oxford University Press.

Bashir, Elena. 1986. Beyond split-ergativity: Subject marking in Wakhi. In Ann M. Turley (ed.), *Papers from the General Session. Chicago Linguistic Society (CLS)*, 22:1(1):14–35.

Bashir, Elena. 2009. Wakhi. In Gernot Windfuhr (ed.), *The Iranian languages*, 825–861. London: Routledge.

Beck, Simone. 2013. Backgrounding and foregrounding, prominence, and highlighting in Afghan Wakhi. MA thesis. University of Gloucestershire, Cheltenham, UK.

Erschler, David. 2010. On optionality in grammar: The case of East Iranian almost Wackernagel clitics. Paper presented at the Syntax of the World's Languages IV, Lyon, September 23, 2010.

Fuchs, Zuzanna. 2015. Second position and "floating" clitics in Wakhi. In Anna E. Jurgensen, Hannah Sande, Spencer Lamoureu, Kenny Baclawski, and Alison Zerbe (eds.), *Proceedings of the Forty-first Annual Meeting of the Berkeley Linguistics Society, February 7–8, 2015*, 133–154. Berkeley: Berkeley Linguistics Society.

Grünberg, Alexander L., and I. M. Stéblin-Kamensky. 1976. *Vakhanskij jazyk.* [Wakhi language]. Moscow: Nauka.

Halpern, Aaron. 1995. *On the placement and morphology of clitics*. Dissertations in linguistics. Stanford: CSLI.

Hughes, Todd R. 2011. Wakhi agreement clitics. MA thesis. University of Florida, Gainesville.

Klavans, Judith L. 1995. *On clitics and cliticization: The interaction of morphology, phonology, and syntax*. New York: Garland Publishing.

Koopman, Hilda. 1996. The spec head configuration. *UCLA working papers in syntax and semantics*, 1:37–64.

Kroeger, Paul. 2005. *Analyzing grammar: An introduction*. Cambridge: Cambridge University Press.

Lewis, M. Paul, Gary F. Simons, and Charlie D. Fennig. 2013. *Ethnologue: Languages of the world*. Dallas: SIL International. http://www.ethnologue.com.

Nevis, Joel A. 1988. *Finnish particle clitics and general clitic theory*. Outstanding Dissertations in Linguistics. New York: Routledge.

Wackernagel, Jacob. 1892. Über ein Gesetz der indogermanischen Wortstellung. *Indogermanische Forschungen*, 1:333–436.

Zwicky, Arnold M. 1977. *On clitics*. Bloomington: Indiana University Linguistics Club.

5

Complex Converbal Predicates in Afghan Turkmen

Nathaniel Shaver
SIL Global

Abstract

In this paper, I examine the syntactic properties of converbal or -IB constructions[1] in Afghan Turkmen,[2] where the designation -IB refers to *-ip/-up* or *-ib/-ub* suffixed verbs.[3] Although, -IB constructions might be described as having coordinate syntax (formed by more than one clause), further examination shows that some -IB constructions exhibit conjoined syntax (multiple predicates within a minimal clause). I provide evidence for the conjoined nature of certain -IB constructions in Afghan Turkmen through a variety of grammatical tests. Next I note that, in Turkic languages, mono-clausal -IB constructions have been analyzed as 1) constructions formed with a main verb and a semantically bleached verb functioning as an auxiliary or 2) as complex predicates formed with a main verb and a light verb.[4] I follow the second analysis. Finally, I offer several tests that distinguish between auxiliaries and light verbs.

---

[1] There are a number of overlapping terms in this paper. -IB verbs, converbs, and gerunds refer to the same thing. Historically, Turkic linguistics has preferred the term gerund over these others (Clifton 2002:i).

[2] During the Soviet era, Yomut and Teke dialects of Turkmen were selected for standardization in Turkmenistan (Rasekh 2016a:1). This paper will refer to these simply as Turkmen. Afghan Turkmen refers to the language spoken across the border in northern Afghanistan that is primarily made up of speakers from the Ä:rsa:rı dialect (2016b:1).

[3] This paper is dedicated to the memory of Simone Beck. Her legacy of sacrificial service and advocacy for the less powerful languages of Afghanistan continues to promote their betterment, even in her absence. You are dearly missed, Simone. Many thanks to the Afghan Turkmen community. They were always happy to answer questions and offer feedback throughout the course of this research. Their patient collaboration greatly improved the quality of this paper and removed many errors. I accept sole responsibility for any remaining mistakes.

[4] The term *light verb* is not without its problems. Since Jespersen (1964:117) first coined the term, it has been used to refer to a verb in a number of construction types. These include a V+V and N+V, as well as verb constructions where the verb has no semantic content and either the heavy verb or the noun is the main predicate. The way I employ it throughout this paper is a construction where both the light and heavy verbs contribute to the lexical predicate (Butt and Geuder (2001:333). This has some overlap with the notion of cosubordination in Role and Reference Grammar (Van Valin and LaPolla (1997:117).

5.1 Introducing converbal constructions

A converb, also known as an -IB verb, refers to a verb that receives very little marking aside from the final *-ip/-up, -ib/-ub* suffix.[5] These verbs occur frequently in Turkic languages, often in groups of two or more in a given sentence. The minimal marking on -IB verbs is typically resolved by the final finite verb, which receives tense, person, and number marking.[6] Clark (1998a:350) describes converbs as "non-final verbs that express action which adds to or clarifies the action of the main verb." Example (1) appears in Clark (1998b:356).

(1) Ялкап   болса   еринден   туруп,   хошлашып   чыкып
    Yalka:p bolθo   yerinden   turup,   hošlošup   čıkıp
    Y.   then   there-ABL   stand-CVB,   welcome-CVB   go.out-CVB
    гитди
    gitdi
    go.PST.3SG
    And Yalkap stood up and went out to welcome them.

Here, three -IB verbs *turup, hošlošup,* and *čıkıp* appear together with the final verb *gitdi*. Despite having the same marking, Clark notes that the three -IB verbs function differently. He categorizes *turup* as a clause-chaining gerund and *hošlošup,* as adverbial. The third, *čıkıp*, combines with the finite verb *gitdi* to form a complex predicate. Clark's claim is that, in spite of their identical marking, converbs have a variety of functions. Different functions suggest that these converbs exhibit various types of syntactic structures. In this paper, I examine whether converbs are a part of single clause or multi-clause constructions. Aside from pragmatic inference, how might one determine this? In fact, a number of grammatical tests exist that can be used for such a task.

5.2 Varieties of converbal constructions in Turkic languages

A glance at the literature quickly reveals that various types of -IB constructions have been identified (Soper (1996); Johanson (1995); Bowern (2004); Clark (1998); and Hoey (2013)).

Soper (1996) identifies three types. The first type **coordinates actions**, where the -IB verb modifies the action of the inflected verb. This would be the same function as *čıkıp* in example (1). The second type is **sequential/connected actions** where the two verbs stand in equal relationship. This is how *turup* is functioning in example (1). In the third type, the *second verb* (inflecting)

---

[5] Depending on the Turkic language, the final consonant is either voiced *-ib/-ub*, or voiceless *-ip/-up*. In Afghan Turkmen, the final consonant is /p/, while the final vowel is influenced by vowel harmony. For example, the converb of *turmak* 'to stand' is *turup*, but the converb of *gitmek* 'to go' is *gitip*. Despite the difference in voicing of the final consonant in Afghan Turkmen, I will continue to refer to them as -IB verbs or constructions rather than -IP constructions.

[6] Occasionally, a sentence may have only converbs, leaving the inflectional marking to be resolved through pragmatic inference.

is comparable to an **auxiliary or directional** giving more information about the -IB marked verb. Example (14) illustrates this variety where the final verb *otyrdu* gives more information about the converb *juwdurup*.

Johanson (1995:314–315) describes four types of -IB constructions that differ in degree of grammaticalization.[7] The first type **coordinates** clauses and has different subjects ('When Ali came, Osman was surprised.'). The second is also **coordinating**, but has one subject, who performs multiple actions ('When Ali came, he was surprised.'). The third is **conjoined**, having one subject but two predicate cores ('Ali brought a book.' [take-CVB bring]). The fourth is a **single predicate** ('Ali kept on reading a book.' [read-CVB stand/stop]). These predicates range from two lexically independent verbs 'came' and 'surprised' that possess two subjects (less grammatical) in the first type, to the fourth type that Johanson calls a single predicate comprised of two verbs with only one subject.

While Soper and Johanson note the possibility of different converbal constructions, they treat them the same syntactically. However, Bowern argues that Soper's type three and Johanson's type four have an underlying syntax that differs from that of coordinating -IB constructions (Bowern 2004:4). She describes these as complex predicates which denote a single event and behave as a single syntactic unit. These complex predicates are formed by a main verb and a light verb.

While Soper, Johnson, and Bowern draw from a variety of Turkic languages, I am specifically interested in examining **conjoined** converbal constructions in Afghan Turkmen. That is, converbal constructions that are syntactically monoclausal. Before beginning this discussion in section 5.3, I rule out the varieties of -IB constructions that are **coordinating** (those that have multi-clausal syntax).

5.3 Varieties of converbal constructions in Afghan Turkmen

Both Hoey (2013:58) and Clark (1998:350–356) offer the following varieties of -IB constructions in Turkmen: sequential, simultaneous, and manner. Hoey adds a fourth variety he calls "relative anteriority". I will examine each of these in turn beginning with **sequential** as seen in example (2).

(2) tur-up   el   ýüzüm   ýuw-up   mekdeb-e git-dim
    get.up-CVB hand face-1SG.POSS wash-CVB school-DAT go-PST.1SG
    'I woke up, washed my hands and face, and went to school.'

Coordinating and conjoined -IB constructions do not exhibit the same syntactic qualities. One way that they differ is that, in conjoined constructions, the converb immediately precedes the main (finite) verb without intervening words or grammatical elements. However, in example (2) we find intervening items. *El ýüzüm* comes between the -IB verbs *turup* and *ýuwup*, while *mekdeb-e* comes between *ýuwup* and the final finite verb *gitdim*. Having intervening items suggests a multi-clause syntax (coordinating).

---

[7] Heine and Narrog define grammaticalization "as the development from lexical to grammatical forms, and from grammatical to even more grammatical forms" (2015:407).

Furthermore, multiple intonation curves provide evidence of a multi-clausal structure. The curved lines in example (2) and following show where slight pauses occur during articulation.[8] One would expect a single articulation curve if (2) were mono-clausal, since there is a correspondence between no pauses during articulation and tighter syntax. Single event, complex predicates fall under one intonation curve (Durie 1997:291) and (Kroeger 2004:229).

Next, we examine the **simultaneous** -IB construction variety. Example (3) comes from Hoey (2013:58).

(3) syr-yp   aýdym aýt-ýa:r
    shave-CVB song tell-PRS.3SG
    'He's shaving and singing.'

Here, the intonation curve indicates that there is no pause during articulation. Although, *aýdym* might appear to be an intervening item between the converb *syryp* and the finite verb, it is not. This is a light verb construction formed by a N+v, much the same as in Dari where *to talk* is 'speech+hit'. The converb and the light verb predicate appear immediately adjacent to one another making a conjoined analysis plausible for this variety.

Next, we consider the **manner** -IB construction variety. The converb modifies the main verb, indicating the manner of action. There are two possible interpretations that are shown in (4) and (5).

(4) Гүлүп   гитди
    Gül-üp   git-di.
    laugh-CVB   go-PST.3SG   (coordinate-structure)

(5) Гүлүп   гитди
    Gül-üp   git-di.
    laugh-CVB   go-PST.3SG   (conjoined)
    'She went away laughing.'

This example could either receive a single event reading (5) (conjoined structure) or a multiple event reading (4) (coordinate structure) with either one or two intonation curves respectively.

The final -IB variety is **relative anteriority**. Relative anteriority denotes two events, one of which has been completed prior to the event in focus.

(6) okuw tamamla:-p   uniwersited-e gi:r-ip-dir
    school complete-CVB   university-DAT enter-PRSM-PST.3SG
    'Having finishing school, he has entered university.'

The intonation curve and intervening material suggest that this example has multi- rather than mono-clausal syntax. In these four examples, the manner and simultaneous -IB varieties are the most likely to exhibit conjoined syntax.

5.4 Mono-clausality tests for complex predicates

Up to this point, I have drawn on examples from Turkmen of Turkmenistan. The examples in the remainder of this paper come from Afghan Turkmen. I use

---

[8] These intonation curves do not represent tone. They represent pauses corresponding to clausal boundaries.

5.4 Mono-clausality tests for complex predicates

a variety of tests to demonstrate the mono-clausal nature of these converbal predicates.

5.4.1 Reflexive and non-reflexive pronouns

In his *Lectures on Government and Binding*, Chomsky (1981:188) proposes two relevant principles that allow us to test clause boundaries using reflexive and non-reflexive pronouns. He states, "A) An anaphor is bound in its governing category. B) A pronominal is free in its governing category." By anaphors, Chomsky means reflexives and reciprocals. Alternatively, we might say A) a reflexive pronoun and its antecedent must be clause mates of the same minimal clause and B) a non-reflexive (regular pronoun) and its antecedent cannot be clause mates of the same minimal clause. Example (7) shows that principle A) holds true in Afghan Turkmen.[9]

(7) (mɛn) œz-ym-i/ *mɛn-i ɣur-at-dɯm
 (1SG) self-1SG-ACC/ *1SG-ACC dry-CAUS-PST.1SG
 'I dried myself/*me.'

(من) اؤزؤمي/*مني غۇراتدىم.

The reflexive pronoun *œzymi* is grammatical since its antecedent '1SG' is marked on the verb and is in the same minimal clause. Alternatively, the regular pronoun *mɛni* is ungrammatical because its antecedent would be in the same minimal clause.

If we extend principle A) to a situation where a converbal predicate occurs, it still holds true. In example (8), the converb *ɣuradɯp* and the inflecting verb *otyrtɯm* are co-predicators within the same minimal clause.

(8) œz-ym-i/ *mɛn-i ɣurad-ɯp ot-yr-tɯm
 self-1SG-ACC/ *1SG-ACC dry-CVB sit-STV-PST.1SG
 'I was drying myself/*me.'

اؤزؤمي/*مني غۇرادىپ اۆتىرتىم.

As is the case for a simple predicate (7), the reflexive pronoun *œzymi* is also grammatically correct for the converbal predicate (8). This would indicate that 'myself' and its antecedent, 'I', are clause mates of the same minimal clause, in spite of the two predicating items. While the presence of a reflexive in a clause with multiple predicating items is not absolutely conclusive, its presence points toward a mono-clausal analysis.

Next, we see that Principle B) holds true in Afghan Turkmen as well. A regular pronoun (non-reflexive) and its antecedent may NOT co-occur in the same minimal clause.

---

[9] Due to dialect differences between Turkmen and Afghan Turkmen, certain vowels differ. The process I followed during transcription was to work from Arabic Script into IPA. Many words retain the same vowels, but others like *œzymi* differ. In Northern Turkmen, the correct IPA equivalent spelling is *œzymɛ*.

(9) (ol) mɛn-i/ *œz-ym-i ɣur-at-dɯ
    (3SG) 1SG-ACC/ *self-1SG-ACC dry-CAUS-PST.3SG
    'He dried me/*myself.'

(اؤل) مني/*اؤزؤمي غۇراتدي.

Example (9) is the same as (7), but the final verb has been changed to 3SG instead of 1SG. The pronoun *mɛn-i*, and its antecedent are no longer clause mates of the same minimal clause, since the antecedent presumably refers to someone already introduced in the discourse. The regular pronoun is grammatically correct here.

Principle B) also holds true in a situation where a converbal predicate occurs. In example (10), the regular pronoun is used in a subordinate clause, since its antecedent occurs in the matrix clause.

(10) (sɛn) ata-ŋ sɛn-i/ *œz-yŋ-i juw-up
     (2SG) father-2SG-POSS 2SG-ACC/ *self-2SG-ACC wash-CVB
     otɯra-nɯ-na bɛgɛn-diŋ-mi?
     sit-POSS-DAT be.happy-PST.2.SG-Q
     'Were you happy (that) your father was washing you/*yourself?'

(سن) آتاڭ سني/*اؤزؤڭي يوووپ اۇتىرانڭنا بگندیڭمي؟

In example (10), the converbal predicate *juwup otɯranɯna* occurs in the subordinate clause. The antecedent to the 2SG-ACC, 'you', lies outside the subordinate clause. Accordingly, the regular rather than the reflexive pronoun is grammatical. The presence of the regular pronoun does not indicate monoclausality. Instead, it provides evidence of a clause boundary corresponding to the subordinate clause. Chomsky's Principles provide helpful parameters for testing clause boundaries.

5.4.2 Causatives

In addition to reflexive and non-reflexive pronouns, causatives may be used to test the syntactic makeup of converbal predicates. Three types of causatives exist, periphrastic, lexical, and morphological. The syntax of these three may be affected by three semantic qualities 1) degree of control, 2) direct vs. indirect causation, and 3) physical manipulation vs. verbal directive. There is a strong correlation between direct causation and morphological causatives (Kroeger 2004:193). This paper only interacts with morphological causatives.

Like applicatives, causatives are a valence-increasing function. However, where applicatives add a new object, causatives introduce a new subject. Introducing a new subject creates a problem for languages because typically a subject already exists. Due to the Uniqueness Condition, both the old and new subjects cannot receive the same grammatical marking.[10] Patterns emerge for how languages handle this situation.

---

10 The Uniqueness Condition states that "no argument relation may be assigned more than once within a single functional structure" (Kroeger 2004a:20). This means that "any single clause may contain no more than one SBJ or OBJ" (2004b:224).

5.4 Mono-clausality tests for complex predicates

Turkic languages have a morphologically productive causative. Most verbs can be made into a causative by adding the suffix *-tɯ/-dɯ*. Although causative morphology increases the valency of a verb, it does not affect the number of clauses present. An intransitive verb becomes transitive with causative morphology. Example (11) demonstrates this.

(11) (a) Nɑwid-Ø jɯqɯ-l-dɯ.
Nawid-NOM fall-REFL-PST.3SG
'Nawid fell.' (intransitive)

نويد يېقېلدي.

(b) Hɑsɑn-Ø Nɑwid-i jɯqɯ-tɯ-dɯ.
Hasan-NOM Nawid-ACC fall-CAUS-PST.3SG
'Hasan made Nawid fall.' (transitive)

حسن نويدي يېقېتدي.

The subject of the intransitive sentence (11a) becomes the ACC marked undergoer/causee of (11b) which has been made transitive by the causative suffix *-tɯ* of the verb *jɯqɯ-tɯ-dɯ*. Meanwhile, the causer/actor takes NOM case in (11b).

When the subject of (11a) became the causee/object of (11b), it was able to take ACC case because there was no ACC-marked object. Example (12) shows what happens to the causee when a transitive sentence with an ACC-marked object becomes causative.

(12) (a) (mɛn) œz-ym-i juw-dɯm
1SG-NOM self-1SG-ACC wash-PST.1SG
'I washed myself.' (transitive)

(من) اؤزؤمي يۇودېم.

(b) Nɑwid-ø mɑŋ-a œz-ym-i juw-dɯr-dɯ
Nawid-NOM 1SG-DAT self-1SG-ACC wash-CAUS-PST.3SG
'Nawid made me wash myself.' (ditransitive)

نويد ماڭا اؤزؤمي يۇودېردي.

The causative verb *juwdurdu* takes two objects in (12b), 'me' and 'myself'. The object of the transitive sentence (12a) *œzymi* remains the ACC-marked object of (12b), while the subject of the transitive verb 1SG-NOM *mɛn* (12a) becomes the DAT-marked second-object/causee of (12b).

We see a pattern emerging. The causee will take the next available grammatical relation. Dryer partially addressed this by noting that languages fall into two groups with regard to how they express the ditransitive root of a verb like *give* < agent, recipient, theme > (1986:821–824). The recipient will either be realized as the primary object (OBJ), and the patient as the secondary object (OBJ$_2$). Or as is the case with Afghan Turkmen, the theme is realized as the primary object while the recipient is realized as the secondary object (OBJ$_2$).

Figure 5.1 displays these two patterns.[11]

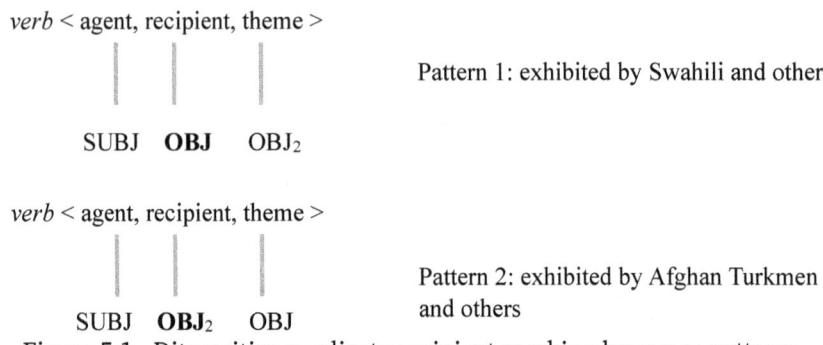
Figure 5.1. Ditransitive predicate recipient-marking language patterns.

Baker (1988) applies Dryer's patterns to causative constructions. Languages following Pattern 2 where the recipient is expressed as OBJ₂ will strongly tend toward expressing a causee as OBJ₂. Figure 5.2 displays this correlation.

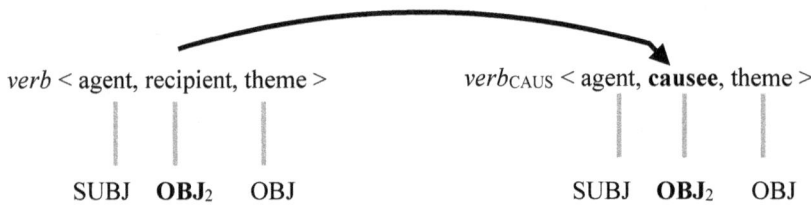
Figure 5.2. Recipient and causee correspondence in Pattern 2 languages.

Comrie (1989a) provides a framework within which to fit Dryer and Baker's observations. It is known as the Hierarchy of Grammatical Relations: subject > direct object > indirect object > oblique object. This hierarchy predicts how a causee will be expressed. "The causee occupies the highest (leftmost) position on this hierarchy that is not already filled" (1989b:176). Thus, 'me' is marked as DAT (OBJ₂) in example (12b) since the direct object (OBJ) slot is already taken by the ACC marked (OBJ) *æzymi*. Kroeger (2004:193) provides a helpful visual of Comrie's Relational Hierarchy, which I modify in figure 5.3.

Subcategorization of basic (underived) verb	Grammatical relation of CAUSEE	Subcategorization of derived causative verbs
{SUBJ}	OBJ ⟶	{SUBJ, OBJ}
{SUBJ, OBJ}	OBJ₂ ⟶	{SUBJ, OBJ, OBJ₂}
{SUBJ, OBJ, OBJ₂}	OBL ⟶	{SUBJ, OBJ, OBJ₂, OBL}

Figure 5.3. Prediction of the causee's grammatical relation.

Comrie's prediction of the causee's grammatical relation offers another possibility for testing the syntactic makeup of Afghan Turkmen converbal

---

[11] Figures 5.1 to 5.3 are recreated and modified with permission from Dr. Kroeger.

5.4 Mono-clausality tests for complex predicates

predicates. When we compare the causee in a simple causative sentence and the causee in a converbal causative predicate, we see that they both receive the same grammatical relation. This provides evidence that the converb and finite verb are acting as a single complex verbal unit.[12] We review (12) in (13), paying closer attention to the grammatical relation of the causee.

(13) (a) (mɛn)   œz-ym-i   juw-dɯm
         1SG-NOM self-1SG-ACC wash-PST.1SG
         'I washed myself.'

         (من) اؤزؤمي يؤودۇم.

   (b) Nawid-ø   **maŋ-a** œz-ym-i   juw-dɯr-dɯ
       Nawid-NOM **1SG-DAT** self-1SG-ACC wash-CAUS-PST.3SG
       'Nawid made **me** wash myself.'

       نوید مانا اؤزؤمي يؤودۇبردي.

The transitive verb in (13a) would receive the following subcategorization *wash* {SBJ, OBJ}. Adding the causative suffix *-dɯr* to *juwdɯm* in (13b) increases its valency making it a ditransitive verb. This derived verb would receive the following subcategorization *wash*$_{CAUS}${agent$_{SBJ}$, causee$_{OBJ_2}$, patient$_{OBJ}$}. Comrie's hierarchy correctly predicts that the causee in (13b) will receive OBJ$_2$ grammatical relations. The actor in (13a) *mɛn* becomes the causee in (13b) *maŋ-a* and receives DAT (OBJ$_2$)-marking, while the patient, *œzymi*, is marked as ACC (OBJ) in both (13a) and (13b).

The causee follows the same pattern in a converbal predicate as seen in example (14).

(14) Nawid-ø   **maŋ-a** œz-ym-i   juw-dɯr-ɯp   otir-dɯ
     Nawid-NOM **1SG-DAT** self-1SG-ACC wash-CAUS-CVB sit-PST.3SG.
     'Nawid was making **me** wash myself/*me.'

     نوید مانا اؤزؤمي/*مني يؤودۇبرىپ اؤتبردي.

Example (14) is identical to (13b) except for the addition of the converbal predicate *juwdɯrɯp otyrdɯ*. Like (13b), the causee is marked as OBJ$_2$. The complex predicate would receive the following subcategorization (*wash*$_{CAUS}$ + *sit*){agent$_{SBJ}$, causee$_{OBJ_2}$, patient$_{OBJ}$}. In spite of the additional verb, no more arguments are added to the subcategorization of the simple predicate *wash*$_{CAUS}$ (13b). The two verbs in (14) are mutually governing. V1 receives causative marking, while person, number, and tense are marked on V2.[13] Yet, in actuality, the various markings affect the entire complex predicate not just

---

[12] Recall that the Uniqueness Condition only constrains grammatical relations within a single clause. If a construction was multi-clausal, more than one NOM-marked subject and ACC-marked object could occur. The fact that the causee of a simple causative and converbal predicate causative receive the same grammatical relation indicates that they are both constrained by the Uniqueness Condition. Hence, they are both mono-clausal.

[13] V1 refers to the first verb of a complex predicate and V2 to the second.

each individual verb. The interdependent marking on these verbs, combined with identical marking of the causee in (13) and (14), suggests a much tighter syntactic structure than could be present in multi-clausal constructions.

5.4.3 Passivization and intonation curves

So far, I have used pronouns and causative constructions to test converbal predicates. Next, I discuss what patterns converbal predicates follow when they undergo passivization.

We saw earlier that causatives increase the valency of verbs by adding a new subject core argument. In contrast, passives may be described as detransitivizing or as a valence-decreasing process. That is, a passive removes a core argument from a verb. A ditransitive verb becomes transitive, a transitive verb becomes intransitive.

Afghan Turkmen allows a verb to undergo both causative and passive processes at the same time. If a new subject argument gets added by a causative, which argument is taken away by the passivizing processes? This is what we will examine next. Passivizing processes provide an opportunity to test the syntactic qualities of converbal predicates by comparing them with passivizing patterns of simple predicates. Aissen (1974:327–330) demonstrates that a morphologically productive Turkish causative Ss behaves the same as simplex Ss with respect to passivization and relativization. The same holds true for Afghan Turkmen.

In Afghan Turkmen, the passive is morphologically productive and is formed by adding the suffix *-il*. For example, *uruʃdurmaq* 'to fight' becomes *uruʃdurulmak* 'to be fought'. When the base verb of a causative construction is intransitive, the **causee** becomes the subject of its passive counterpart.

(15) (a) Hɛr gyn Nawid **toqlar-ɯ** uruʃ-dɯr-jor
Every day Nawid **chickens-ACC** fight-CAUS-IPFV.3SG
'Every day, Nawid is causing the **chickens** to fight.'
(intransitive-base verb)

هرگۆن نوید تۆوقلاري اۆرۆشدیریۆر.

(b) **Toqlar** gyn-da Nawid tarafyndan
Chickens day-LOC Nawid by
uruʃ-dɯr-ɯl-jor
fight-CAUS-PASS-IPFV.3SG
'The **chickens** are caused to fight every day by Nawid.'
(intransitive causative + passive verb)

تۆوقلار گۆنده نوید طرفیندان اۆرۆشدیریلیۆر.

In example (15a), the causee, *toqlarɯ* 'chickens-ACC', becomes the subject of the passive sentence in (15b).

However, if the base verb of a causative construction is transitive, the **basic patient** *rather than the causee* is promoted to the passive SBJ.

5.4 Mono-clausality tests for complex predicates

(16) (a) Gyn-dɑ Mɑtin-ɑ kɛtɑb-ɯ gœr-kɛz-jor-tɯm
day-LOC Matin-DAT book-ACC see-CAUS-IPFV-PST.1SG
'Every day, I kept on showing Matin the *book*.' (show = cause to see) (transitive-base verb)

گۆنده متینه کتابی گۆرکزیۆرتم.

(b) *Kɛtɑb* mɛn tɑrɑfɛmdɛn Mɑtin-ɑ
book 1SG by Matin-DAT
gœr-kɛz-il-jor-tɯ
see-CAUS-PASS-IPFV-PST.3SG
'The *book* was being shown to Matin by me.' (transitive CAUS + PASS verb)

کتاب من طرفمدان متینه گۆرکزیلیۆرتی.

In (16a), the basic patient (in this case the stimulus), *kɛtɑb-ɯ* 'book-ACC', is promoted to the passive subject of (16b), rather than the causee *Mɑtin-ɑ*. These patterns of passive subject promotion are illustrated in figure 5.4.

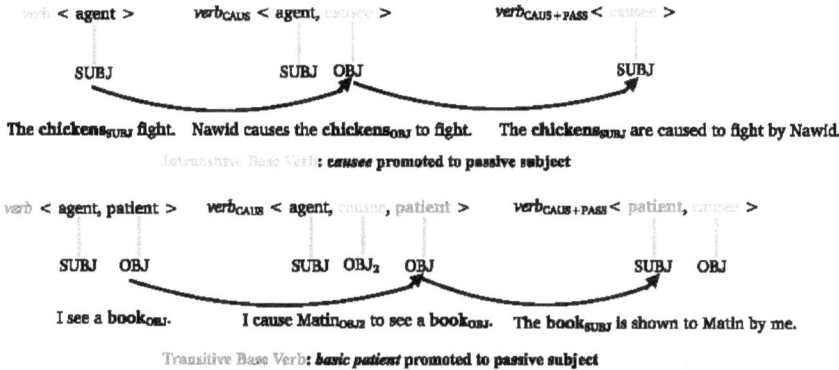

Figure 5.4. Passive promotion patterns for intransitive and transitive base verbs.

The same patterns of passive subject promotion occur for causative converbal predicates, providing evidence of mono-clausality. Example (15) is repeated in (17), but includes a converbal predicate.

(17) (a) Hɛr gyn Nawid **toqlar-ɯ** uruʃ-dɯr-ɯp jœri-jor
Every day Nawid **chickens-ACC** fight-CAUS-CVB walk-IPFV.3SG
'Every day, Nawid is causing the chickens to continue fighting.' (intransitive base verb)

هرگۆن نوید توۆقلاری اوروشدرپپ یۆریپۆر.

(b) **Toqlar** gyn-da Nawid tarafɯndan uruʃ-dɯr-ɯl-ɯp
Chickens day-LOC Nawid by fight-CAUS-PASS-CVB
jœr-il-jor-tɯ
walk-PASS-IPFV-PST.3SG
'The **chickens** were being caused to fight every day by Nawid.' (intransitive CAUS + PASS verb)

توۆقلار گۆنده نوید طرفیندان اوروشدرپلپپ یۆریلیۆرتی.

Example (17a) follows the pattern of (15) where the **causee** is promoted to the passive subject of (17b). The presence of the two verbals in (17a) does not disrupt this pattern. The original subject 'Nawid' is demoted to an oblique argument, *Nawid tarafunden*, which may be deleted without affecting the grammaticality of the sentence.

Likewise the pattern of passive promotion stays the same for a transitive-base verb and its converbal predicate counterpart. This is illustrated in example (18).

(18) (a) Gyn-da Matin-a kɛtab-ɯ gœr-kɛz-ip otɯr-jor-ɯn
Day-LOC Matin-DAT book-ACC see-CAUS-CVB sit-IPFV-1SG
'I daily keep on showing Matin the *book*.' (transitive base verb)

گۆنده متینه کتابی گۆرکزیپ اۆتریۆربن.

(b) *Kɛtab* mɛn tarafɛmdɛn Matin-a gœr-kɛz-ɯl-ip
Book 1SG by Matin-DAT see-CAUS-PASS-CVB
otɯr-jor-tɯ
sit-IPFV-PST.3SG
'The *book* was being shown to Matin by me.'
(transitive CAUS + PASS verb)

کتاب من طرفمدان متینه گۆرکزیلیپ اۆتریۆرتی.

In (16b) the *basic patient*, **rather than the causee**, was promoted to the passive subject. The same pattern is observed with the converbal predicate counterpart in (18). The basic patient '*book*' and not the causee '**Matin**' is promoted as the passive subject in (18b).

These complex predicates follow the same patterns of passive promotion as their non-complex counterparts. If the causee, the DAT marked OBJ$_2$ *Matin-a*, were promoted to the passive subject, the sentence would be ungrammatical

5.4 Mono-clausality tests for complex predicates

(*Matin men tarafemden ketab-i görkezilip otirýorty). In fact, the inability to promote a DAT object to passive SBJ is true for causative Ss and simplex Ss (Aissen 1974:330). In Afghan Turkmen, we can add to Aissen's observation by saying that simplex Ss, causative Ss, and causative$_{complexpred}$ Ss all behave the same with regard to passivization when the causative$_{complexpred}$ belongs to a mono-clausal, complex converbal construction.

Furthermore, the intonation curves show that there are no pauses during the articulation of these examples. This is consistent with grammatical theories such as Role and Reference Grammar that see pauses corresponding to syntactic separation. Van Valin (2005:6) describes how elements that are internal to a simple sentence but clause-external are set off by a pause. These include items that are in either the Right/Left Displaced Position. They are separated both syntactically and phonologically from the clause.

Additionally, in discussing the correlation between linguistically coded information and articulation, Givón (1990:24) argues that the "temporal-physical distance between chunks of linguistically coded information correlates directly to the conceptual distance between them." Pauses in speech signal syntactic separation. He goes on to discuss complex predicates which have a single-event interpretation saying, if these "reflect a unique strategy of cognitive segmentation of 'events', then pauses of the type that characteristically appear – in non-serializing languages such as English – at the boundaries of main/finite verbal clauses will also appear in serial-verb languages at serial clause boundaries." In example (18), although the absence of pauses does not prove the absence of clause boundaries, their presence would certainly imply syntactic separation.

5.4.4 The problem of unmarked coordination

Before continuing with other grammatical tests, it is necessary to discuss the problem of unmarked coordination. Afghan Turkmen exhibits coordination among noun phrases, elements within a noun phrase, and among verb phrases (Hoey 2013a:75). The same coordinators are used for all of these. They include the Arabic/Persian *we, hem(-de)* 'and', and *emma:, ýö:ne* 'but' as well as the *-dA* focus particle of Turkic origin (2013b:75). While an overt marker of coordination may appear between clauses, unmarked coordination with the -IB suffix is quite common. Recall examples (4) and (5), *Gülüp gitdi*, could either be understood as having conjoined syntax (mono-clausal) 'He/she left laughing,' or having unmarked coordinate syntax (multi-clausal) 'He/she laughed (and) left.' This is problematic since the two forms have identical marking.

When coordinate markers appear between verbs, two or more S constituents occur as daughters of and co-heads of a higher S (Kroeger 2004:40). This is depicted in figure 5.5.

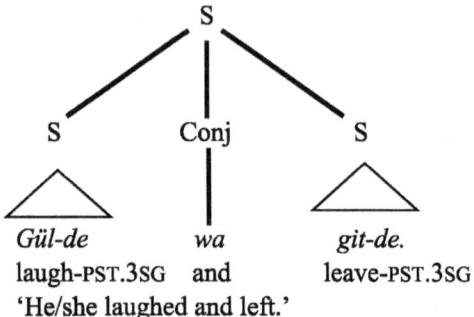

Figure 5.5. S-STRUCTURE of marked coordinate clauses in Afghan Turkmen.

Anywhere an overt coordinating conjunction occurs between two Ss, we can expect multi-clausal syntax. Unmarked coordination has the same S-STRUCTURE, but without the overt conjunction. In example (5), the -IB suffix along with intonation signals the coordinate syntax. Notice in figure 5.5, the finite form of both verbs occurs. This allows for the presence of *wa*. The sentence would be ungrammatical if a *wa* was inserted between a converb and a finite verb *Gülüp wa gitdi* even if a coordinate statement was intended.

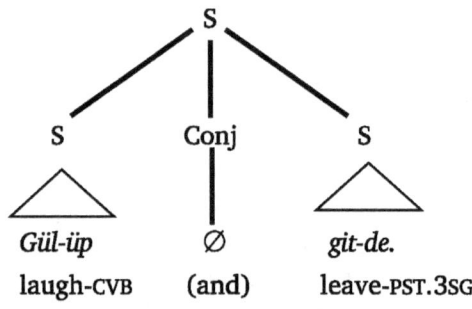

Figure 5.6. S-STRUCTURE of unmarked coordinate clauses in Afghan Turkmen.

In order to demonstrate that converbal predicates are mono-clausal, it is necessary to show that they do not exhibit unmarked coordination. A number of tests may be employed to distinguish predicates with unmarked coordination (figure 5.6) from complex predicates with conjoined syntax. These tests include 1) scope of negation, 2) licensing of negative concord items, and 3) filler gap constructions.

5.4.5 Scope of negation and licensing of negative concord items

The predicating items of a complex predicate are restricted in how they function together. One of these restrictions deals with polarity. The verbs in a complex predicate must share the same polarity (Durie 1997:291). It would be ungrammatical to assert the truth of one verb while negating the other (Kroeger 2004a:230). Observe what happens when we test this in example

5.4 Mono-clausality tests for complex predicates

(19). In unmarked coordination, it is possible to negate either verb. But in a conjoined predicate, it is possible to negate only one of the verbs (Kroeger 2004b:231).

(19) (a) (Ol) nɑ:n ij-ip jɑt-ir
3SG food eat-CVB lay-STV.3SG
'He is eating food.' (conjoined)

(اؤل) نان ایىپ یاتیر.

(b) (Ol) nɑ:n ij-**mæn** jɑt-ir
3SG food eat-NEG.CVB lay-STV.3SG
'He is not eating food.' (conjoined)

(اؤل) نان ایمأن یاتیر.

(c) (Ol) nɑ:n ij-ip jɑt-mɯz
3SG food eat-CVB lay-NEG.3SG
He ate food (but) did **not** lie down. (unmarked coordination)

#(اؤل) نان ایىپ یاتمىز.

It is possible to negate the value of the first verb (V1) in (19b) while still maintaining the conjoined reading.[14] However, if we negate the second verb (V2) (19c), the sentence proves to be infelicitous and would be understood as a multi-clausal statement. If both V1 and V2 are negated, *(Ol) nɑ:n ijmæn jɑtmɯz* 'He never goes to sleep (and not)/without) eating,' V1 and V2 are also no longer conjoined. Speakers prefer to rearrange this statement as *(Ol) jɑtmɯz, nɑ:n ijmæn*. This places *nɑ:n* between the verbal elements and clarifies that it is a multi-clausal statement.

Licensing of a negative concord item (NCI) can demonstrate whether or not a construction is unmarked coordination. Following Kuno (2007), Sugar (2018:4) says "an NCI expresses negation in tandem with a sentential negation marker." Furthermore, he notes that NCIs seem to be subject to the Clausemate Condition, meaning that they must appear in the same minimal clause as the negator that licenses it.[15] We see how this works out in example (20).

---

[14] While other Turkic languages allow the negative -IB form *ima(i)p*, Afghan Turkmen prefers to use the form ending in *-man* to negate the -IB form (for example, *ijip* is negated as *iman*). Clark (1998:344) notes this as a possible negative form of the past participle. He also offers the example on page 356 that follows the pattern of a verb being repeated, followed by the question particle where one is positive and one is negative. This construction communicates uncertainty. In this example, the negative -IB verb follows the *-man* form of the negative participle. *Gelipmi gelmänmi bilemdo:k.* 'We don't know whether she's coming or not.'

[15] Sugar cites Oyakawa (1975), Muraki (1978), and Kato (1985).

(20) (a) Hɛr gyn Nawid **hitʃ** toqlar-ɯ uruʃ-dɯr-**man**
Every day Nawid no chickens-ACC fight-CAUS-NEG.CVB
jœri-jor-tɯ
walk-IPFV-PST.3SG
'Every day, Nawid was causing no chickens to continue fight.'

هرگۆن نويد هيچ تۆوقلاري اۇرۇشدۇرمان يۆرييۇرتي.

(b) Hɛr gyn Nawid **hitʃ** toqlar-ɯ uruʃ-dɯr-ɯp
Every day Nawid no chickens-ACC fight-CAUS-CVB
jœri-**mi**-jor-tɯ
walk-NEG-IPFV-PST.3SG
'Every day, Nawid is causing no chickens to continue fighting.'

هرگۆن نويد هيچ تۆوقلاري اۇرۇشدۇرپ يۆريمييۇرتي.

In example (20), either V1 *uruʃdɯrmaq* 'to cause to fight' (20a) or V2 *jœrimek* 'to walk' (20b) may be negated to license the NCI *hitʃ* 'no'. Either verb may license *hitʃ* because V1 and V2 along with the direct object *toqlar-ɯ* are in the same clause. A verb that is separated by a clause boundary may not license the NCI. Such is the case with the sentence, **Nawid 'hɛr gyn mɛn hitʃ toqlar-ɯ uruʃ-dɯr-ɯp jœri-jor-dɯm,' di-ma-dɯ* *"'Every day, I was causing no chickens to fight,' Nawid said" (intended). An NCI and its licensing verb may not be separated by a clause boundary. Example (20) demonstrates that this converbal predicate is not unmarked coordination (multi-clausal) since either V1 or V2 are able to license the NCI.

5.4.6 Filler gap

Filler gap tests also demonstrate whether or not a construction exhibits unmarked coordination. Kroeger (2004:223) describes coordinate structures as "extraction islands," meaning they cannot contain a gap. In languages where this constraint applies, "neither object can be extracted from the coordinate structure." He offers an example from Sranan (Sebba 1987) 'Kofi shot Amba and killed Kwaku' and notes that, in this coordinate structure, it is not possible to extract either 'Amba' or 'Kwaku'. (*'Who did Kofi shoot Amba and kill?'). Complex converbal predicates, on the other hand, allow extraction of either object. Example (21) demonstrates this.

5.4 Mono-clausality tests for complex predicates

(21) (a) Mɛn Matin-dɛn kɛtab-ɯ bir oglan-a
1SG matin-ABL book-ACC a boy-DAT
gœr-kɛz-dir-ip ot-yr-tɯm.
show-CAUS-CAUS-CVB sit-STV-1SG.PST
'I made Matin keep on showing a boy the book.'

من متیندن کتابی بیر اوغلانا گؤرکزدیریپ اوتیرتیم.

(b) Mɛn Matin-dɛn bir oglan-a naːmɛ gœr-kɛz-dir-ip
1SG matin-ABL a boy-DAT what show-CAUS-CVB
ot-yr-tɯm?
sit-STV-1SG.PST
'I made Matin keep on showing a boy the what?'

من متیندن بیر اوغلانا نأمه گؤرکزدیریپ اوتیرتیم؟

(c) Mɛn Matin-dɛn kɛtab-ɯ kim-ɛ gœr-kɛz-dir-ip
1SG matin-ABL book-ACC who-DAT show-CAUS-CVB
ot-yr-tɯm?
sit-STV-1SG.PST
'I made Matin keep on showing who the book?'

من متیندن کتابی کیمه گؤرکزدیریپ اوتیرتیم؟

In example (21), it is possible to extract either object by using 'what' in (21b) and 'who' in (21c). The scope of negation, licensing of negative concord items, and filler gap tests demonstrate that these converbal predicates are not unmarked coordination, rather they are complex predicates exhibiting mono-clausal syntax.

5.4.7 Uniqueness of tense and aspect marking

Complex predicates must share tense, aspect, modality, and polarity (Durie 1997:291). Alternatively put, it is not possible for the two verbs in a complex predicate to be marked with differing tense and aspect markers. When we compare (16a) and (16b), we see that *-tɯm* indicates past tense for both verbs in (16b). When the tense marker is not present (16a), both verbs are present tense. Likewise, in (16b), the imperfective aspect marked on the final verb governs both verbs.

In this section, I have used a variety of grammatical tests to show the mono-clausal nature of conjoined converbal predicates. I also discussed the problem of distinguishing between unmarked coordination and complex predicates. In the next section, I discuss two analyses proposed for the verbs in a converbal predicate.

5.5 Auxiliary or light verb

A debate exists regarding the classification of V2 in certain converbal predicates. Some authors categorize the final verb as a semantically bleached verb that functions as an auxiliary. This analysis explains the converbal predicate's monoclausality in terms of V2 being an auxiliary rather than a main verb. One such author, Sugar (2018), draws on parallels from languages that allow V2s to be passivized themselves or select passivized complements, to propose a clausal spine for Uyghur with two locations for *-(ip)* converbs and two locations for bleached V2 auxiliaries.

In contrast to the auxiliary analysis, Bowern (2004:13) suggests that the V2 in a conjoined converbal predicate should be analyzed as a light verb. She argues that, while there are quite a number of light verbs in Turkic languages, they fall into only four types: 1) event structure, 2) selection criteria, 3) word order, and 4) interrogative marking. She adapts Lin's (2001) proposal that "different languages license differing degrees of lexicalization of light verb structures," by proposing a new tier to accommodate one of the four light verb types.

One way to decide which of these two analyses better explains the data is by looking at the characteristic properties of auxiliaries to see if the V2 in a conjoined converbal predicate exhibits them or not.

5.6 Characteristic properties of auxiliaries

In *The Category AUX as a Language Universal*, Steele (1978) provides some characteristic properties of auxiliaries that occur cross-linguistically. These include:

1. The presence of a surface unit separate from the main verb.
2. The AUX unit expressing modality, aspect, or tense.
3. The AUX and the main verb occurring in the same clause; that is, the main verb is not (at any point in the derivation) subordinate to the AUX.

Kroeger (2004:251–254) expounds on Steele's list of characteristic properties. He notes that auxiliaries do not function as independent semantic predicates. This means that 1) they do not take their own arguments, 2) their semantic content is grammatical rather than lexical, 3) they typically express elements such as tense, aspect, mood, voice, and polarity, 4) they do not assign semantic roles, and 5) they do not determine the number of arguments in a clause. These criteria may be used to distinguish auxiliaries from light verbs. I argue that V2s in conjoined converbal predicates do not exhibit these characteristics, suggesting a light verb rather than an auxiliary analysis.

5.6.1 Auxiliaries are grammatical rather than lexical

For V2 to be a bleached auxiliary, it cannot add any semantic content to the predicate. However, we see that the V2 retains semantic content in a converbal predicate. For instance, the final verb must be changed to *jatmaq* 'to lay',

5.6 Characteristic properties of auxiliaries

durmaq 'to stand', or *jœrimɛk* 'to walk' in example (22) to correspond with differing postures or motions of the actor.

(22) œz-ym-i/   *mɛn-i   ɣura-dɯp   ot-yr-tɯm
      self-1SG-ACC /*1SG-ACC   dry-CVB   sit-STV-1SG.PST
      'I was drying myself (sitting).'

اؤزیمی/*منی غورادیپ اؤتیرتیم.

If the actor were standing drying himself/herself, it would be infelicitous to use 'sit', 'walk' or 'lay' as V2.

5.6.2 Auxiliaries do not assign semantic roles

An auxiliary may not assign semantic roles. In example (23), the causative marking on V2 may affect the semantic roles. While the causative typically is marked on the converb (V1) and this marking governs both verbs, V2 also receives causative morphology in example (23).

(23) gyn-da   (mɛn)   Matin-a   œz-ym-i/   *mɛn-i   bir
      day-LOC   (1SG-NOM) Matin-DAT   self-1SG-ACC/ *1SG-ACC   A
      darak   al-dɯr-ɯp   dara-ta-jor-ɯn.
      comb   take-CAUS-CVB   comb-CAUS-IPFV-1SG
      'Every day, (I) am making Matin comb myself/*me (take up a comb, comb me).' (single event)

گۆنده (من) متینه اؤزؤمی/*منی بیر داراق آلدیریپ داراتیؤن.

Due to its causative nature, V2 is at least partially responsible for assigning the *agent* semantic role to 'I'. This would not be possible if V2 was a bleached auxiliary.

5.6.3 Auxiliaries and number of arguments in a clause

Auxiliaries do not determine the number of arguments in a clause. If V2 is a bleached auxiliary, it should not affect the number of arguments in a clause.

(24) (a) œz-ym-i/   *mɛn-i   ɣura-dɯp   ot-ɯr-tɯm
           self-1SG-ACC/ *1SG-ACC   dry-CVB   sit-STV-1SG.PST
           'I was drying myself.'

(من) اؤزؤمی/*منی غورادیپ اؤتیرتیم.

      (b) œz-ym-i/   *mɛn-i   *1SG-ACC   dry-CVB   bol-dɯm
           self-1SG-ACC/ *1SG-ACC   *1SG-ACC   dry-CVB   bol-dɯm
           *'I became dry.'

(من) *اؤزؤمی غورادیپ بؤلدیم.

Megerdoomian (2001:5) offers a test for a Persian complex predicate, where changing V2 (light verb) changes the transitivity of the sentence. This same test may be repeated with Afghan Turkmen providing evidence that V2 is a light verb. If the final verb in (24) is changed to *bolmak* 'to be, become', the sentence becomes ungrammatical. Even though everything before *bolmak* remains the same, the unaccusative nature of *bolmak* reduces the number of arguments in the sentence. So the subcategorization of *yuradɯp otɯrmak* 'to dry' <agent, patient> would differ from the subcategorization of *yuradɯp bolmak* 'to become dry' <patient>. Accordingly, the sentence would read *(Men) yuradɯp boldɯm* 'I became dry.' The core meaning of the predicate remains the same (that is, an individual changing state from wet to dry), but the choice of V2 changes the transitivity of the complex predicate, thus affecting its argument structure.

5.6.4 Auxiliaries have dependent status

Auxiliaries 1) typically cannot appear as the only verb in an independent clause and 2) they must normally co-occur with a regular (non-auxiliary) verb. This main verb determines transitivity, subcategorization, and selectional restrictions within the clause. However, we see that the V2 of a converbal predicate may exist alone in an independent clause.

(25) (a) soŋ   mɛn-Ø   inglis   kurs-ɯ   al-ɯp
         Then 1SG-NOM English course-ACC take-CVB
         baʃla-dɯm.
         begin-PST.1SG.
         'Then, selecting (one) I began an English course.'

سۏڭ من انگليسي کورسي آلېپ باشلادېم.

(b) soŋ   mɛn-Ø   inglis   kurs-ɯ   baʃla-dɯm.
    Then 1SG-NOM English course-ACC begin-PST.1SG.
    'Then, I began an English course.'

سۏڭ من انگليسي کورسي باشلادېم.

In example (25), the converbal predicate *alɯp baʃladɯm* may simply become *baʃladɯm* with the V2 serving as the matrix verb. Although the meaning changes slightly in (25b), the fact remains that the V2 appears as the only verb in an independent clause.

5.6.5 Auxiliaries have defective paradigms

Auxiliaries are often morphologically defective in some way, lacking regular inflected forms for tense, agreement, etc. This is not the case for the V2 in Afghan Turkmen converbal predicates. Taking the previous example, the final verb has a wide range of possible conjugations. Table 5.1 displays only some of the inflection possibilities.

Table 5.1. Non-defective paradigm of V2 in Afghan Turkmen

Vernacular	Inflection
aluıp baʃlamuıdum	Negative past indefinite
aluıp baʃlajordum	Past continuous
aluıp baʃlajorun	Present indefinite
aluıp baʃladjak	Future definite
aluıp baʃladjakdum	Unrealized past
aluıp baʃlaran	Future indefinite
aluıp baʃladur	Subjunctive present perfect tense

Considering these inflection possibilities showing a wide variety of tense and agreement marking, one could hardly say that V2 has a defective paradigm. Since V2 fails to exhibit several of the key properties one would expect of auxiliaries, the light verb analysis is the preferred option.

5.7 Conclusion

In this paper, I examined the syntactic properties of Afghan Turkmen converbal predicates. I distinguished between multi-clausal and mono-clausal types using a variety of grammatical tests. Next, I discussed how the two verbs in a converbal predicate have been analyzed. First, one group of authors describes V2 as a semantically bleached auxiliary. A second group describes V2 as a light verb. I followed the second analysis and offered several tests demonstrating that V2s in the Afghan Turkmen converbal predicates do not exhibit the characteristic properties of auxiliary verbs.

This investigation opens up areas for further inquiry which include the following questions.

1. What other syntactic description could be given to Afghan Turkmen converbal predicates? Are any complex predicates in Afghan Turkmen comprised of three or more verbs?
2. How do a number of grammatical approaches (Government and Binding Theory, Lexical Functional Grammar, Role and Reference Grammar, etc.) explain complex predicates and how might examples from Afghan Turkmen enhance or detract from these explanations?
3. What effect does the reflexive *-ʃ* have on converbal predicate marking? Notice in example (17b) the passive *-il/-ul* was marked on both V1 and V2. Why is this the case?
4. Finally, what is the relationship between Afghan Turkmen converbal predicates and Serial Verb Constructions (SVCs)? Particularly, is there any connection between converbal predicates and what Aikhenvald (2006:21) describes as Asymmetrical SVCs?

References

Aikhenvald, Alexandra. 2006. Serial verb constructions in typological perspective. In Alexandra Y. Aikhenvald and R. M. W. Dixon (eds.), *Serial verb constructions: A cross-linguistic typology*, 2:1–68. Oxford: Oxford University Press.

Aissen, Judith. 1974. Verb raising. *Linguistic Inquiry*, 5(3):325–366.

Baker, Mark C. 1988. *Incorporation: A theory of grammatical function changing*. Chicago: University of Chicago Press.

Bowern, Claire. 2004. (Some notes on) light verbs and complex predicates in Turkic. *MIT Working Papers in Linguistics*, 44:33–48.

Butt, Miriam, and Wilhelm Geuder. 2001. On the (semi)lexical status of light verbs. In Norbert Corver, Henk van Riemsdijk, Harry van der Hulst, and Jan Koster (eds.), *Semi-lexical categories: The function of content words and the content of function words*, 324–370. Berlin: De Gruyter Mouton.

Chomsky, Noam. 1981. *Lectures on government and binding*. Studies in Generative Grammar 9. Dordrecht: Foris.

Clark, Larry. 1998. *Turkmen reference grammar*. Turcologica 34. Wiesbaden: Harrassowitz.

Clifton, John M. 2002. Introduction. In John M. Clifton and Deborah A. Clifton (eds.), *Comments on discourse structures in ten Turkic languages*. Dallas: SIL International.

Comrie, Bernard. 1989. *Language universals and linguistic typology*. Chicago: University of Chicago Press.

Dryer, Matthew S. 1986. Primary objects, secondary objects, and antidative. *Language*, 62(4):808–845.

Durie, Mark. 1997. Grammatical structures in verb serialization. In Alex Alsina, Joan Bresnan, and Peter Sells (eds.), *Complex predicates*, 10:289–354. Stanford: CSLI.

Givón, T. 1990. Verb serialization in Tok Pisin and Kalam: A comparative study of temporal packaging. In John W. M. Verhaar (ed.), *Melanesian Pidgin and Tok Pisin: Proceedings of the First International Conference of Pidgins and Creoles in Melanesia*, 19–56. Studies in Language Companion Series 20. Amsterdam: John Benjamins. https://doi.org/10.1075/slcs.20.03giv.

Heine, Bernd, and Heiko Narrog. 2015. Grammaticalization and linguistic analysis. In Bernd Heine and Heiko Narrog (eds.), *The Oxford handbook of linguistic analysis*, 407–428. Oxford: Oxford University Press.

Hoey, Elliot Michael. 2013. Grammatical sketch of Turkmen. MA thesis. University of California, Santa Barbara.

Jespersen, Otto. 1964. *Essentials of English grammar*. Tuscaloosa: University of Alabama Press.

Johanson, Lars. 1995. On Turkic converb clauses. In Martin Haspelmath and Ekkehard König (eds.), *Converbs in cross-linguistic perspective: Structure and meaning of adverbial verb forms – adverbial participles, gerunds*, 313–347. Berlin: De Gruyter Mouton.

Kato, Yasuhiko. 1985. *Negative sentences in Japanese.* Sophia Linguistica 19. Tokyo: Sophia University.

Kroeger, Paul. 2004. *Analyzing syntax: A lexical-functional approach.* Cambridge: Cambridge University Press.

Kuno, Masakazu. 2007. Focusing on negative concord and negative polarity: Variations and relations. PhD dissertation. Harvard University, Cambridge, MA.

Lin, Jonah. 2001. Light verb syntax and the theory of phrase structure. PhD dissertation. University of California, Irvine.

Megerdoomian, Karine. 2001. Event structure and complex predicates in Persian. *Canadian Journal of Linguistics,* 46:97–125.

Muraki, Masatake. 1978. The *sika nai* construction and predicate restructuring. In John Hinds and Irwin Howard (eds.), *Problems in Japanese syntax and semantics,* 155–177. Tokyo: Kaitakusha.

Oyakawa, Takatsugu. 1975. On the Japanese *sika nai* construction. *Gengo Kenkyu,* 67:1–20.

Rasekh, Muhammad Salih. 2016. A study of the Turkmen dialects of Afghanistan phonology – morphology – lexicon – sociolinguistic aspects. PhD dissertation. Humboldt University, Berlin.

Sebba, Mark. 1987. *The syntax of serial verbs.* Amsterdam: John Benjamins.

Soper, John. 1996. *Loan syntax in Turkic and Iranian.* Bloomington: Eurolingua.

Steele, Susan. 1978. The category AUX as a language universal. In Joseph H. Greenberg, Charles A. Ferguson, and Edith A. Moravcsik (eds.), *Universals of human language: Word structure,* 3:7–45. Redwood City: Stanford University Press.

Sugar, Alexander. 2018. A restructuring analysis of Uyghur bleached V2 constructions. In Betül Erbaşi, Sozen Ozkan, and Lara Mantenuto (eds.), *Proceedings of the 3rd Workshop on Turkish, Turkic, and the Languages of Turkey (Tu+3).* Los Angeles: UCLA Working Papers in Linguistics.

Van Valin, Robert D., Jr. 2005. *Exploring the syntax-semantics interface.* Cambridge: Cambridge University Press.

Van Valin, Robert D., Jr., and Randy J. LaPolla. 1997. *Syntax: Structure, meaning, and function.* Cambridge Textbooks in Linguistics. Cambridge: Cambridge University Press.

6

"How Have You Appreciated the Uzbek Language?": The Role of Language in Afghan Uzbek Identity Formation

Joseph Stark
Samarkand International University of Technology

Abstract

The author conducted an ethnographic study using grounded theory tools to examine Afghan Uzbek identity formation in Northern Afghanistan. The study involved twenty participants (seventeen men and three women), people from ages 25 to 65 of different economic statuses, and of nine different city/village origins and was conducted over a period of eight months from 2017–2018. The findings indicated that the study participants formed their identity through the tension between being a distinct ethnic group on the one hand, and sharing religion, geography, and traditions with other groups in Afghanistan on the other – all the while aspiring to legitimacy or "partnership" within Afghanistan as Uzbeks. Participants described two distinct boundary markers for "being Uzbek," namely speaking Uzbek and having an Uzbek father. This chapter focuses on the role of language for these boundary markers. In so doing, the study indicates the importance of language for those engaging in any form of work among minority groups in Afghanistan.

6.1 Introduction

Teacher Qadir is fluent in English, has a master's degree from a foreign university, and is married to a Tajik, but in an interview about Uzbek identity, he points to the value of the Uzbek language. For him, it is of utmost of importance that he "appreciate" the Uzbek language. In an interview conducted in 2018 as part of a larger study on Uzbek identity formation in Afghanistan, he told me:

> You ask, "How have you appreciated the Uzbek language?" Look at us, at the time of President Dawood [1973–1978], we didn't have permission to learn Uzbek or read books in Uzbek and we had to burn the Uzbek books but with this kind of exile we've still preserved our language. We have preserved our culture. We speak in Uzbek. And we write in Uzbek. They couldn't do anything to us [to stop the preservation of our language and culture.] … We have to appreciate this, right? We've stayed here and we've gotten master's degrees and we talk in our mother's tongue, and in order to remember our mother's traditions, we search hard. … I'm proud to be an Uzbek. But for the last two hundred years, we have lots of problems in our country, especially Afghanistan Uzbeks. Even [for] thirty or forty years we could not study in Uzbek. We could not find any book in Uzbek. But we still didn't lose our language

or our culture or traditions. Still right now we have departments to train Uzbek teachers. We are doing good to train Uzbek teachers to build and spread the Uzbek language. I am happy. I am proud.

Language, particularly its preservation in the home and academic settings, proved a key marker for Teacher Qadir's description of his identity as an Afghan Uzbek.

This study focused on Uzbek-speakers in Northern Afghanistan. A number of studies were produced about Afghan ethnic groups in the 1970s and 1980s and some of them had relevance to Uzbeks in particular (Barfield 1982; Naby 1984; Shalinsky 1982, 1994; Tapper 1983, 1991). But only a few studies on Uzbeks have been published since then (Azoy 2012; Baldauf 2015; Baldauf 2017; Giustozzi 2005; Rasuly-Paleczek 2010; Williams 2007; 2013). This study fills a large gap in current studies by providing insights on identity formation particularly among Uzbek speakers in Afghanistan through direct interviews and participant observation.

The findings indicated that Uzbek participants of the study formed their identity through the tension between being a distinct ethnic group on the one hand, and sharing religion, geography, and traditions with other groups in Afghanistan on the other – all the while aspiring to legitimacy or "partnership" within Afghanistan as Uzbeks. For the purposes of this compendium, in honor of our colleague's efforts at linguistic development in Afghanistan, I will focus on the role that language in particular played in Uzbek identity formation. Three key elements have relevance for this issue. First, participants described the sense of loss they had experienced with regard to education opportunities in the country, often because they spoke a minority language, and because they sensed a devaluing of their language within society. Second, participants described speaking Uzbek as one of two key markers for indicating Uzbek identity. And third, participants, like Teacher Qadir above, indicated an intentional effort to preserve and promote the Uzbek language as a way of maintaining legitimacy within the Pashtun-dominated Afghanistan. This chapter will address these three points after a brief summary of the research project's methodological approach and overall findings. It will close with a brief summary of relevant theoretical issues related to identity formation and language as a symbolic boundary marker.

6.2 Methods of data gathering

The research was conducted over an eight-month period from 2017 to 2018 with participants in Northern Afghanistan, primarily in the Uzbek-dominated provincial capital of Sheberghan. The study involved twenty participants (seventeen men and three women), people from ages 25 to 65 of different economic statuses, and associated with nine cities/villages. I used an ethnographic framework that was supplemented by the analytical tools of grounded theory (Charmaz and Mitchell 2001; Charmaz 2006; Wolcott 2008). Data was gathered from Uzbek-speaking participants, using interviews, participant observation, and archival study. I used a combination of purposeful sampling of interviewees based upon existing relationships and snowballing techniques to find and interview participants. I interviewed Uzbek speakers with at least one parent who self-identified as an ethnic Uzbek. Because identity issues were the focus of the study, however, I discovered that some Uzbek speakers distinguished themselves separate from Uzbek ethnicity. Initial interviews were unstructured and informal as I sought an initial understanding of the phenomenon as well as appropriate ways to ask about it (Merriam and Tisdell 2016). Using an unstructured approach with probes allowed participants to volunteer information in accord with their interest and preferences. Grounded theory tools for coding and theory development were used for analyzing the data (Charmaz 2006). The study aimed for fundamental trustworthiness through an extended time in the field, triangulation in the use of varied forms of data collection, thick descriptions, and peer reviews. Finally, I conducted the study in keeping with my sponsoring university's (Biola University) ethical protocols, and the university ethical board provided approval before I began field work. Throughout this work, I have used pseudonyms for participants so as to preserve their anonymity and protect them from any adverse effects of the interviews.

6.3 Summary of the study's key findings

The primary research question for the overall study was, "How do members of an Uzbek Muslim community in Afghanistan negotiate their identity?" I found that the Uzbek participants in the study formed their identity through the tension between being a distinct ethnic group on the one hand and sharing religion, geography, and traditions with other groups in Afghanistan on the other. Within this tension, they asserted a desire for legitimacy or "partnership" within Afghanistan as Uzbeks. This involved a recognition of their rights as a people within the country that did not erase or undermine the heritage of their language and history.

Within the findings, I discerned three main theoretical patterns, namely the sense of shared components with other people/citizens of Afghanistan, the assertion of distinct language, history, and identity and finally, the aspiration for legitimacy within Afghanistan. The key findings are pictured in figure 6.1.

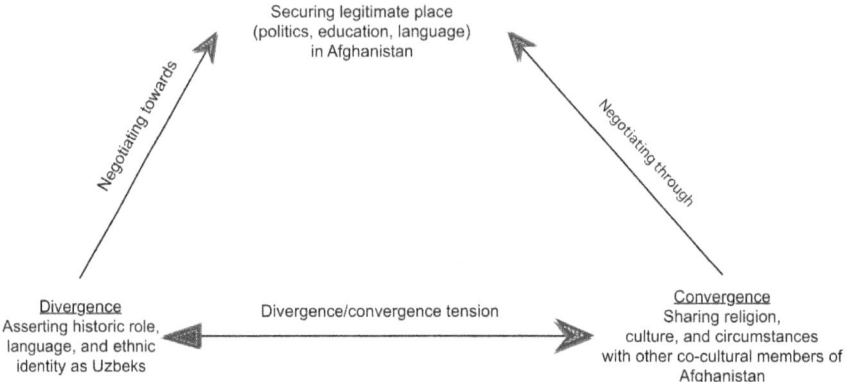

Figure 6.1. Patterns of convergence/divergence tension in Afghan Uzbek identity formation.

In the first case, participants emphasized that they were united with other people groups of Afghanistan through their shared religion, culture, and circumstances. They often began the interview by emphasizing these commonalities and then secondarily describing differences. The primary categories they described as being shared were religion, marriage (particularly to Tajiks or Farsiwans), and difficulties.

In terms of asserting their historic role, language, and identity, participants distinguished themselves by emphasizing certain components they considered distinctive to being Uzbek. These elements included a sense of exclusion from their place of legitimacy within the country through past and current experiences of losing wealth, territory, recognized history, educational opportunities, esteem for their language, legitimate identity, and their just portion as members of civil society. Participants, however, emphasized positive elements that they found integral to being Uzbek. This included a recognition of Uzbek as a distinct and major ethnic group within Afghanistan. It also included, as this chapter will detail, the primary importance of speaking Uzbek, and having an Uzbek father. Other elements, such as association with other Uzbeks, the feeling of being Uzbek, characteristics, an Uzbek atmosphere, and cultural traditions of food, clothing, and holidays also contributed to positive identity formation. Participants distinguished themselves from other ethnic groups. They did not emphasize differences with the Tajik or Farsiwan communities, but they did draw strong distinctions between themselves and Turkmen, Pashtun, and Hazaras. Finally, participants described some different family network groups (*qawm*) based on regional associations or historic tribal associations.

Finally, participants also described an aspiration for legitimacy within Afghanistan. Participants described shared components with other members of Afghanistan while also distinguishing themselves as a unique ethnic people (*millyet*). The two elements of shared participation with other members of Afghanistan and distinct elements as an ethnic people were in tension but led to an aspiration for legitimacy within Afghanistan. They sought a restoration of the loss they had experienced, not through a restoration of empire, but by a legitimate place in the political process of Afghanistan. As this chapter will indicate, one of the ways they pursued that legitimacy was through a recognition of the importance of preserving and recognizing the Uzbek language.

6.4 Losing education and language

The first area of identity formation that emerged in the study was the dramatic sense of loss that the Uzbek participants described. Though participants detailed multiple areas of life and history in which they had experienced loss – rights, territory, privilege, and opportunity – this section will detail the two with relevance to issues of language, namely the loss of educational opportunities and the loss of their language's value.

Losing educational opportunities. Participants described the loss of educational opportunities within Afghanistan. In some cases, participants described this as explicit government policy to promote the Pashtun language and diminish opportunities for Uzbeks. In other cases, educational opportunities were limited by the lack of educational opportunities in the Uzbek language itself.

Government policies that encouraged or required the Pashtun language in the classroom were perceived as one way that educational opportunities have been limited for Uzbeks. Samim, who was educated in the 1980s, experienced a time when opportunities for Uzbeks were growing. But he was able to describe policies prior to the 1980s that involved "forced" [*jabir*] learning of Pashtun by all school administrators. Moreover, he explained how, during the time of President Dawood (1973 to 1978),[1] a number of the teachers in the Uzbek-dominated city of Maimana were from Pashtun areas.

Sardor reckoned with the reality that village children without any exposure to a language other than Uzbek struggled in school when they had to begin school in Pashtun or Farsi:

> Because of the work of the Pashtuns, we couldn't really study in school. And our father couldn't study because of them. I'm not saying it was by force. The teachers at the school spoke Pashtun. For an Uzbek, it's really hard to speak Pashtun. When you just came from America, and you don't know Uzbek, and someone says, "Speak Uzbek," how well are you going to speak? You won't be able to speak. And you won't understand what they say. ... Our not learning comes from the hands of the Pashtuns. ... The Pashtuns did this.

Sardor, in short, indicated the domination of Pashtun within the educational system as hindering Uzbek learning and advancement.

The limitations in language and their impact on educational opportunities for learning on the part of Uzbeks came out repeatedly in multiple interviews. Osef described Uzbeks as being "behind" [*past qolgan*]. Nasir described them as one of the "forgotten" peoples [*marum*], and Shiqibo used other similar words to say they had been "left behind" [*orqib ketgan; uzoq qolgan*]. Sardor, Raza, and Baqir all admitted that their fathers had a role in their lack of education

---

[1] Dawood (alternative spelling Daoud) was president from 1973 to 1978, but Rasanayagam (2003) describes Dawood as expanding the government education system during his time as Prime Minister (1953 to 1963).

and did not encourage the children to pursue education. But there was a sense among the participants of shared fault between the lack of Uzbek family involvement and explicit government policy in Afghanistan that hindered their opportunities.

Though participants frequently talked about historical policies that prevented opportunities for Uzbeks during the 1960s and 1970s, they applied this sense of loss to present issues as well. Teacher Mustafo complained that the government did not publish their Uzbek books or send the university's trained Uzbek teachers to the village to teach Uzbek children. He recognized an increasing of opportunity that had opened up for Uzbeks beginning with the Saur Revolution of 1978. The government allowed the Uzbeks a radio and television program and allowed them to publish one page of a newspaper. In the present time, they valued the ability to develop an Uzbek language department at the local university, but he and Basir both complained that the greater opportunities were just the beginning of what was necessary to try to provide adequate training and education for their people.

Losing the value of the Uzbek language. Lost opportunity in education and cultural development fed into another theme that emerged from the participants, namely, the diminished value of the Uzbek language within their communities. Sardor mentioned an intentional effort on the part of the government to spread the Pashtun language, and Teacher Mustafo talked about the government transplanting Uzbeks to the South of the country. Their forced move to Pashtun communities led to their loss of their Uzbek language. No participant, however, talked in terms of a broad loss of the Uzbek language within Northern Afghanistan. Even though one participant, Teacher Fahim, admitted that some Uzbeks lost their language, he did not seem troubled by it.

Rather, the sense of loss came in terms of the prestige given to the Uzbek language. Teacher Fahim explained,

> And so for most families, they speak Uzbek in their homes. But there are some families that even with the father being Uzbek and the mother being Uzbek, they speak Dari or they speak Farsi. They think Farsi is a modern language, but Uzbek does not own a high position [in society]. So, unfortunately, even in my own hometown, even my own in-laws, their mother and father are Uzbek, but they speak Farsi. So about this subject, I know these two or three reasons. The influence of the atmosphere. The influence of the neighbors. A modernizing perspective — the perspective on the languages and thinking that Uzbek is not a modern language. They think that because they don't know Farsi it must be rich and they think that Uzbek is a poor language.

Teacher Fahim highlighted the "atmosphere" of the community - a term that participants used repeatedly to indicate an environment of language and culture with or without pressure to conform. But he also pointed to a "modernizing perspective." Uzbek is seen as the poorer language and the language that lacks influence.

This latter point intersects with the issues related to education. At present (in contrast to what participants indicated about the 1970s), the education system is bent towards Dari, as one of the two national languages. Dari is the common language of the North, the language of education and the language of government. Teacher Farid and Shiqibo both described how people could hide their knowledge of Uzbek in certain contexts and so emphasize their knowledge of Dari so as to retain status and even jobs, particularly in non-Uzbek cities like Mazar-i-Sharif and Kabul. Shiqibo explained how this happens early on in life, "For example, the children go to school and speak Uzbek and the kids laugh." And Teacher Qudrat expressed his frustration at how this system applied to him as he sought to get a master's degree. In his opinion, he had yet to be accepted in his applications for scholarships to foreign universities because he did not know Pashto.

Participants, then, expressed frustration and concern that they as a community missed out on educational opportunities because their first language was Uzbek and that the language of Uzbek itself was looked down upon. In terms of identity formation, then, language played a key role in the sense of loss as Uzbeks that the participants described.

6.5 Asserting positive identity as Uzbek people

In the previous section, I described the sense of loss that the Uzbek participants described in the interviews, particularly with respect to education opportunities and devaluing of the Uzbek language. In this section, I draw out the role of language as a positive expression of Uzbek identity formation and its relationship to paternal bloodlines.

Defining Uzbek. Throughout the research, participants indicated a coherent sense of communal identity for Uzbeks. They indicated this primarily by describing Uzbeks as a distinct ethnic group [*millyet*] within the broader community of Afghan citizens [*millat*]. There was some confusion, however, between the terms for ethnic group [*millyet*] and family network [*qaom*]. In the end, I found that *qaom* was the informal term for ethnic distinction, while *millyet* was the more formal term. Additionally, *qaom* had implications of closeness and blood relationships that *millyet* did not always carry. Figure 6.2 gives a visual representation of the relationship between *millat*, *millyet*, *qaom*, and language.

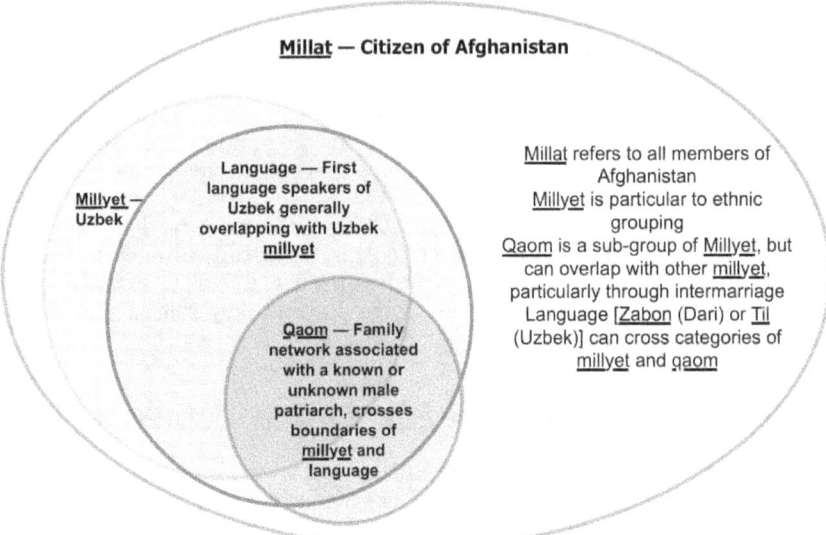

Figure 6.2. The relationship between *millat* (nationality), *millyet* (ethnic group), *qaom* (family network), and *til* (language).

To distinguish themselves as a distinct ethnic group [*millyet*], participants indicated two dominant markers. One was the ethnicity of the father. The other, the focus of this section, was the language spoken in the home (Uzbek). In both cases, these were permeable boundary markers; there were exceptions to these boundary markers that meant they could be crossed. This section will focus on the peculiar role that language played in identity formation and its relationship to paternal bloodlines.

Defining the permeable markers of language and paternal bloodlines for being Uzbek. When I arranged for interviews with participants and explained that I was researching the Uzbek people, I was surprised by the almost immediate description of dialect differences by the participants. They told me about different terms used in different provinces of Afghanistan (areas in Afghanistan with significant Uzbek speakers are pictured in figure 6.3). They commented on the mixture of Dari with Uzbek. They talked, in other words, about language. This was a repeated phenomenon: language was the first marker that participants mentioned when discussing what it meant to be Uzbek. But as the research continued, the picture became more complex. Hence, to indicate this complexity this subsection discusses the two main intersecting and permeable boundary markers of language and paternal bloodlines in defining Uzbek.

In the first place, most participants assumed that Uzbeks speak Uzbek. Habiba, for instance, could not imagine that an Uzbek born within the geographical boundaries of Afghanistan could grow up not speaking Uzbek. She said, "If someone is Uzbek and grows up in Afghanistan, it's 100 percent certain that he will know Uzbek." Sardor put it similarly. When asked if any Uzbeks could not speak Uzbek, he said, "I don't think there's those kinds. ...

6.5 Asserting positive identity as Uzbek people

They definitely speak Uzbek at home. They definitely speak Uzbek at home with their kids."

Figure 6.3. Areas of Afghanistan with significant Uzbek speakers indicated by shading.[2]

This pattern of describing an Uzbek home as one in which Uzbek was spoken, at least to some members, was consistent. Basir explained, "Because my father is Uzbek, we speak Uzbek at home with my mother. My father is Uzbek and my mother. And so we speak Uzbek with everyone." Teacher Qadir, despite having a Tajik wife, noted, "Generally, we speak Uzbek in the home. With my brothers, sister, mother and father, I speak Uzbek. I speak Uzbek also with my children." And Azizullah put it simply, "Our whole family speaks Uzbek."

The preference for Uzbek in the home meant that identifying another person often involved recognizing the fluency of his or her Uzbek. When I asked Tadris how he knew another person was Uzbek he said, "If he speaks Uzbek, I know right away from one word if he's Uzbek or a Farsi speaker. I can tell from his accent. I can tell from the way someone speaks." The importance of speech generally overrode any physical characteristics that people might identify as

---

[2] The map also indicates cities that participants of the study associated with, namely, Maimana, Andkhoy, Aqcha, Sheberghan, Sar-e Pul, Mazar-e Sharif, Kunduz, and Taloqan from the region of Takhar. *Note*: Ethnic group location approximations based on Dupree (2002:5).

non-Uzbek. So, for instance, Shiqibo explained that though her brother's face does not look Uzbek, "people know he's Uzbek" if he speaks Uzbek.

The importance of speech extended beyond the speaking of Uzbek alone, however, into how one spoke Farsi. Shiqibo had difficulty convincing people that she was Uzbek because of the "smoothness" of her Dari. Osef was unknown for a long time at his workplace as an Uzbek because he worked hard to make sure his Dari sounded like that of a Farsi speaker. And Tadris also described how others believed he was a "Farsi speaker [*Farsiwan*], not an Uzbek" because of how well he spoke Farsi. Basir summarized a common perception, though, that "even if an Uzbek speaks Farsi, people know that he's from the Uzbek *qaom*. ... We know who is Uzbek through our accents."

Language, then, was one way of distinguishing the Uzbeks of Afghanistan from the Uzbeks of Uzbekistan while also showing their commonality. Participants commonly noted how the accent and mixture of languages was different for the Uzbekistan Uzbeks. The Uzbeks of Uzbekistan mixed Russian in their language, Sardor pointed out, while the Uzbeks of Afghanistan mixed Farsi into their language. This led to there being a difference between the two languages, however small. The convergence/divergence tension of identity was evident on this front as well. Basir explained it, "We are partners in the way that we speak. And so we say, 'Uzbekistan's Uzbeks and Afghanistan's Uzbeks.'" In this sense, language provided both a shared identity with the Uzbeks of Uzbekistan (because they are mutually understandable) but also enough difference to distinguish the two groups.

Though participants mentioned ways that they identified a person as Uzbek through language, they also disputed language as being the sole identifier of being Uzbek. The other major factor to emerge was the ethnic identity of the father.

Hamid indicated some of the tension behind these two boundary markers when I asked him about children of an Uzbek father primarily speaking Farsi in the home (as was the case with his family). He replied at length:

> H: I'm not very interested in this kind of talk and I won't defend it. They are all Afghanistan's languages. If someone speaks Uzbek, it's for their own benefit. If someone speaks Farsi, it's for their own benefit. So it's not important to me, "I'm Uzbek and I speak Uzbek." Learn Farsi. Learn Uzbek. Learn Turkmen. Learn Pashtun [with emphasis]. There's a benefit to this. It's good to learn languages. Now my children think, "My dad is Uzbek," but he speaks Farsi. There's no difficulty with this. But there are others in Afghanistan that put a lot of value on this. They say, "Oh they should speak Uzbek at home." It doesn't matter for me—if it's Uzbek or Farsi. They are all Afghanistan's languages.
> JS: But if someone asks your children what *qaom* they are from, what will they say?
> H: They say Uzbek.

Hamid's response reflects the tension I found in Uzbek identity formation between shared elements with other members of Afghanistan and distinct elements of being Uzbek. For him, all of the languages of Afghanistan are valuable as "Afghanistan's languages." Hence, he would not allow the speaking of the Uzbek language in the home to be the defining mark of a person being Uzbek. He also was not troubled that Uzbek would be devalued in his own

6.5 Asserting positive identity as Uzbek people

home if he spoke Farsi with his children. He simply recognized the educational value of Farsi for his children as one of "Afghanistan's languages." In his case, his bloodline relationship with his children defined them as Uzbek, rather than the primary language that they speak at home.

So, even as language was emphasized as a crucial marker for identity, participants still made the point that it was the father's ethnicity that defined the child's ethnicity. This perspective primarily had to do with the national identity cards [*taskara*]. Azizullah explained, for instance, that the *millyet* identity listed on the identity card was determined by the father. So, if the father was Uzbek the identity card would say, "Uzbek." If Arab, it would say "Arab." If Tajik, it would say "Tajik." This political designation, then, could be distinguished from the language spoken at home. In describing some cousins that spoke Farsi primarily at home, Tadris explained "Wherever they go it will still be written on their identity card that their father is Uzbek, even though they speak Farsi." Teacher Qadir affirmed this point when describing Uzbeks that primarily spoke Farsi, "Their identity card, if their father was Uzbek, will say Uzbek."

The identity cards, however, were not the only issue raised. Others simply referred to paternal bloodlines as being the defining marker. Baqir explained, "Let's say I'm Uzbek and I get a wife from the Turkmen. [The children] will become Uzbek from the father, or if the father is Pashtun, they'll become Pashtun." Sartor described the same point:

> JS: So, in your reckoning how is someone Uzbek?
> S: If their father is Uzbek. Even if the mother is from a different *qaom*, if the father is Uzbek, they'll be Uzbek. If they speak Uzbek, if they have an Uzbek identity card ... and their grandfather is Uzbek. And they are from Uzbek ancestors, they'll be Uzbek. So for instance, there are some, which are from a different *qaom*. So for example in our village. They come and they've taken a wife from among us. They do a wedding and they take a wife. And some of them even speak Uzbek. Because the wife is Uzbek. Even if the father is from another language, they speak Uzbek. And the kids speak Uzbek. But the people will ask, "What are you originally?" And if the father is Turkmen, they'll say Turkmen. If the father is Tajik, they'll say Tajik. If they are from the Arabs, they'll say Arab.

Sartor's explanation provided a helpful bridge between the role of the identity card as a generational indicator of paternal bloodlines and the cultural ascription of identity within a community. Even if the family spoke primarily Uzbek, the bloodline association trumped language for him.

This perspective, however, was contested in experience even if it seemed to be clear ideally for most of my participants. I interacted with two counter-cases to this perspective during my research period. During a visit at Eid-i-Ramadan, for instance, I talked with one man whose father was Uzbek but whose family primarily interacted in Farsi. He self-identified as a Tajik. Kabir, another interview participant, identified himself as being in a similar situation and explained the rational. For him, the issue had primarily to do with the "strength" of his mother. His father was Uzbek and his mother was Tajik, but "my mom was stronger than my dad. So I followed my mom." This meant that his dominant language was Farsi, rather than Uzbek. So he tended to identify himself as a Tajik, but not exclusively so. Sometimes, perhaps when convenient socially, he identified himself as "Uzbek." In this sense, he considered himself "two veined," a term that Sardor also used to describe those with Uzbek and Tajik parents.

Marriage also played a role in defining ethnic associations. Shiqibo is married to a Tajik man and described all of her children as being "Tajik" because of their father's ethnicity. I asked her, however, if she still identified herself as Uzbek. She explained:

> If someone says, "What is your mother-tongue?" I say, "Uzbek." If they say what is your family or what are your children or what is their mother's tongue, I say "Dari." But about myself personally, others say, "Uzbek." They call my husband "Tajik" or "Dari."

Marriage changed the dominant dynamic for Shiqibo. Though she personally identified as an Uzbek, her family was seen as "Dari-speakers" or Tajik. Even with this, however, she retained her ethnic identity as an Uzbek because of her mother tongue and her father's bloodlines.

In summary, participants named two primary ways of identifying themselves and others as Uzbeks: speaking the Uzbek language and having an Uzbek father. Neither of these identity markers was absolute, however, as participants and observation in the community revealed exceptions. Hence, they were permeable boundary markers that could be crossed within the community. The permeable and overlapping nature of these two markers is pictured in figure 6.4. In the next section, I describe the importance of language in current efforts to assert Uzbek legitimacy within Afghanistan.

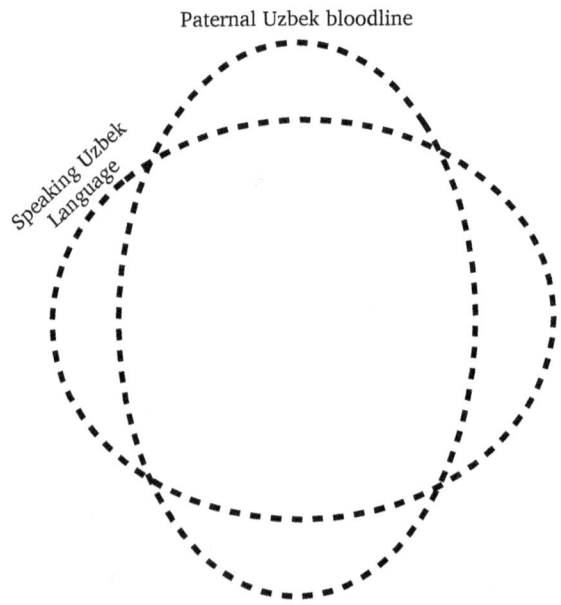

Figure 6.4. Uzbek language use and paternal Uzbek bloodlines compose Uzbek identity markers.

6.6 Fighting to assert Uzbek identity, culture, and language

The importance of language for Uzbek identity formation also emerged in how participants expressed their desire for legitimacy for the Uzbek people within a united Afghanistan. In particular, some participants cited explicit efforts to assert a place for their culture and particularly their language.

Participants, particularly the more academic members of this study, detailed a concentrated effort on their part and the part of other Uzbeks to retain and honor Uzbek language and culture within Afghanistan. In the introduction, I pointed out Teacher Qadir's claim to "appreciate the Uzbek language." He emphasized in this description the role that getting master's degrees, speaking his mother tongue and remembering his mother's tradition played in this act of appreciation. For Teacher Qadir, the Uzbek people had worked hard to retain and then develop the capacity of education and resources within Uzbek. He described opposition to this for a number of years but celebrated the recent success.

Multiple participants, not just the academics, described these developments of increasing freedom to work and publish in the Uzbek language since the late 1970s. Teacher Mustafo described how they had been given permission to have a half-hour radio program in Uzbek in the 1970s and then one page in Uzbek in the *Yulduz* newspaper. As he explained this, Teacher Qudrat commented with a tone of irony, "One! They gave us permission for one! That's how much permission we had" (see Naby 1984; Williams 2013). According to Teacher Mustafo's reporting of the process, however, he and his colleagues seized the few opportunities that came along. They studied at the university in Kabul and even sacrificed the prestige of studying medicine and more honored subjects so as to be in the social science departments and advance the interests of the Uzbek language and literature. Teacher Mustafo, who felt he had sacrificed his own reputation in the process, explained, "If I have to be beheaded for the sake of my mother tongue, that's fine. But my people [*millyetim*] should understand 'Who am I?'"

Teacher Mustafo gave two additional stories about accommodation to Pashtun domination in order to advance the honor and prestige of the Uzbek language and people. He wrote a historical grammar of the Uzbek language but was not able to publish it in Kabul. Eventually, he produced all of his credentials in Pashtun, and it was approved. Unfortunately, the book itself was not allowed to be published in the Uzbek language. Additionally, he described a prominent Uzbek academic who had qualified for a scholarship in the United States forty years ago. After being turned away at the airport multiple times to make his trip, he eventually changed one letter in his name on his passport from "Kul" [an Uzbek name] to "Gul" [a Pashtun name]. The difference between the two letters is only one small line. He was then allowed to leave. When he returned from his studies, he proudly proclaimed that he was no longer "Gul" but "Kul" again. Teacher Mustafo confided, "Now, we're telling you the truth about these matters. These things are painful for us." But the pain was mixed with a sense of pride at their accomplishments and efforts to increase the prestige of their language and people.

Samim, who was not from the university, described the same process of development in terms of the opportunities that had opened up for education in Uzbek.

> [The Uzbeks] got a program on the radio station. And then in that form, they got to print books and had a subject in the schools. Before that, there weren't other languages allowed. And then after the civil war, they gave them permission to have one hour of their language as one subject. So, then even during the civil war, there was a time when they studied Uzbek from the first class till the 12th or 11th class. They finished in the 11th class and then didn't do it in the 12th class. So, then there was a program announced that said they needed to graduate from the 12th grade and go into a university faculty program. They said that there should be an Uzbek department and they should enter into that college degree program. Now, there is such a university and there is an Uzbek faculty. And they can study the Uzbek language, English language, and Turk language.

Participants, in short, described a dramatic shift from being an unrecognized language group to one that had its own department at a major university. They saw this as limited progress. In keeping with this, Basir explained that the Afghan President Ashraf Ghani had recently restated during a visit to Uzbekistan that "Uzbek is the third official language of Afghanistan." Though he expressed disappointment that the government had not done all it could to publish books in Uzbek, he also credited a ten-year effort on the part of Uzbek leaders to achieve this recognition.

Fundamentally, participants described an aim to provide a clear position of legitimacy for Uzbek. Whereas on the formal level they had made progress, they saw continued effort as necessary on the popular level. Teacher Fahim described how people still considered Uzbek a "poor language" despite how historic and rich it truly was. With their current opportunity, those working in this field sought to explain and develop that. Fahim continued,

> The government has created this opportunity. There's this department, and we research and work and develop a warm atmosphere for our language, in other words to explain our language to other peoples. And to explain our culture to others. It's not to make enemies of others. That's not our desire.

No participant expressed interest in Uzbeks dominating or controlling the country. But they repeatedly stated how they wanted recognition or, as I have put it, legitimacy as a language and people within the country.

As I lived in the community, I saw other signs of efforts to establish the legitimacy of the Uzbek language. Local authors have self-published books of poetry in Uzbek. While I was conducting research, Ibrohim (2017) published an Uzbek-Dari dictionary that was distributed through local bookstores. Two predominantly Uzbek television stations have operated in the Northwest of the country, *Botir* television, and most recently *Bek* television. And with the ease of distribution through social media, Uzbek songs can be found on YouTube. One, sung by a popular local artist, Suhrab Elyar Chavoosh, declared, in an ode to the Uzbek language called "Mother Tongue," "I love you more than my life. With you my pride increases" (Madridista 2014a). Another song, called "Wake up," called on Uzbek people to "Wake up and raise your head from sleeping ... Sacrifice yourself for your people!" (Madridista 2014b). All of these popular efforts seemed to be part of on-going efforts to establish legitimacy for Uzbek language and people.

In summary, participants described themselves in an ongoing effort to establish or restore their position of prestige and legitimacy as Uzbeks within Afghanistan. They did not aspire to rule the country as they once did centuries ago. Rather, they wanted a place of legitimacy in which they were equal partners in Afghanistan with equal recognition of their language, culture, and ethnic identity. Some of them described themselves as activists in this cause. Others simply noted the process in positive ways. All the participants seemed to share this as a concern and as part of how they formed their identity as Uzbeks.

6.7 Interaction with other literature

The findings of the study indicated the important role of language in identity formation among Uzbeks. This section provides brief interactions with other literature on the issue of identity formation and particularly the role that symbolic boundaries play in identity formation.

Frederic Barth's studies (1969a, 1969b, 1994) on ethnicity and emphasis on boundary formation, rather than culture, as the primary ways of marking out ethnic identity proved particularly salient in analyzing the data from this study. Phoenix in her description of "Ethnicities" summarizes the importance of this point: "It is now generally accepted that there is no one-to-one correspondence between ethnicity and culture; that ethnic groups are internally differentiated and that ethnic identities are based on socially constructed differences—rather than definite, fixed differences" (2010:297). In short, ethnicity is not self-evident. It is constructed based on a variety of issues. Those issues include the fact that ethnic identities can be "multiple, potentially contradictory, and situationally variable" (2010:378). The research of the previous chapter coheres with this understanding.

Sciortino expands on Barth's ideas by emphasizing the role of symbolic boundaries in marking out identity and ethnicity. He notes that, as a discreet category, ethnicity mostly involves issues of descent, particularly the "attribution of meaning to ancestral origin and descent" (2012:378). But even as paternity in particular played a symbolic role in marking out Uzbek identity, so did language. Yet, in keeping with the comments of Phoenix (2010) and Sciortino (2012), those ascribed characteristics of Uzbek identity were not absolute. Indeed, participants sometimes indicated contradictions in their formulation of the roles these particular characteristics played, claiming, for instance, that Pashtuns and Mongols could become Uzbeks over time but ascribing an essential characteristic of *Uzbekness* that lingered over multiple generations.

The most striking finding, then, in terms of symbolic boundaries, was the role of language in identity formation. As a minority group within the country, this had the strongest salience for members in terms of self-identity. The role of symbolic boundaries, then, emerged in the discussions about language. In their description of a "communication theory of identity," Hecht, Warren, Jung and Krieger (2005:257) suggest how the dominating context often plays a role in bringing forward salient themes. In particular, they note how majority co-culturals may assume that minority communities are ready to sign the contract of how to relate to the larger culture without actually receiving the assent of those minority communities. Uzbek participants felt pressure to conform linguistically to the majority culture, as if there was a "ready-to-sign" contract (p. 267) to which they had not agreed. That contract included the assumed mode of communication (Dari or Pashto) and the value placed on the dominant languages. Both resistance to this communal contract as well as recognition of its salience seems to be part of what brought forward language as a primary consideration in identity formation.

6.8 Summary and applications

This study of twenty Uzbek-speaking participants indicated the crucial role that language played in identity formation among Afghanistan Uzbeks. Participants described senses of loss in terms of the value of their language in the broader society and the educational opportunities afforded them. But they also emphasized the role speaking Uzbek had in identifying themselves and others as Uzbeks. Some described an intentional political and academic effort to carve out a place for their own Uzbek identity and language as legitimate parts of Afghan society.

These findings suggest the importance that language has for work within Afghanistan. Despite some anxiety about my foreign identity and religion, participants valued and respected me for speaking Uzbek. They opened up to me, often sharing deeply from the pains of past and present experience. The value of learning another language as an expression of respect for a people can hardly be overestimated. Military personnel, civil servants, business people, and aid workers continue to come to Afghanistan to help the people in its aspirations for development and peace. It is crucial for those serving in Afghanistan to spend time, energy, and money learning the language of the people they seek to serve and partner with. Those working in areas with significant populations that speak languages other than Dari should also invest in learning other languages. This will help to give these other language groups and *millyet* a voice in influencing the peaceful development of the country.

The study also identified some key areas for further study. For one, a similar study on identity formation among Turkmen, particularly because they share Turkic roots but distinguish themselves strongly from Uzbeks, would be of considerable value. Secondly, my study was limited primarily to city-dwellers or those who had strong associations with the city. I was unable to interview rural Uzbeks without city associations and particularly Uzbeks who had little to no contact with foreigners. A study of such Uzbeks would be incredibly valuable in understanding other forms of Uzbek identity formation. Finally, this study was focused on the northern area of the country. There are large Uzbek populations in the northeast part of the country, where Shalinsky (1994) did her study of Uzbek *mohajrin* 'migrants'. Studies of the distinct elements of Uzbek identity formation in that area of the country could supply further insight into the different aspects that geographical difference and history play in identity formation.

References

Azoy, G. Whitney. 2012. *Buzkashi: Game and power in Afghanistan*. Third edition. Long Grove: Waveland.

Baldauf, Ingeborg. 2015. Uzbek oral histories of migration and war. In Nile Green (ed.), *Afghan history through Afghan eyes*, 235–256. Oxford: Oxford University Press.

Baldauf, Ingeborg. 2017. Female sainthood between politics and legend: The emergence of Bibi Nushin of Shibirghan. In Nile Green (ed.), *Afghanistan's Islam: From conversion to the Taliban*, 207–224. Oakland: University of California Press.

Barfield, Thomas J. 1982. *The Central Asian Arabs of Afghanistan: Pastoral nomadism in transition*. Austin: University of Texas Press.

Barth, Fredrik. 1969a. Introduction. In Fredrik Barth (ed.), *Ethnic groups and boundaries: The social organization of culture difference*, 9–38. Oslo: Universitesforlaget.

Barth, Fredrik. 1969b. Pathan identity and its maintenance. In Fredrik Barth (ed.), *Ethnic groups and boundaries: The social organization of culture difference*, 117–134. Oslo: Universitesforlaget.

Barth, Fredrik. 1994. Enduring and emerging issues in the analysis of ethnicity. In Hans Vermeulen and Cora Govers (eds.), *The anthropology of ethnicity: Beyond 'Ethnic groups and boundaries'*, 11–32. Amsterdam: Het Spinhuis.

Charmaz, Kathy. 2006. *Constructing grounded theory: A practical guide through qualitative analysis*. Introducing Qualitative Methods Series. London: SAGE.

Charmaz, Kathy, and R. G. Mitchell. 2001. An invitation to grounded theory in ethnography. In Paul Atkinson, Amanda Coffey, Sara Delamonte, John Lofland, and Lyn Lofland (eds.), *Handbook of ethnography*, 160–174. London: SAGE.

Dupree, Louis. 2002. *Afghanistan*. Oxford: Oxford University Press.

Giustozzi, Antonio. 2005. The ethnicisation of an Afghan faction: Junbesh-i-Milli from its origins to the presidential elections. Working Paper 67. Crisis States Programme. Working Papers Series 1. London: Development Studies Institute (DESTIN): http://eprints.lse.ac.uk/13315/1/WP67.pdf.

Hecht, Michael L., Jennifer R. Warren, Eura Jung, and Janice L. Krieger. 2005. The communication theory of identity: Development, theoretical, perspective, and future directions. In William B. Gudykunst (ed.), *Theorizing about intercultural communication*, 257–278. Thousand Oaks: SAGE.

Ibrohim, R. 2017. *Farhang Uzbeki-Dari* [Dictionary for Uzbek to Dari]. Mazar-i-Sharif, Afghanistan: Saqafat.

Madridista, A. 2014a. Bosh Kutar Uyqudan [Wake up from sleep] [video file]. https://www.youtube.com/watch?v=VuZyVSkeNqw. Accessed 2019. (The video is no longer available.)

Madridista, A. 2014b. Suhrab Elyar - Ona Til Onam Tilisan [Mother tongue, you are my mother tongue (by Suhrab Elyar)] [video file]. https://www.youtube.com/watch?v=JCE09oj2y9c. Accessed 2019. (The video is no longer available.)

Merriam, Sharan B., and Elizabeth J. Tisdell. 2016. *Qualitative research: A guide to design and implementation*. Fourth edition. The Jossey-Bass Higher and Adult Education Series. San Francisco: Wiley.

Naby, Eden. 1984. The Uzbeks in Afghanistan. *Central Asian Survey*, 3(1):1–21.

Phoenix, Ann. 2010. Ethnicities. In Margaret Wetherell and Chandra Talpade Mohanty (eds.), *The SAGE handbook of identities*, 297–320. London: SAGE.

Rasanayagam, Angelo. 2003. *Afghanistan: A modern history – monarchy, despotism or democracy? The problems of governance in the Muslim tradition*. New York: I. B. Tauris.

Rasuly-Paleczek, Gabriele. 2010. Alignment politics and factionalism among the Uzbeks of north-eastern Afghanistan. In Robert L. Canfield and Gabriele Rasuly-Paleczek (eds.), *Ethnicity, authority, and power in Central Asia: New games great and small*, 77–94. London: Routledge.

Sciortino, Giussepe. 2012. Ethnicity, race, nationhood, foreignness, and many other things: Prolegomena to a cultural sociology of difference-based interactions. In C. Alexander Jeffrey, Ronald N. Jacobs, and Philip Smith (eds.), *The Oxford handbook of cultural sociology*, 365–389. Oxford: Oxford University Press.

Shalinsky, Audrey C. 1982. Islam and ethnicity: The northern Afghanistan perspective. *Central Asian Survey*, 1(2–3):71–83.

Shalinsky, Audrey C. 1994. *Long years of exile: Central Asian refugees in Afghanistan and Pakistan*. Lanham: University Press of America.

Tapper, Nancy. 1983. Acculturation in Afghan Turkistan: Pashtun and Uzbek women. *Asian Affairs*, 14(1):35–44.

Tapper, Nancy. 1991. *Bartered brides: Politics, gender, and marriage in an Afghan tribal society*. Cambridge: Cambridge University Press.

Williams, Brian Glyn. 2007. Writing the Dostumname: Field research with an Uzbek warlord in Afghan Turkistan. In *Central Eurasian Studies Review*, 6(1/2):2–8. https://centraleurasia.org/wp-content/uploads/2018/04/Vol.6_no.12_fulljournal_CESR.pdf.

Williams, Brian Glyn. 2013. *The last warlord: The life and legend of Dostum, the Afghan warrior who led US Special Forces to topple the Taliban regime*. Chicago: Chicago Review.

Wolcott, Harry F. 2008. *Ethnography: A way of seeing*. New York: AltaMira.

7

The Questions of *pa* – A Munji Contemplative Question Particle

Paul Williamson
SIL Global

7.1 Introduction

The purpose of this paper is to describe and explain the use of a Munji particle which marks contemplative questions. The grammatical marking of this subset of questions is a distinctive feature of the Munji language and provides an example of how languages categorize questions.

7.2 Background

The Munji language is spoken in the Kuran wa Munjan district of Badakhshan province in Afghanistan. There are about 5,300 Munji speakers (Beyer and Beck 2011). Munji is classified as a Southeastern Iranian Pamir language.

7.3 Question formation in Munji

The default word order in Munji is SOV. Syntactically, questions are formed either by putting a question word *in situ* or by putting a question word in the focus position directly before the verb. Example (1) shows an indicative sentence which could serve as the answer to the questions in examples (2) and (3).

(1) ahmad-an   və nayın[1] cıkevda
Ahmad-OBL.M.SG OBJ bread cook.PST.3SG
'Ahmad cooked the bread.'

Question word placed *in situ:*

(2) **kaj**   və nayın cıkevda
who.OBL OBJ bread cook.PST.3SG
'Who cooked the bread?'

Question word in the focus position directly before the verb:

(3) və nayın **kaj**   cıkevda
OBJ bread **who.OBL** cook.PST.3SG
'**Who** cooked the bread?'

---

[1] For the examples in this paper, Munji nouns are direct case and masculine unless labelled otherwise.

Munji also uses polar questions which may be answered with "Yes" or "No." These questions are syntactically the same as statements but are uttered with a rising intonation on the end of the clause. With rising intonation on the clause, sentence (4) functions as a polar question:

(4) ahmad-an və naɣɪn cɪkevda
ahmad-OBL.M.SG OBJ bread cook.PST.3SG
'Did Ahmad cook the bread?'

7.4 The meaning of the *pa* particle

Munji also uses a particle, namely *pa*, for certain types of questions. Grammatically, the *pa* particle may occur in any question clause. It is only on the discourse level that its use can be judged felicitous or infelicitous. The *pa* particle shows that the speaker intends to communicate a question to the addressee, but the speaker does not expect the addressee to know the answer. In other words, *pa* is not used in rhetorical questions when the answer to the question is apparent to either the speaker or the addressee—or at least that is how the speaker is presenting things. It is as if the speaker is saying: "I (the speaker) don't know the answer to this question, and I don't expect you (the addressee) to know the answer either. But I'm inviting you to think about this with me." Therefore, I have labelled this interrogative particle as the "contemplative question marker" (CQ). In sentences (5) to (7), the speaker does not expect the addressee to know the answer to the question. If the speaker did expect the addressee to know the answer, then the *pa* would be infelicitous. The free translation sometimes uses the words "I wonder" or "I wonder if" to help carry the meaning of this contemplative question marker.

(5) ali be-kɔr ast **pa**
Ali without-work be.PRS.3SG CQ
'I wonder if Ali is busy?'

(6) fɪkər kind kə dəm ʃti ast **pa**
think do.PRS.3SG COMP in.NR what be.PRS.3SG CQ
'He is thinking, "I wonder what is inside this?"'

(7) mən pizɔçi ku ʃi **pa**
1SG.OBL sheep where go.PST.3SG CQ
'I wonder where my sheep went?'

7.5 Semantic restrictions on the use of *pa*

In some contexts, the use of *pa* is infelicitous or semantically ill-formed. Namely, the speaker cannot use *pa* if he wants to communicate that he believes the addressee likely knows the answer to the question. Without using *pa*, he communicates that he expects an answer. This applies in situations where the addressee would obviously know the answer, as in a question like "Where were you yesterday?" One assumes that most people would know the answer to

7.5 Semantic restrictions on the use of pa

that question. Thus, while *pa* would technically be grammatical, the sentence would be infelicitous.

(8) wəziɾ   ku   vi-aj   (*pa)
    yesterday where be.PST-2SG   (CQ)
    'Where were you yesterday?'

Since the contemplative question marker *pa* also communicates that the speaker himself does not know the answer to the question, it makes it unfit for use in some rhetorical questions. In many rhetorical questions (as in example (9)), the speaker ostensibly communicates that the listener has sufficient contextual information to fill in an answer to the question. But the *pa* particle communicates just the opposite, namely, that neither the speaker nor the listener knows the answer to the question. By way of illustration, in one traditional Munji folktale a prince realizes that his father is against him and says to himself:

(9) mən   tɔt   kə   nɔmən duʃmən ʒə   ʔidiɾ maɾdəm-an
    OBL.1SG father COMP to.me enemy from other people-OBL.SG
    ʃti   tawaqu
    what expectation
    'When my own father is an enemy to me, what can I expect from other people?' (Grjunberg 1972:116)

This rhetorical question is a strong way for the storyteller to let the listener know that the prince has no hope of anyone helping him. For this context, *pa* cannot be used because it would shift the way in which this sentence is understood. So even though *pa* would be grammatical, it would change the meaning as example (10).

(10) mən   tɔt   kə   nɔmən duʃmən ʒə   ʔidiɾ maɾdəm-an
     OBL.1SG father COMP to.me enemy from other people-OBL.SG
     ʃti   tawaqu   **#pa**
     what expectation cq
     'When my own father is an enemy to me, **I wonder** what can I expect from other people?'

But in the context of the story, the prince is not wondering; he knows that he can only expect others to also be his enemy. Thus, the *pa* particle would be infelicitous in this sentence.

Sentence (11) provides another example where the *pa* particle would not be used. In this case, a speaker is asking a question with an obvious answer to make a point.

(11) aga wes və zaxm-ə   t͡ʃɪ-kɔr-am   də waxt ʒə
     if now OBJ field-F.SG NEG-plant.PRS-1PL in time of
     ləɾi-ɔ-wan   ʃti   ɣɾv-am
     cut.with.sickle.PST-INF-OBL.M.SG   what get.PRS-1PL
     'If we don't plant now, what will we get at harvest?'

The speaker is not asking his audience to contemplate this with him, but rather he is communicating to his listeners what both he and they know very well. Without planting, they will harvest nothing.

Although not grammatically required, in every case when a speaker is wondering about something, the *pa* particle is appropriate and natural. For example, in situations when someone is asking a question of himself, the *pa* particle usually occurs. The logic is this: If one is asking himself a question, of course the answer is not immediately apparent; otherwise, he would not be asking. Thus, in sentence (12) the speaker is perplexed about what to do next. In this case, the use of *pa* is fitting and natural.

(12) wes zə ʃti kən-əm **pa**
now 1SG what do.PRS-1SG CQ
'Now what will I do?'

7.5.1 The pragmatic use of *pa*

Thus far, we have seen that the *pa* particle signals that the speaker is **wondering** about something and by implication **inviting** the listener to join him in contemplation. This is the basic meaning of this particle and explains the majority of its occurrences. A common example is how *pa* is used when people are talking to themselves. For a long time, my own research only showed natural examples of *pa* for this kind of self-dialogue. But, of course, it seemed unlikely that a language would have a word that people *only* use when talking to themselves! Certainly, people use it in self-address, but its function is to invite others to observe one's own thought processes. The speaker's wonder, confusion, and ponderings are laid out before the listener.

Speakers also use the explicit assertions of the *pa* particle in layered, and nuanced ways. As with any linguistic form, the grammar merely shows what is explicitly asserted, but it does not show what the person actually thinks or how he intends to be understood. With the *pa* particle the speaker makes an explicit assertion that has two parts: 1) "I am wondering about this topic" and 2) "I don't expect you to know the answer." Along with this is often the implication that the speaker is inviting the listener to join in this contemplation in some way. Thus, *pa* may show a real invitation, or it may be a polite way to frame a request for information.

By way of example, if a person's pen is missing, and he wants to ask a co-worker about it, he may use the *pa* particle even though he is certain the co-worker knows the answer to the question. To ask the question without the *pa* particle would make it sound like an accusation of theft, but that would be impolite and bring tension to the relationship. Thus, as in example (13), the speaker may use the *pa* particle to assert that he is merely wondering about this and asking the other person to join him in contemplating the pen's whereabouts.

(13) mən qalam ku ʃi pa
1SG.OBL pen where go.PST.3SG CQ
'I wonder where my pen went?'

7.5.2 The syntax of *pa*

The default position for *pa* is clause-final, and this is where *pa* occurs most of the time. However, it may occur after any constituent in the sentence to show emphasis. So, in addition to expressing a contemplative meaning, the *pa* particle is also used to show focus.

Note that in example (14) the focus is on what the person is going to do in the immediate future, so the emphasis is on the word "now."

(14) wes **pa** zə ʃti kən-əm
now CQ 1SG what do.PRS-1SG
'**Now** what will I do?' (Grjunberg 1972:102–103)

In example (15), the focus of the question is on the reason for the crying, not on the action or response of the crying:

(15) t͡ʃɪ-vzɔn-əm kə ja t͡ʃi **pa** xʃit
NEG-know.PRS-1SG COMP 3SG.mid why CQ cry.PRS.3SG
'I don't know [the answer to the question]: **Why** is she crying?'

Examples (15), (16), (17), and (18) illustrate the clause level syntax for *pa*.

(16) Unmarked word order:
mən pizɔçi ku ʃi **pa**
1SG.OBL sheep where go.PST.3SG CQ
'I wonder where my sheep went?'

(17) Emphasis on 'where':
mən pizɔçi **ku pa** ʃi
'I wonder **where** my sheep went?'

(18) Emphasis on 'my sheep':
mən pizɔçi pa ku ʃi
'I wonder **my sheep** went?'

The *pa* particle puts focus on the whole marked constituent. In example (18), this is the whole noun phrase *mən pizɔçi* "my sheep." To put emphasis on the possessive pronoun, the speaker must break up the original noun phrase into two separate noun phrase constituents. Then *pa* may be used to put focus on the possessive pronoun, as in example (19).

(19) Emphasis on 'my':
mən **pa** wə pizɔçi ku ʃi
1SG.OBL CQ 3SG.far sheep where go.PST.3SG
'I wonder where **my** sheep went?'

The *pa* particle is always ungrammatical in clause-initial position:

(20) Ungrammatical:
pa mən pizɔçi ku ʃi
for: 'I wonder where my sheep went?'

7.6 Summary and conclusion

The Munji *pa* particle functions as a contemplative question marker. It asserts that the answer to a question is not immediately apparent to either the speaker or the addressee. It is used to invite dialog, solicit advice, or to exclaim about one's own wonder or confusion. Syntactically, *pa* may move from its default position, clause final, and occur directly after any constituent to show focus. The use of *pa* is infelicitous for rhetorical questions or when the speaker is expressing an assumption that the addressee knows the answer to a question. Pragmatically, *pa* is used in certain social situations for polite requests or to soften questions used in socially sensitive situations.

References

Beyer, Daniela, and Simone Beck. 2011. A linguistic assessment of the Munji language of Afghanistan. *Language Documentation & Conservation*, 6:38–103.

Grjunberg, Alexander L. 1972. *Languages of the eastern Hindukush: The Munji language*. Leningrad: Nauka.

Language Index

Afghan Turkmen [tuk]   xxi, 140–143, 145–146, 148, 151, 153, 157–159
Arabic [ara]   95, 151
Burushaski [bsk]   102, 108, 111
Dameli [dml]   90, 98
Dari [prs]   xx, 52, 85–88, 90, 113, 142, 168–170, 172, 174, 176, 178
Darwazi [prs]   86, 88, 90, 95, 97, 102, 109
English [eng]   52, 86, 120–121, 125–126, 151, 163, 176
French [fra]   131
Gawar-Bati [gwt]   86, 90, 93, 95, 100, 102–103
Gojri [gju]   86–87, 89–90, 93, 100, 104
Ishkashimi [isk]   xx, 53, 85–86, 91–92, 94–95, 97, 102, 109
Kalkoti [xka]   90
Kashmiri [kas]   94, 110
Kazakh [kaz]   92
Khowar [khw]   98, 105
Kipchak [uzn]   92
Kyrgyz [kir]   85, 87, 92, 94, 109
Munji [mnj]   xvii, xx– xxi, 53, 85–87, 91, 95–96, 100, 100, 104–108, 181–182, 186
Nuristani [ask, wbk, xvi, bsh, prn, wbk]   83, 85, 88–89, 93, 103
Nuristani Ashkun [ask]   87, 89, 96–96, 103–104
Nuristani Kalasha [wbk]   86, 98
Nuristani Kamviri [xvi]   89
Nuristani Kati [bsh]   86–87, 89
Nuristani Kati Eastern [bsh]   99
Nuristani Kati Western [bsh]   94
Nuristani Prasun [prn]   86, 89, 93, 97, 108–109, 111–112
Nuristani Waigali [wbk]   86, 89, 94, 100–101, 106–107, 109
Ormuri [oru]   92
Palula [phl]   90
Parachi [prc]   85, 86, 92, 97, 99
Pashai [aee, glh, psi, psh]   87, 93, 98, 110
Pashai Alasai [glh]   107, 109, 112
Pashai Alingar [psi]   98, 98
Pashai Alishang [glh]   94, 109
Pashai Amla [psi]   86, 98, 101
Pashai Aret [aee]   86, 98, 100
Pashai Chalas [aee]   96, 86, 98, 104
Pashai Korangal [aee]   86, 98, 100, 107
Pashai Sanjan [glh]   86, 104, 107, 109, 112
Pashai Shemal [aee]   86, 98, 100
Pashto [pbt]   xx, 53, 86–88, 90, 92, 95, 109, 112
Persian [prs]   110, 151
Roshani [sgh]   85, 87, 91–92, 95–96
Sanglechi [sgy]   xx, 53, 85–86, 91–92, 95–97
Sawi [sdg]   85, 86, 90, 93, 97

Shughni [sgh]   xx, 53, 85–87, 91–92, 95, 104
Shumashti [sts]   87
South Siberian Turkic [clw, atv, alt, tyv among others]   92
Tirahi [tra]   87
Tregami [trm]   87
Turkic [41 languages]   97
Uzbek [uzb]   xvii, xxi, 87, 92, 106, 109
Wakhi [wbl]   xvii, xix– xx, 53, 72, 86–87, 91, 95, 97, 103–104, 126
Wotapuri-Katarqalai [wsv]   87
Yidgha [ydg]   91

SIL Global Publications

Publications in Linguistics Series
ISSN 1040-0850

155. *Central Sinama–English dictionary*, compiled by A. Kemp Pallesen, Anne Carol Pallesen, Lydia James, and Jeremiah Joy James. 2024, 823 pp., ISBN 978-1-55671-499-3 (pbk), 978-1-55671-500-6 (ePub).

154. *A grammar of Digo: A Bantu language of Kenya and Tanzania*, revised edition, by Steve Nicolle. 2023, 436 pp., ISBN 978-1-55671-437-5 (pbk), 978-1-55671-492-4 (ePub).

153. *The geometry and features of tone*, second edition, by Keith L. Snider, 2020, 198 pp., ISBN 978-1-55671-414-6.

152. *Kankanaey: A role and reference grammar analysis*, by Janet L. Allen, 2014, 402 pp., ISBN 978-1-55671-296-8.

151. *Understanding Biblical Hebrew verb forms: Distribution and function across genres*, by Robert E. Longacre and Andrew C. Bowling, 2015, 642 pp., ISBN 978-1-55671-278-4.

150. *Sudanese Arabic–English, English–Sudanese Arabic: A concise dictionary*, by Rianne Tamis and Janet L. Persson, 2013, 415 pp., ISBN: 978-1-55671-272-2.

149. *A grammar of Digo: A Bantu language of Kenya and Tanzania*, by Steve Nicolle. 2013, 462 pp., ISBN 978-1-55671-281-4.

148. *A grammar of Bora with special attention to tone*, by Wesley Thiesen and David Weber. 2012, 555 pp., ISBN 978-1-55671-301-9.

147. *The Kifuliiru language, volume 2: A descriptive grammar*, by Roger Van Otterloo, 2011, 612 pp., ISBN 978-1-55671-270-8.

146. *The Kifuliiru language, volume 1: Phonology, tone, and morphological derivation*, by Karen Van Otterloo, 2011, 512 pp., ISBN 978-1-55671-261-6.

SIL Global Publishing Services
7500 W Camp Wisdom Road
Dallas, TX 75236-5629 USA
publications@sil.org

www.ingramcontent.com/pod-product-compliance
Lightning Source LLC
LaVergne TN
LVHW021711060526
838200LV00050B/2606